OECD Studies on Water

Water Governance in Peru

OECD
BETTER POLICIES FOR BETTER LIVES

Please cite this publication as:
OECD (2021), *Water Governance in Peru*, OECD Studies on Water, OECD Publishing, Paris, *https://doi.org/10.1787/568847b5-en*.

ISBN 978-92-64-95569-1 (print)
ISBN 978-92-64-42988-8 (pdf)

OECD Studies on Water
ISSN 2224-5073 (print)
ISSN 2224-5081 (online)

Photo credits: Cover © Ministerio del Ambiente del Perú.

Corrigenda to publications may be found on line at: *www.oecd.org/about/publishing/corrigenda.htm*.

Preface

As part of the OECD Programme on Water Governance, we are very proud to introduce the report Water Governance in Peru. This report is the result of a two-year Policy Dialogue with 175 stakeholders across all levels of government in Peru, as well as from public, private and non-profit sectors.

Water is the most cross-cutting natural resource we have. It plays a key role in all forms of development, poverty alleviation, public health and hygiene, agriculture and food security, environment, energy generation, as well as land use and urban planning. Moreover, water is key to economic growth and, as such, managing the risks of too much, too little and too polluted waters – while fostering the conservation of ecosystems – is essential to people's well-being.

2021 coincides with Peru's 200 years of independence. It is also a time when it faces the economic and social impacts of COVID-19, as well as competing demands for water resources. Furthermore, water supply is unevenly distributed across the country, resulting in significant gaps in service delivery. Two-thirds of Peruvians live in the Pacific hydrographic region, which provides only 1.7% of water availability in the country and is also suffering from glacier retreat that is exacerbated by climate change. For these reasons, the integrated and sustainable management of water resources is a top priority, as well as a development opportunity.

The Policy Dialogue underlying this report facilitated a consensus among water stakeholders on key issues related to overcoming governance gaps, strengthening the regulatory framework for the provision of sanitation services and providing economic instruments for an effective and efficient water resources management.

The recovery from COVID-19 presents a unique window of opportunity for Peru to leverage this report's policy recommendations and outline a vision for the future where environmental sustainability is a major feature of the country's development strategy. Such a vision should call for action to trigger changes in the current water policy paradigm, acknowledging and highlighting the ecological, economic, and social value of water.

To consolidate its water governance systems, Peru will need to mobilise joint and effective actions to achieve Sustainable Development Goal 6 on "Clean Water and Sanitation". Local, provincial, regional, and national governments will be called upon to work together towards this collective objective, while also recognising the key role of the private sector and civil society in the implementation of necessary reforms. Furthermore, implementing these actions will require aligning policies across different ministries and policy sectors, and mobilising economic instruments to manage water risks and protect watersheds.

By implementing these policy recommendations and raising their profile within the national community and globally, Peru can enhance water security and provide good quality water services to all. The OECD stands ready to support Peru design, develop, and deliver better water governance policies for better lives.

Ángel Gurría
OECD Secretary-General

Gabriel Quijandría Acosta
Minister of Environment, Peru

Foreword

Water Governance in Peru adds to the rich compendium of country, region, city or thematic reviews published as part of the *OECD Studies on Water* over the past 15 years. This report expands the global outreach of OECD's work, adding to regional analyses of water governance in OECD countries (2011), Latin America and the Caribbean (2012), Asia-Pacific (2021) and African Cities (2021), as well as national water governance policy dialogues in Mexico (2013), The Netherlands (2014), Jordan (2015), Tunisia (2015), Brazil (2015 and 2017), Argentina (2019), and the metropolitan water governance policy dialogue in Cape Town, South Africa (2021).

In the past 30 years, access to basic health services has increased in Latin America and the Caribbean, especially for the 21% of the urban population living in slums, informal settlements or precarious housing. However, much remains to be done to achieve clean access to water and sanitation for all, and the COVID-19 pandemic has magnified pressing and emerging challenges including the lack of access to basic handwashing facilities in part of the territory. On the economic front, GDP in Latin America and the Caribbean region is projected to contract by 9.1%, while unemployment could reach 13.5% in 2021, with 37% of the LAC population expected to live below the poverty line. Peru is no exception to this regional context, but GDP is projected to return to pre-crisis levels in 2022 and aggregate growth in the recovery period will continue to be driven by water-intensive sectors, such as agriculture.

Over the past decade, Peru has significantly raised water security in its political agenda, but wider governance failures have jeopardised policy continuity and delivery. Recent political and social turmoil have had an impact on the effective implementation of public policies, including water and sanitation. This report can support forward-looking water policies, to achieve global commitments and tackle pressing megatrends, such as climate change.

Acknowledgements

This report was prepared by the OECD Centre for Entrepreneurship, SMEs, Regions and Cities (CFE) led by Lamia Kamal-Chaoui, Director, as part of the Programme of Work and Budget of the Regional Development Policy Committee. It is the result of a 2 year policy dialogue with 175 stakeholders across all levels of government in Peru, as well as from public, private, and non-profit sectors (Annex D).

The policy dialogue and the underlying report were co-ordinated by Oriana Romano, Head of the OECD Water Governance Programme, under the supervision of Aziza Akhmouch, Head of the Cities, Urban Policies and Sustainable Development Division in the CFE. The report was drafted by a core team comprised of Oriana Romano and Elisa Elliott Alonso, Junior Policy Analyst in the CFE (Chapter 1 and Annexes), Gonzalo Delacámara, Head of the Water Economics Department, Madrid Institute for Advanced Studies (IMDEA) (Chapter 2), Gérard Bonnis, Senior Policy Analyst, OECD Environment Directorate (Chapter 3), as well as Anna Pietikainen, Senior Policy Analyst and Martha Baxter, Policy Analyst, in the OECD Directorate on Public Governance (Chapter 4). Ander Eizaguirre, Juliette Lassman and Melissa Keri-Dikeni, Junior Policy Analysts in the OECD Water Governance Programme, CFE provided inputs for the analysis and contributed with desk research.

The OECD Secretariat is grateful for the high-level political impetus and commitment from the Minister of the Environment Gabriel Quijandría Acosta, as well as his predecessors in the early stages of the policy dialogue, namely Elsa Patricia Galarza Contreras, Fabiola Muñoz Dodero and Lucía Ruiz Ostoic. Special thanks are herein conveyed to the Peruvian local team from the Ministry of Environment, led by Luis Marino Nava, General Director of Economy and Environmental Financing and coordinated successively by Yolanda Zuñiga Fernandez, and Analia Alejandra Aramburu Inga, Policy and Public Management Advisors, for the excellent coordination and collaboration throughout the policy dialogue. The Secretariat is also very thankful to the member institutions of the multilateral commission set up to foster multi-sectoral consultation in the process, namely the Ministry of Agricultural Development and Irrigation (*Ministerio de Desarrollo Agrario y Riego, MIDAGRI*), the Ministry of Energy and Mining (Ministerio de Energía y Minas, MINEM), the Ministry of Foreign Affairs (*Ministerio de Relaciones Exteriores, RREE*), the Ministry of Health (*Ministerio de Salud, MINSA*), the Ministry of Housing, Construction and Sanitation (*Ministerio de Vivienda, Construcción y Saneamiento, MVCS*), the Ministry of Production (*Ministerio de Producción, PRODUCE*), the Ministry of the Environment (*Ministerio del Ambiente, MINAM*), the National Water Authority (*Autoridad Nacional del Agua, ANA*), Peru's water regulator (*Superintendencia Nacional de Servicios de Saneamiento, SUNASS*), the Presidency of the Council of Ministers (*Presidencia del Consejo de Ministros*) and the Technical Body for the Administration of Sanitation Services (*Organismo Técnico de la Administración de los Servicios de Saneamiento, OTASS*).

Furthermore, the policy dialogue benefitted from valuable insights from several peer reviewers who contributed through their valuable expertise and country experience, participated in onsite and virtual missions and provided international best practices as well as guidance on the report. They are herein gratefully acknowledged, namely Peter Gammeltoft, former Head of Unit for Water at the European Commission, Jaime Fernando Melo Baptista, former Chairperson of the Portuguese Regulatory Authority of Water and Waste Services (ERSAR) and President of the Board of Directors of LIS-Water –(Lisbon

International Centre for Water, Portugal), Gonzalo Delacámara, Head of the Water Economics Department, Madrid Institute for Advanced Studies (Spain) and Patrick Frenel, former Head of Geographical Services, Water Agency Loire-Bretagne (France).

As part of an inclusive and bottom-up consultation process, the draft report was shared for comments with stakeholders from Peru (see Annex D) who were engaged throughout the policy dialogue via interviews and webinars, as well as with the members of the OECD Water Governance Initiative. Interim findings and progress results were also presented and discussed at the 12th and 13th meeting of the OECD Water Governance Initiative (20-21 June 2019, Berlin, Germany and 9-10 January 2020, Paris, France). The report was submitted for approval by written procedure to the Regional Development Policy Committee on 19 February 2021 under cote CFE/RDPC/WGI(2021)3. Special thanks are extended to François Iglesias and Pilar Philip for preparing the report for publication, and to Eleonore Morena for editing and formatting the report.

Table of contents

Preface 3

Foreword 4

Acknowledgements 5

Abbreviations and acronyms 11

Executive summary 16

1 Water resources in Peru: The state of play 19
- Key data 20
- Water and the economy 21
- Water and social inclusiveness 24
- Water and environment 26
- Managing water under uncertainties 27
- References 28
- Notes 30

2 Multi-level water governance in Peru 33
- The legal framework for water resources management 34
- Institutional mapping of water roles and responsibilities 36
- Assessment of multi-level water governance 47
- Ways forward to strengthen multi-level water governance 59
- References 69
- Additional references 72
- Notes 72

3 Economic instruments for water risk management 77
- Payments for ecosystem services 78
- Environmental charges 88
- Public financial support for river rehabilitation 96
- Economic instruments for water resources management and policy coherence 96
- Ways forward to strengthen the use of economic instruments for greater water security 98
- References 112
- Additional references 115
- Notes 115

4 Regulatory framework for water supply and sanitation services in Peru 117
Peru's water supply and sanitation (WSS) services 118
Sector structure 119
Institutional framework 121
Legislative and planning tools for WWS services 125
Ways forward to strengthen the regulatory framework 126
Governance of SUNASS 132
Ways forward to enhance the governance and performance of the economic regulator 142
References 145
Notes 147

Annex A. The Ica River Integrated Basin 149
References 159

Annex B. The Olmos River Basin 161
References 171

Annex C. The Chillón, Rímac and Lurín River Basins (Chirilú) 173
References 183

Annex D. List of stakeholders consulted during the policy dialogue 185

FIGURES

Figure 1.1. Total demand for water resources in Peru in 2018, by use 20
Figure 1.2. Main crop exports in Peru in 2018 22
Figure 1.3. Share of the population with access to water and sewerage from the public network, by department 25
Figure 2.1. Composition of the National Water Resources Management System in Peru 35
Figure 2.2. Institutional mapping for water resources management in Peru 38
Figure 2.3. Institutional mapping for water Supply and Sanitation in Peru 44
Figure 2.4. Progress in the creation of River Basin Councils 46
Figure 2.5. OECD Principles on Water Governance 48
Figure 3.1. The logics of a PES Instrument 79
Figure 3.2. Revenues from charges on water abstraction and discharge of treated wastewater 95
Figure 4.1. Access to safely managed drinking water services is low in Peru compared to the LAC region 118
Figure 4.2. Satisfaction rates with the quality of water in Peru 119
Figure 4.3. Market structure of WSS services providers in Peru 120
Figure 4.4. Responsibilities in the WSS sector in Peru 123
Figure 4.5. Number of active water operators in the water and sewerage sector supervised by water regulators 134
Figure 4.6. Regulators funded through budget appropriations, fees or both 136

Figure A A.1. The Ica River Integrated Basin 151
Figure A A.2. Distribution of agricultural use of water resources in the Ica Valley according to size of land owned 152
Figure A A.3. Extreme events associated with climate change in the Ica department, 2003-13 153
Figure A B.1. The Olmos River Basin 163
Figure A B.2. PEOT implementation timeline 164
Figure A B.3. Main crops in the old Olmos Valley, in percentage of area cultivated 165
Figure A B.4. Institutional mapping of the Olmos River Basin 167
Figure A C.1. The Chirilú River Basin 175
Figure A C.2. Total surface and groundwater volume, in hm^3 175

TABLES

Table 3.1. Creation of MERESE and GRD/ACC reserve funds by the water companies 84
Table 3.2. Activities covered by MERESE reserve funds of water companies 86
Table 3.3. Water abstraction charge (REUA) rates 93
Table 3.4. Fixed water abstraction charge (REUA) 93
Table 3.5. Rates of charges on the discharge of treated wastewater (REVART) 94
Table 3.6. Charges collection 95
Table 3.7. Inter-basin water transfers in Peru 100
Table 3.8. The Quiroz-Chira Water Fund project 105
Table 3.9. Summary of actions to strengthen policy coherence between the economic instruments 111
Table 4.1. Regulatory functions for water in Peru 122
Table 4.2. SUNASS strategic objectives, according to the OECD input-process-output-outcome framework 135
Table 4.3. Benchmarking indicators to measure utility performance 139

Table A A.1. Rates of poverty, malnutrition and access to water and sanitation services in the Departments of Ica and Huancavelica 153
Table A A.2. Players involved in water governance in the Ica River Integrated Basin 154
Table A B.1. Rates of poverty and access to water and sanitation in the departments of Lambayeque and Piura 166
Table A B.2. Players involved in water governance in the Olmos River Basin 168
Table A C.1. Comparing Lima's resilience to other Latin American capitals 176
Table A C.2. Composition and main objectives of the Chirilú River Basin Council 179

BOXES

Box 1.1. Characteristics of the agricultural sector in Peru 21
Box 1.2. Social conflicts and Indigenous communities 23
Box 1.3. Sanitation policy efforts in Peruvian rural areas 26
Box 2.1. Regional and co-operation planning tools for water management in Peru 40
Box 2.2. The OECD Principles on Water Governance 47
Box 2.3. River basin organisations: Experiences from France and Spain 50
Box 2.4. The National Water Agency of Brazil (ANA) 60
Box 2.5. The National Delta Programme in the Netherlands 61
Box 2.6. Co-ordination mechanisms across levels of government in Peru 63
Box 2.7. Brazil's National Water Management Pact 65
Box 3.1. Inter-basin water transfers in Peru 100
Box 3.2. New York City Watershed Protection Program 101
Box 3.3. OECD Principles on Water Governance applied to water charges in Brazil 107
Box 3.4. River rehabilitation policy in Switzerland 110
Box 3.5. Synergies between water and climate policies in New Zealand 112
Box 4.1. Portugal's 20-year "Strategic Cycle of Public Water Policy" 127
Box 4.2. Examples of co-ordination among regulatory agencies 128
Box 4.3. Paying for water in Peru: Charges, tariffs and family fees 129
Box 4.4. Scotland's Outputs Monitoring Group 141

Box A A.1. Key data for the Ica River Integrated Basin 150
Box A A.2. International experiences for water management 158
Box A B.1. Key data for the Olmos River Basin 162
Box A B.2. Timeline of the Olmos Irrigation Project (PEOT) 163
Box A C.1. Key data for the Chirilú River Basin 174
Box A C.2. Payment for ecosystem services (PES) in the Chirilú Basin 178

Follow OECD Publications on:

- *http://twitter.com/OECD_Pubs*
- *http://www.facebook.com/OECDPublications*
- *http://www.linkedin.com/groups/OECD-Publications-4645871*
- *http://www.youtube.com/oecdilibrary*
- *http://www.oecd.org/oecddirect/*

Abbreviations and acronyms

ALA	*Administraciones Locales de Agua,* Local Water Administration Authorities
AAA	*Autoridades Administrativas del Agua*, Administrative Water Authorities
ANA	*Autoridad Nacional del Agua*, National Water Authority
ANPs	*Áreas Naturales Protegidas,* Natural Protected Areas
AQUAFONDO	*Fondo de Agua para Lima y Callao*, Water Fund for Lima and Callao
ARD	*Agencias Regionales de Desarrollo,* Regional Development Agencies
ATM	*Área Técnica Municipal,* Municipal Technical Areas
CAC	*Centros de Atención al Ciudadano*, Citizen Service Centres
CBC	Central America Bottling Corporation
CCA	Climate Change Adaptation
CEPLAN	*Centro Nacional de Planeamiento Estratégico*, National Centre for Strategic Planning
CHRC	*Consejo de Recursos Hídricos de Cuenca*, River Basin Council
CONCYTEC	*Consejo Nacional de Ciencia, Tecnología e Innovación Tecnológica*, National Council of Science, Technology and Innovation
COVID-19	Coronavirus Disease 2019
CRHC	*Consejos de Recursos Hídricos de Cuenca,* River Basin Councils
DATASS	Rural WASH Information System
DGAA	*Dirección General de Asuntos Ambientales*, Directorate-General for Environmental Issues
DGPPC	*Dirección General de Programas y Proyectos en Comunicaciones* , DG Programmes and Building and Sanitation Projects
DGPRCS	DG Policies and Regulation on Building and Sanitation
DICAPI	*Dirección General de Capitanías y Guardacostas*, Directorate General for Captaincy and Coast Guard of Peru
DIGESA	*Dirección General de Salud Ambiental e Inocuidad Alimentaria,* Directorate-General for Environmental Health and Food Safety
DIRESA	*Dirección Regional de Salud,* Regional Health Directorate
DP	Delta Programme
DRR	Disaster Risk Reduction
DWQR	Drinking Water Quality Regulator for Scotland

EPs	*Empresas Prestadoras del Servicio de Saneamiento,* Water and Sanitation Service Providers
UN	United Nations
EQS	Environmental Quality Standards
ETS	Emissions Trading Scheme
FAO	Food and Agriculture Organization
FONAVI	*Fondo Nacional de Vivienda,* National Housing Fund
FONCODES	*Fondo de Cooperación para el Desarrollo Social*, Co-operation Fund for Social Development
FORASAN	*Fondo Regional del Agua*, Regional Water Fund
GDP	Gross domestic product
GETRAM	*Grupo Especializado de Trabajo Multisectorial*, Specialised Multi-sectoral Task Forces
GGGI	Global Green Growth Institute
GHG	Greenhouse Gas Emission
GIS	Geographic Information Systems
GORE	*Gobierno Regional-Ejecutivo,* Executive Regional Government
GWP	Global Water Partnership
IDB	Inter-American Development Bank
IFC	International Finance Corporation
IGA	*Instrumento de Gestión Ambiental*, Environmental Management Instruments
ILO	International Labour Organization
IMDEA	*Institutos Madrileño de Estudios Avanzados*, Madrid Institute for Advanced Studies
INDECI	*Instituto Nacional de Defensa Civil,* National Civil Defense System
INDECOPI	*Instituto Nacional de Defensa de la Competencia y de la Protección de la Propiedad Intelectual*, National Institute for the Defence of Competition and the Protection of Intellectual Property
INEI	*Instituto Nacional de Estadistica e Informatica*, National Institute of Statistics and Information Technology
INRENA	*Instituto Nacional de Recursos Naturales,* National Institute on Natural Resources
JASS	*Juntas Administradoras de Servicios de Saneamiento,* Sanitation Services Administration Boards
JUASVI	*Junta de Usuarios de Aguas Subterráneas del Valle de Ica,* Board of Groundwater Users of the Ica Valley
JUSH	*Junta de Usuarios del Sector Hidráulico*, Board of users of the hydraulic sector
LAC	Latin America and the Caribbean
LMCC	*Ley Marco sobre Cambio Climático,* Framework Law for Climate Change

MANRHI	*Mancomunidad Regional Huancavelica e Ica*, Ica-Huancavelica Regional Association
MEF	*Ministerio de Economía y Finanzas,* Ministry of Economy and Finance
MERESE	*Mecanismo de Retribución por Servicios Ecosistémicos*, Ecosystem Services Compensation Mechanism
MIDAGRI	*Ministerio de Desarrollo Agrario y Riego,* Ministry of Agricultural Development and Irrigation
MIDIS	*Ministerio de Desarrollo e Inclusión Social,* The Ministry of Development and Social Inclusion
MINAGRI	*Ministerio de Agricultura y Riego*, Ministry of Agriculture and Irrigation
MINAM	*Ministerio del Ambiente,* Ministry of the Environment
MINEM	*Ministerio de Energía y Minas*, Ministry of Energy and Mining
MINSA	*Ministerio de Salud,* Ministry of Health
MIRR	*Margen Izquierda del Río Rímac,* Left bank of the Rímac River
MVCS	*Ministerio de Vivienda Construcción y Saneamiento*, Ministry of Housing, Construction and Sanitation
NDC	Nationally Determined Contribution
NGOs	Non-Governmental Organisations
NIWS	Natural Infrastructure for Water Security
O&M	Operation and Maintenance
OECD	Organisation for Economic Co-operation and Development
OEFA	*Organismo de Evaluación y Fiscalización Ambiental*, Agency for Environmental Assessment and Enforcement
OMG	Output Monitoring Group
ONDS	*Oficina Nacional de Dialogo y Sostenibilidad*, Office for Dialogue and Sustainability
OSINERGMIN	*Organismo Supervisor de la Inversión en Energía y Minería,* Supervisory Body for Investment in Energy and Mining
OTASS	*Organismo Técnico de la Administración de los Servicios de Saneamiento*, Technical Agency for the Administration of Sanitation Services
PADH	*Plan de Aprovechamiento de Disponibilidades Hídricas,* Water Use Plan
PCM	*Presidencia del Consejo de Ministros,* Presidency of the Council of Ministers
PDMC	Concerted Municipal Development Plans
PEI	*Plan Estratégico Institucional*, Organisational Strategic Plan
PEN	Peruvian Sol, National currency
PENRH	Política y Estrategia Nacional de Recursos Hídricos, National Water Resources Policy and Strategy
PEOT	*Proyecto Especial Olmos Tinajones,* Special Project Olmos Tinajores
PES	Payments for ecosystem services
PETACC	*Proyecto Especial Tambo Ccaracocha,* Tambo-Ccaracocha Special Project

PGRHC	*Plan de Gestión de Recursos Hídricos de Cuencas*, Water Resources Management Plan
PHES	Payments for Hydrological Ecosystem Service
PIFA	*Portal Interactivo de Fiscalización Ambiental,* Portal for Environmental Enforcement
PMO	*Plan Maestro Optimizado,* Optimised Master Plan
PNRH	*Plan Nacional de Recursos Hídricos*, National Water Resources Plan
PNS	*Plan Nacional de Saneamiento,* National Sanitation Plan
PNSR	*Programa Nacional de Saneamiento Rural*, National Rural Sanitation Programme
PNSU	*Programa Nacional de Saneamiento Urbano*, National Urban Sanitation Programme
POMDIH	*Plan de Operación, Mantenimiento y Desarrollo de Infraestructura Hidráulica,* Operation, Maintenance and Development Plan of the Hydraulic Infrastructure
PPP	Public-Private Partnership
PRODUCE	*Ministerio de Producción*, Ministry of Production
PRONASAR	*Programa Nacional de Agua y Saneamiento Rural,* National Rural Water Supply and Sanitation Project
RAT	*Régimen de Apoyo Transitorio*, Transitional Support Scheme
REUA	*Retribuciónes Económicas por el Uso del Agua,* Water abstraction charges
REVART	*Retribuciónes Económicas Por El Vertimiento De Aguas Residuales Tratadas,* Charges On The Discharge Of Treated Wastewater
RIA	Regulatory impact assessment
RREE	*Ministerio de Relaciones Exteriores*, Ministry of Foreign Affairs
RT	Roundtable
SAGE	*Schéma d'aménagement et de gestion de l'eau,* Water development and management plan
SANIPES	*Organismo Nacional de Sanidad Pesquera,* National Fisheries Health Agency
SDAGE	*Schéma directeur d'aménagement et de gestion de l'eau,* Master plan for water development and management
SDGs	United Nations Sustainable Development Goals
SEDAPAL	*Servicio de Agua Potable y Alcantarillado de Lima,* Lima Drinking Water and Sewerage Service
SENACE	*Servicio Nacional de Certificación Ambiental para las Inversiones Sostenibles,* National Environmental Certification Service for Sustainable Investment
SENAMHI	*Servicio Nacional de Meteorología e Hidrología del Perú,* National Meteorological and Hydrological Service
SEPA	Scottish Environment Protection Agency
SERNANP	*Servicio Nacional de Áreas Naturales Protegidas por el Estado,* National Service of Natural Areas Protected by the State

SFCS	*Sistema de Fortalecimiento de Capacidades,* Sanitation Sector Capacity-building System
SGSD	Secretariat of Social Management and Dialogue
SIAS	*Sistema de información en agua y saneamiento*, Water and Sanitation Information System
SINAGERD	*Sistema Nacional de Gestión de Riesgos de Desastres*, National System of Disaster Risk Management
SNACE	*Servicio Nacional de Certificación Ambiental para las Inversiones Sostenibles,* National Environmental Certification Service for Sustainable Investments
SNGA	*Sistema Nacional de Gestión Ambiental*, National Environmental Management System
SNGRH	*Sistema Nacional de Gestión de Recursos Hídricos,* National Water Resources Management System
SNIP	*Sistema Nacional de Inversión Pública,* National System of Public Investment
SUNASS	*Superintendencia Nacional de Servicios de Saneamiento*, National Superintendence of Sanitation Services, Peru's water and sanitation regulator
SUNAT	*Superintendencia Nacional de Aduanas y de Administración Tributaria,* National Superintendence of Customs and Tax Administration
TNRCH	*Tribunal Nacional de Resolución de Controversias Hídricas,* National Court for the Adjudication of Water Disputes
TPS	Tradeable Permit Systems
UNFCCC	United Nations Framework Convention on Climate Change
UPGC	*Unidad de Prevención y Gestión de Conflictos,* Conflict Prevention and Management Unit
USAID	United States Agency for International Development
VMCS	*Vice Ministerio de Construcción y Saneamiento*, Vice Ministry of Construction and Sanitation
WASH	*Agua, Saneamiento e Higiene*, Water, Sanitation and Hygiene
WFP	World Food Programme
WHO	World Health Organization
WICS	Water Industry Commission for Scotland
WRMMP	Water Resources Management Modernisation Project
WSS	Water supply and sanitation
WTO	World Trade Organization
WWTP	Wastewater treatment plant
IWRM	Integrated Water Resources Management

Executive summary

While the COVID-19 virus has hit Peru particularly hard, with 1.4 million confirmed cases as of March 2021, the pandemic has further emphasised the importance of water and sanitation for health, the environment and the economy. From a health standpoint, the pandemic has taken a strong toll on Peru, the fifth-most affected country in the LAC region with about more than 45 000 deaths to date. On the economic front, in the first half of 2020, Gross domestic product (GDP) declined by 11.4%. Projections show that GDP will not return to pre-crisis levels before 2022, and aggregate growth will continue to be driven by water-intensive sectors, such as agriculture. Regarding the environment, high levels of rainfall in certain areas and inadequate drainage systems have created a dual health risk with the overflowing and flooding of untreated wastewater, which, in turn, hinder proper hygiene conditions that can prevent the spread of the virus.

Although Peru has made good progress in water management, significant water security challenges remain in terms of floods, droughts, pollution and universal access to drinking water and sanitation. Peru is currently not on track to meet the targets of the United Nations (UN) Sustainable Development Goal (SDG) 6 "Clean water and sanitation" by 2030. According to the most recent data (2017) from the UN Water monitoring system, only 50% of the population use a safely managed drinking water service (SDG indicator 6.1.1) and 43% use a safely managed sanitation service (SDG indicator 6.2.1a). Overall, 3 million Peruvians (9.2% of the population) lack access to water services and 8.2 million Peruvians (25.2%) lack access to sewerage services, with a large urban-rural divide. Between 2000 and 2020, floods affected an estimated 4 million people, while 10 moderate to extreme drought events occurred in 20 departments between 1981 and 2018. The inadequate management of solid waste and informal and illegal mining affect water quality, leading to severe public health issues, and social conflicts, including with indigenous communities.

In response to these challenges, the National Sanitation Policy 2017-21 set out Peru's objective to achieve sustainable, universal access to water and sanitation, with the underlying goal of expanding coverage, improving water quality and promoting the sustainable use of sanitation services. In addition, Peru's nationally determined contribution (NDC) aims to achieve the Paris Agreement of the UNFCCC targets by 2025 and 2030 through 30 adaptation measures on water to be implemented in a shared responsibility with regional and local governments. These measures include the modernisation of the granting of water use rights in basins especially vulnerable to climate change, incorporating climatic scenarios, and implementing early-warning systems for floods, droughts, landslides and glacier-related risks.

Over the last decade, Peru has consolidated its legal and institutional framework for water policy, but governance gaps hinder effective implementation. State Policy no. 33/2012 on Water Resources acknowledges that water is part of the public domain and recognises the human right to water and sanitation, following the UN Assembly Declarations in 2010 and 2015. It also highlights the relevance of implementing integrated water resources management in order to guarantee the equitable and sustainable use of water nationwide. The 2009 Water Resources Law sets the legal and institutional framework for water resources management, and a myriad of institutions hold water and sanitation prerogatives in terms of policy design, financing, regulation and implementation. However, coordination failures and capacity gaps across these various institutions hinder the implementation of social, financial and technological solutions to identified water challenges.

Peru has adopted economic and financial instruments for water resources management, but their implementation is lagging. For instance, good practices include the gradual implementation of abstraction charges and payments for groundwater, with some environmental criteria being factored in; the existence of treated wastewater discharges for domestic and industrial discharges; as well as coefficients to reflect water availability and type of use for surface water. However, these instruments are set too low to collect the revenues needed to bridge the current 46 USD million funding gap by 2035. Achieving this goal, would require disclosing more systematically how collected revenues are used and how they contribute to coping with water quantity and quality challenges, while taking into account affordability and distributional effects.

While Peru has set water issues high in its policy agenda, wider governance failures have put in jeopardy policy continuity and delivery. Since 2018, Peru has been subject to political challenges that can largely be traced to the 2016 Odebrecht affair, since when the Peruvian presidency has changed four times. The nationwide political instability has had serious consequences for water and sanitation with four ministers of environment being appointed over the same period and staff turnover in the public administration resulting in shifting priorities and budgets, which were aggravated by the COVID-19 pandemic.

The primary goal of good water governance is to contribute to mastering complexity and fragmentation, which are inherent to water policy. This entails dealing with sectoral policy coordination, improving the data and knowledge base, delivering innovative financing mechanisms, addressing trade-offs across water users, revisiting policy approaches related to water use efficiency, diversifying water supply sources and natural infrastructures, and building capacity. Strengthening water governance in Peru is a means to achieving long-term water security, and aligning individual user behaviour and collective action. In line with the OECD Principles on Water Governance, the report suggests a series of tailored policy recommendations to strengthen the multi-level governance of water policy, the effectiveness of economic instruments, and the regulatory framework for water supply and sanitation services in Peru.

Strengthen multi-level governance

- Progress towards a **holistic and integrated approach** to water resources management for greater water security. The approach should consider integration across sectors and levels of government, as well as strengthen the link between water resources management and water supply and sanitation services, while enhancing the role of ANA as the leading institution.
- Assess the legislative **framework and its implementation**, in order to translate the aspirations of the law into realistic and workable objectives that evolve as institutional capacity develops.
- Ensure **sufficient capacity** in terms of staff and technical expertise at national, regional and local level, including to make the existing 6 River Basin Management Plans (RBMPs) fully operational.
- Strengthen the **information and knowledge base** about current and future risks of water pollution, droughts and floods. Peru needs more granular data and accurate water balances at basin level. Academia and research institutions could support research and technological development on alternative water supply sources for different purposes.
- Enhance **strategic planning for more effective public investment** by matching the "Optimised City Masterplan", which includes investment projects, with the municipal sector plan, which includes urban development projects; but also streamlining investment evaluation procedures within the National Multi-Year Programming and Investment Management System.
- Redesign **economic and financial instruments** so that they not only raise revenue, but also consider water quantity and quality objectives, while taking into account distributional effects. As

such, improving pricing schemes, with emphasis on bulk water pricing would contribute to adapting water availability and demand, especially in the most water-stressed basins.

- Engage **stakeholders** in defining the acceptable levels of water risk. Responsible institutions at national and subnational level need to improve platforms for dialogue such as within River Basin Committees, while guaranteeing adequate representativeness of a variety of stakeholders for policy-making and implementation.

Effectively implement economic instruments for water risk management

- Increase the **use of payments for ecosystem services** (PES) to protect headwaters by, amongst others, carrying out a water risk analysis for an effective use of the funds from the existing Compensation Mechanism for Ecosystem Services (PES) (*Mecanismo de Retribución por Servicios Ecosistémicos*, MERESE); ensuring full adherence to PES projects by populations living in the upper parts of the basin (often farming communities); and enhancing the willingness to pay for beneficiaries of ecosystem services and coherence between the various PES systems.
- Strengthen **economic incentives of abstraction and pollution charges** based on water risks (scarcity, pollution) to develop a "water culture" and support the implementation of the polluter pays and user pays principles in practice.
- Strengthen **policy coherence** between the economic instruments deployed to manage water risks and instruments related to sectoral and environmental policies, such as in the case of agricultural production, renewable energy and policies aimed at promoting carbon sequestration.
- Launch a **policy of "river rehabilitation"** to improve water supply, ensure natural protection against floods and protect nature. This requires estimating the river sections to be restored and the financial support to be mobilised.

Strengthen the regulatory framework towards universal coverage of water supply and sanitation

- Implement a **high-level pact** between all actors involved in the water supply and sanitation (WSS) policy design, implementation, regulation and delivery to present a unified implementation plan for the country's 2030 policy goals.
- Improve **clarity in the allocation of regulatory functions**, such as in the case of regulatory norms and frameworks to ensure financial sustainability and good corporate governance of water and sanitation service companies.
- Improve **data collection and management for the WSS sector**, through defining specific targets with regard to burden reduction on WSS actors for data submission, clarifying sanitation-related data collection responsibilities, and better coordinating public sector data collection and sharing.
- Enhance the **governance and performance of the economic regulator** through: monitoring the evolving role and objectives of SUNASS; ensuring adequate and predictable financial resources; continuing to develop and fully implement the process for the systematic use of regulatory impact assessment; and improving performance monitoring of WSS service provision by SUNASS.

1 Water resources in Peru: The state of play

Water and sanitation are key priorities in Peru for sustainable development and social well-being. However, within the context of climate change and political instability, governance challenges come about with an unprecedented level of uncertainty. The chapter provides key facts and data on water security in Peru, as well as an analysis of how megatrends increasingly challenge water supply for the economy, society and the environment.

Key data

Peru is the eighth water-richest country in the world in terms of freshwater volume and the third in Latin America, after Brazil and Colombia. However, freshwater is unequally distributed across the country: 97% of available freshwater is in the Amazon Hydrographic Region, where the 31% of the population live (INEI, 2018[1]; ANA, 2013[2]). On the other hand, the majority of the population (65%) and economic activities are located in the Pacific Hydrographic Region, despite generating just 1.77% of Peru's available freshwater. Water demand in the capital city of Lima, in the water-scarce Pacific Hydrographic Region, has experienced strong growth due to the significant increase (+51.8%) in its population over the past 25 years (INEI/UNFPA, 2020[3]). Its population consumed 163 litres per capita and per day in 2018, significantly above the 100 litres per capita and per day recommended by the World Health Organization (WHO). Despite the scarce amount of water resources, more than two-thirds of the agricultural gross domestic product (GDP) originates from the Pacific watershed (FAO, 2015[4]). Finally, the Titicaca Hydrographic Region provides 0.32% of total freshwater and hosts 4% of the population (INEI, 2018[1]; ANA, 2013[2]).

The three Hydrographic Regions also differ greatly in terms of volume of groundwater: from 542 998 hm^3 in the Amazon Hydrographic Region (99%) to 4 844 hm^3 in the Pacific Hydrographic Region (0.9%) and 615 hm^3 in the Titicaca Hydrographic Region (0.1%) (ANA, 2013[2]). Overall, groundwater sources represent 25% of water available resources, of which the majority originates from surface water sources (75%) (INEI, 2015[5]). Groundwater is particularly important in the water-scarce Pacific Hydrographic Region, where water from aquifers is mainly used for agriculture and human use. Although some aquifers, notably in the Pacific Hydrographic Region, are closed or overexploited, the overall groundwater balance in the country is positive (an estimated +546 730 hm^3) (ANA, 2013[2]).

Overall, water uses are as follows: in 2018, 29.3% corresponded to consumptive uses, mostly agriculture (74.8 %), and 70.7% to non-consumptive uses, mostly energy (97.7% of total non-consumptive demand), as 81% of electricity in Peru comes from hydraulic sources (ANA, 2019[6]) (Figure 1.1). Tensions related to water use are rising as demand increases, driven by a growing population and economy. In addition, climate change makes water scarcer and affects water security due to melting glaciers: 51% of glaciers in Peru has melted due to climate change in the last 50 years (World Bank, 2021[7]).

Figure 1.1. Total demand for water resources in Peru in 2018, by use

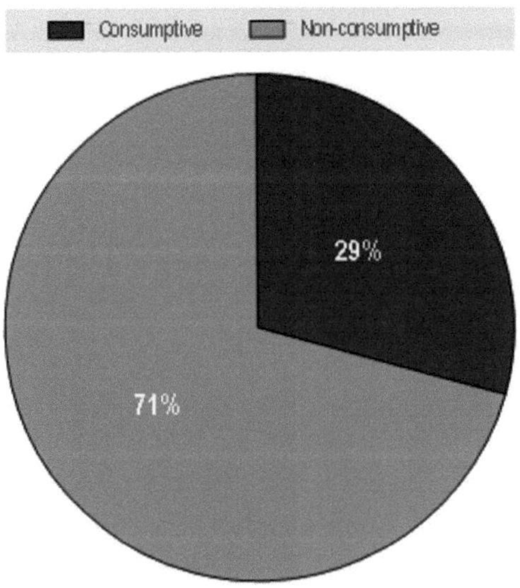

Source: ANA (2019[6]) , ANA REGISTRO 2019.

Water and the economy

Peru is a fast-growing economy, which achieved the status of a middle-income country in 2008. With an annual average GDP growth rate of 6.1%, between 2002 and 2013, Peru doubled its real per capita income and was one of the fastest-growing countries in Latin America and the Caribbean (LAC), with 3.4% annual average GDP growth rate. Between 2014 and 2019, while the GDP growth slowed to an annual average rate of 3.1% reaching 4% in 2019, it was still above other LAC countries such as Colombia (3.0%), Chile (1.1%), or Brazil and Mexico (1.0%). Private investments and consumption, the services sector, as well as the mining and non-traditional agriculture sectors led the economic growth. Nevertheless, it is worth noticing that the service sector, which accounts for almost two-thirds of GDP, include informal activities in commerce, transport, or domestic services (World Bank, 2021[7]) .

The COVID-19 pandemic has deeply affected the Peruvian economy, which contracted by 12% in 2020 (MEF, 2020[8]). This 12% decrease in economic output between 2019 and 2020 made the Peruvian employment rate drop by -25% between the first and second quarter of 2020 (ILO, 2020[9]). The high rate of formal unemployment – around 70% (OECD, 2020[10]) – makes the majority of Peruvian workers particularly vulnerable to crises and the ensuing loss of income. Peru also experienced the strongest fall (-72%) in foreign direct investment (FDI) in the LAC region and a 10% depreciation in its exchange rate. The economic response to COVID-19 highlights the strong increase in non-financial public spending and the progressive recovery of external demand. For the period 2022-24, economic activity is expected to reach an average growth of 4.5% and this economic recovery will be sustained if there is a boost of the accumulation of capital that will come from increased investments (MEF, 2020[8]).

Agricultural production, which accounts for 74.8 % of consumptive water demand and one-third of the Peruvian working population, is of great economic and social importance in Peru (Box 1.1). Overall, agriculture, forestry and fishing contributed 7.0% to the country's overall GDP in 2019 (World Bank, 2021[11]). The Peruvian economy is dependent on the exports of water-intensive commodities, which means that significant increases in prosperity and human well-being are contingent on improved access to drinking water and sanitation. However, the demand for water services has soared in many coastal regions, where the bulk of agricultural production is located, and it is now higher than long-term renewable resources. Hence, water scarcity has worsened over time. The potential for traditional responses to long-term water scarcity, such as new water storage and major diversion projects, may face a number of very significant constraints: the need to ensure upfront capital investment and to finance operational expenses, the emergence of social and territorial conflicts, meaningful environmental damages, etc. Yet the diversity of institutions and approaches in Peru is still biased towards supply augmentation solutions rather than water demand management. New ways forward are to be explored, including joint management of surface and groundwater, relevant efforts towards the diversification of water supply sources, water demand management (including water use efficiency measures), a more integrated approach to water bodies that factors in not only quantitative dimensions but also qualitative and hydro-morphological ones, the promotion of solutions to infrastructural development to complement conventional public works, and a redefinition of a number of financial and economic incentives.

Box 1.1. Characteristics of the agricultural sector in Peru

The great variety of climates and ecological zones allows the production of a wide range of crops. In general, in Peru, three different kinds of agricultural production systems coexist (FAO, 2015[4]):

- **Subsistence agriculture**: Characteristic of the poorest social sectors in rural areas, especially in the Andes Mountains region. The predominant crops are corn, beans, cereals, rustic grasslands, vegetables and other bread crops.

- **Agriculture for local markets**: Rice, potatoes, hard yellow corn, cotton, sugar cane, beans, wheat, fruits, vegetables, etc. This type of agriculture is prevalent in the irrigated valleys of the coast, where sugar cane is produced by companies on a larger scale.
- **Export-oriented agriculture**: With high levels of dynamism in terms of incorporating new technology also to improve water efficiency and agro-commercial management, Peru is rated among the countries with the highest export rate of asparagus (revenues of USD 384 million in 2018), mango (USD 257 million), avocado (USD 724 million) and coffee (USD 680 million), etc. (Figure 1.2). These business activities are mostly carried out on the coast.

Figure 1.2. Main crop exports in Peru in 2018

Percentage of total production for export

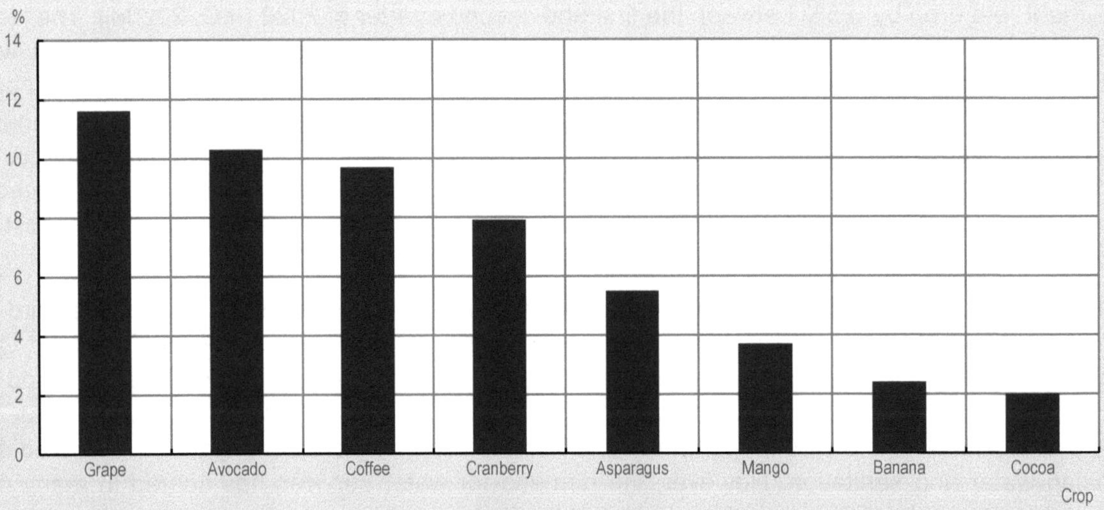

The National Land Classification System (*Sistema Nacional de Clasificación de las Tierras*), according to its Greater Use Capacity (*Capacidad de Uso Mayor*) includes regulations for soil management and conservation. Along the same line, the National Agrarian Policy, in its first axis "Sustainable management of water and soils", contains Policy Axis 1 "Water management", whose objective is to improve the management of water for agricultural use, for which establishes eight strategic guidelines. In general, these guidelines encourage the participation of user organisations, promote water use rights, the identification of water sources, the establishment of an integrated information system on sources, payment for water use and water recharge.

Source: Author's own elaboration based on MINAGRI (2019[12]), *Boletín Estadístico de Comercio Exterior Agrario*, https://www.midagri.gob.pe/portal/boletin-estadistico-de-comercio-exterior-agrario ; Reglamento de Clasificación de Tierras por su Capacidad de Uso Mayor, Decreto Supremo No. 017-2009-AG; Política Nacional Agraria, Decreto Supremo No. 002-2016-MINAGRI.

Mining is also a major driver of Peru's export-oriented economy. Peru is a global producer of copper ore and gold, which respectively amount to 26.9% and 15.9% of Peru's total exports (OECD, 2017[13]). The main mining deposits in the country are located in the heights of the Andes, where the headwaters of the watersheds and areas of water recharge are located. In recent years legal mining has improved processes towards greater environmental protection (OECD, 2017[13]). On the other hand, illegal mining is responsible for negative environmental externalities, which include metal contamination, acid mine drainage, increased sediment levels in streams, soil erosion, nutrient loss and untreated wastewater effluents. It is estimated that in the last 20 years, more than 3 000 tons of mercury have been dumped into Amazonian rivers, contaminating water, aquatic organisms and human populations that consume water and fish (WWF, 2019[14]). Water contamination by anthropogenic activities, wastewater from the various uses, discharges, treatment or reuse of water, among others, is at the centre of a number of conflicts that have emerged as a result of pollution pressures and have involved Indigenous communities (Box 1.2).

Box 1.2. Social conflicts and Indigenous communities

Many social conflicts in Peru stem from water-related issues. As of December 2019, the Secretariat for Social Management and Dialogue (SGSD) identified 143 cases of social conflict at the national level, of which 8.4% (12 cases) were related to water. Although there is leeway for improvement in the methodology used by the Ombudsman to upgrade and update the analysis of complex social conflicts, the Ombudsman's Office registered between January 2011 and December 2014 a total of 153 social conflicts linked to water resources, representing 28.36% of the total number of conflicts over that period (539 cases).

Resolution No. 285-2014-ANA established two types of classification of water conflicts: one in relation to the "theme" of the social conflict linked to the use of water (e.g. dispute over the volume or flow of the water resource; management of the quality of the resource; hydraulic infrastructure and assets associated with water resources); and in relation to the "stage" in which the conflict is prevented and treated. The National Water Authority (ANA) intervenes prior to the emergence of the water conflict and/or in the event of a crisis, or at the time of the open manifestation of the conflict. The intervention at different stages seeks to reduce the intensity of the factors that exacerbate the water conflict and find solutions through mechanisms, guidelines and established spaces for its approach (dialogue, agreement and negotiation).

In 2015, 8% of water conflicts registered with the ombudsman in Peru involved Indigenous communities and 5% involved Indigenous organisations (Ombudsman's Office, 2015[15]). Conflicts are related to: the implementation of irrigation projects; the use of lagoons; the construction of dams; projects that would affect groundwater conduits; or stem from demands of Indigenous organisations for not having been consulted. Law No. 29785, recognised in the International Labour Organization (ILO) Convention 169, develops content, principles and procedures for the right to prior consultation with Indigenous or native peoples regarding legislative or administrative measures that directly affect them. Along the same line, the Regulation of Law No. 30754, the Framework Law on Climate Change (Supreme Decree No. 013-2019-MINAM), incorporates the creation of the Indigenous Peoples' Platform to face climate change, as a space for Indigenous peoples to share their proposals for adaptation and mitigation measures to climate change.

Peru is the third-largest home to Indigenous peoples, after Bolivia and Guatemala, with over 2 000 Indigenous communities belonging to 44 different Indigenous peoples (INEI, 2017[16]) and over 20% of the total population claiming Indigenous heritage (World Bank, 2015[17]). Many of these communities live in the mountainous regions of the Andes and the Amazon Rainforest. 78% of Indigenous people have access to piped water and 68% have access to sewerage (INEI, 2009[18]), significantly below the national average of 89% and 73% respectively (INEI, 2020[19]). The contamination of water resources poses a serious threat to their economic subsistence, as well as their cultural identity, which is ultimately linked to the conservation of the territory they inhabit and that they use both for practical reasons (to obtain resources) as well as symbolic reasons (ritual significance).

The OECD has recognised that the 38 million Indigenous peoples living across 12 OECD countries contribute to stronger regional and national economies and have unique assets and knowledge that address global challenges such as climate change. OECD (2019[20]) suggests to improve Indigenous statistics and data governance; create an enabling environment for Indigenous entrepreneurship and small business development at the local and regional levels; improve the Indigenous land tenure system to facilitate opportunities for economic development; adapt policies and governance to implement a place-based approach to economic development that improves policy coherence and empowers Indigenous communities.

Source: OECD (2019[20]), *Linking Indigenous Communities with Regional Development*, https://doi.org/10.1787/3203c082-en; OECD (2017[13]), "Mining regions and their cities", http://www.oecd.org/cfe/regional-policy/Mining%20discussion%20paper%20FINAL_CM.pdf; ANA (2015[21]), *Conflictos sociales y recursos hídricos, Autoridad*, https://repositorio.ana.gob.pe/handle/20.500.12543/2807; PCM (2020[22]), *Willaqniki N° 12 - 2019: Monthly Report December 2019*; Ombudsman's Office (2015[15]), "Social conflicts and water resources", Defensoría del Pueblo; INEI (2017[16]), *III Censo De Comunidades Nativas 2017: Resultados Definitivos, Tomo 1: Lima*, https://www.inei.gob.pe/media/MenuRecursivo/publicaciones_digitales/Est/Lib1598/TOMO_01.pdf; INEI (2020[19]), *Perú: Formas de Acceso al Agua y Saneamiento Básico*, https://www.inei.gob.pe/media/MenuRecursivo/boletines/boletin_agua_y_saneamiento.pdf.

Water and social inclusiveness

In Peru, there are significant gaps in access to water and sanitation. Fourteen out of 24 departments,[1] home to 91% of the population, have access to public water supply (Figure 1.3) (INEI, 2020[19]). It is estimated that 3 million Peruvians (9.2% of the population) lack access to water services and 8.2 million Peruvians (25.2%) lack access to sewerage services (INEI, 2020[19]). Between 2017 and 2018, only half of the total population that reported consuming water from the public network benefitted from this service 24 hours a day (INEI, 2020[19]). The COVID-19 crisis further emphasised the importance of water and sanitation for health, especially amongst the population living in informal settlements with difficult access to proper sanitation. In certain areas of the country, inadequate draining systems also created a double health risk due to the overflowing and flooding of untreated wastewater, inhibiting proper hygiene conditions to prevent the spread of the virus.

Access to water and sanitation shows a large urban-rural divide. Despite the existence of rural sanitation plans and specific rural sanitation programmes at the national, regional and local levels, 25.3% of the rural population and 4.7% of the urban population does not have access to public water supply networks. Moreover, 22.8% of the population lacked access to public sewerage networks in 2019, of which 9.6% in urban areas and 71.7% in rural areas. This situation has slightly improved since 2013 when close to a third (32.5%) of the population had no access to public sewerage (INEI, 2021[23]). However, according to the most recent data (2017[24]), Peru is far from achieving the SDG 6 on water and sanitation: 50% of the population use a safely managed drinking water service (SDG indicator 6.1.1) and 43% use a safely managed sanitation service (SDG indicator 6.2.1a). Disparities are larger in sanitation, where 89% of the urban population reside in homes with drainage service through a public network (84% inside the home), compared to just 17% of the rural population (UN, 2017[24]). Large urban settlements such as Arequipa, Callao, Lima and Tacna all report rates of improved access to sanitation well above the national average (74.9%), whereas the rural departments of Huancavelica, Huánuco, Loreto and Ucayali all show access to sanitation rates below 45%. As of July 2019, the Ministry of Housing, Construction and Sanitation (*Ministerio de Vivienda Construcción y Saneamiento*, MVCS) has invested and transferred PEN 3 749 million for the execution of 1 610 water and sanitation projects nationwide, from which more than 1 800 000 Peruvians in urban and rural areas are expected to benefit.

Figure 1.3. Share of the population with access to water and sewerage from the public network, by department

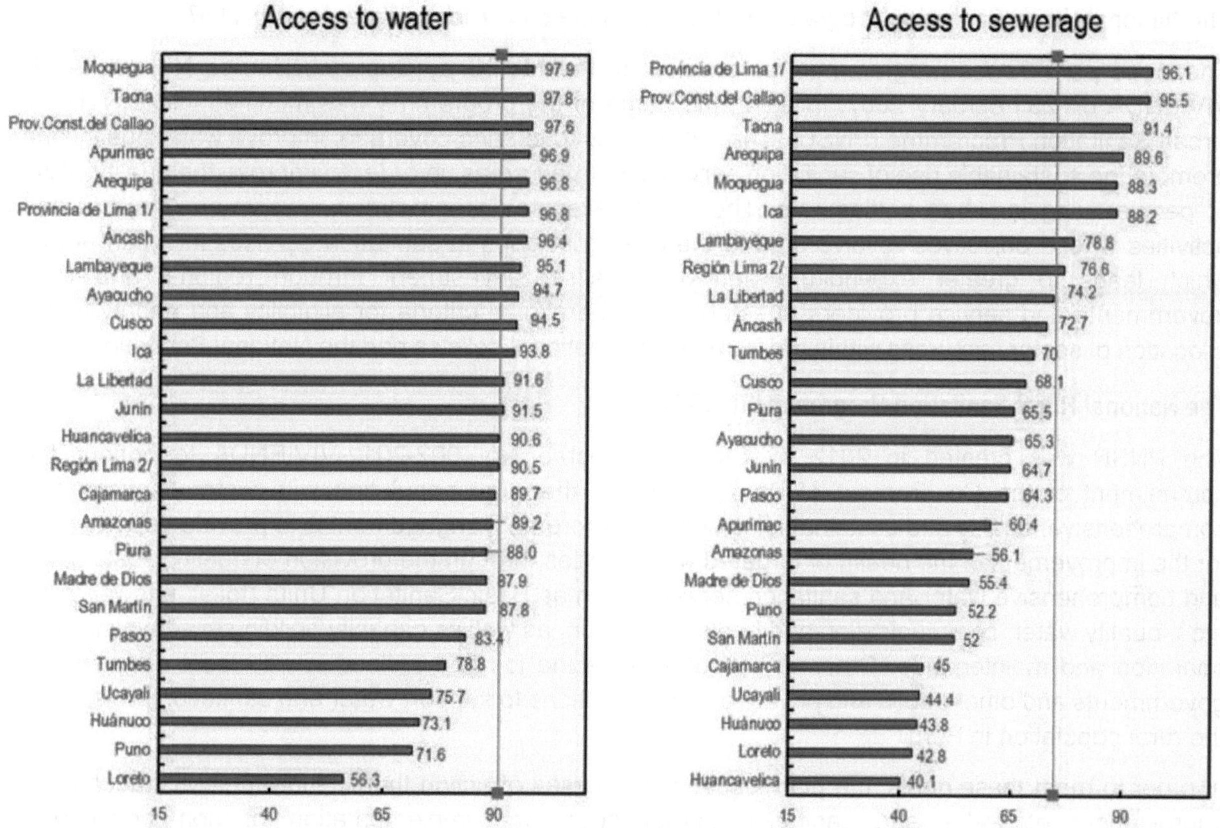

Source: 2019 data in INEI (2020[19]), *Perú: Formas de Acceso al Agua y Saneamiento Básico*, https://www.inei.gob.pe/media/MenuRecursivo/boletines/boletin_agua_y_saneamiento.pdf.

Urban and rural areas also face disparities regarding water quality, with 46.5% of the urban population having access to chlorinated water compared to only 2.2% for rural areas. In 41 hydrographic units (representing 26% of total hydrographic units), some parameters exceed Environmental Quality Standards (EQS) for water caused by the dumping of untreated wastewater, inadequate management of solid waste, environmental liabilities and informal and illegal mining (ANA, 2015[25]). Water quality degradation poses a number of challenges and leads to severe public health issues, although more epidemiological evidence and cost estimates would be needed to assess the full magnitude of the problem. In some areas, prevalently rural, there are high levels of chronic child anaemia. The World Food Programme (WFP) estimated[2] in 2018 that around 50% of childhood anaemia cases were linked to a lack of access to water and sanitation, as well as hygiene (CADE, 2018[26]). In 2017, anaemia affected 43.6% of girls and boys under 36 months.

Bridging gaps in access to sanitation services has become a national priority in Peru. The National Environmental Policy, the National Environmental Action Plan and the National Agenda of Environmental Action have all set the target of treating 100% of urban wastewater effluents by 2021, in line with the National Sanitation Plan (Box 1.3). However, the target is far from being achieved: in 2019, 22 companies registered 0% treatment of their wastewater, 18 of which did not have a wastewater treatment plant (WWTP) (SUNASS, 2020[27]).

Box 1.3. Sanitation policy efforts in Peruvian rural areas

The National Urban Sanitation Programme (PNSU) or *Agua para Todos* (Water for All), 2007

The *Agua para Todos* programme was created by the MVCS by Supreme Decree No. 006-2007-VIVIENDA on 23 February 2007. In 2012, the name of the programme was modified to the National Urban Sanitation Programme (PNSU). The PNSU aims to expand coverage, improve water quality and promote the sustainable use of sanitation services in urban areas, in order to improve the quality of life of people living in urban settlements. The PNSU executes programmes, investment projects and activities whose objectives revolve around the closing of gaps in sanitation services in urban areas, which leads to greater expenditure and decentralised investment through regional and local governments and service providers. It established operational criteria for eligibility and priority in the allocation of sector resources within the framework of national policies and the National Sanitation Plan.

The National Rural Sanitation Programme (PNSR), 2012

The PNSR was created in 2012 by Supreme Decree No. 002-2012-VIVIENDA to honour the commitment of the Government of Peru to provide the rural population with water services and comprehensive, quality and sustainable sanitation. Its foremost engagement is to provide opportunities for the improvement of the health of targeted rural families through the provision of quality, sustainable and comprehensive water and sanitation services such as Basic Sanitation Units (toilet, shower, sink, etc.), quality water, communication and health education, as well as capacity building in administration, operation and maintenance. Other objectives include the joint co-ordination with local and regional governments and other public and private entities of actions to support water and sanitation projects for the rural population in Peru.

In order to meet these goals, the plan focuses on courses of action that include the construction and improvement of water and sanitation infrastructure, the implementation of non-conventional technological solutions for access to drinking water, and capacity building for local and regional public authorities and citizens in different areas (e.g. management and maintenance of sanitation services and investment in sanitation).

Source: MVCS (2019[28]), *Programa Nacional de Saneamiento Rural*, http://pnsr.vivienda.gob.pe/portal/ (accessed on 12 March 2021); MVCS (2012[29]), *Manual de operaciones del programa de saneamiento*.

Water and environment

Peru is the third Latin American country in terms of dryland area, which covers 40% of its surface (MINAM, 2016[30]). In 2011, around 25.75% of the country suffered from desertification, while 3% was already desert. In terms of desertification, 80% of the affected area is concentrated in the Andes region. Of the 128.5 million hectares of national territory, 56.7% (72.9 million hectares) is affected by water erosion (INRENA, 2005[31]). The Coastal (23.8%) and Andes (72.5%) regions are the most affected by severe water erosion, which encourages desertification, aggravated by the scarcity of vegetation cover due to human activities (MINAGRI, 2017[32]). In addition, drainage and salinity issues, occurring along the coastal region, affect at least 25% of cultivated lands (World Bank, 2013[33]).

The country is also undergoing massive deforestation, especially in the Amazon rainforest. Peru is currently the 10th country in the world with the highest forest density, with more than half of the country (673 109 km^2) covered by forests (WWF, 2015[34]). Only Brazil has a larger tropical Amazonian forest area. More than 330 000 people directly depend on national forests for their livelihoods and many more depend on numerous ecosystem goods and services provided by forests, such as carbon fixation and storage, water regulation and the protection of Peru's biodiversity. However, between 2000 and 2014, Peru has lost an average of 118 081 hectares of forest every year (MINAM, 2016[35]). Deforestation is negatively affecting the capacity of the hydrological system to regulate itself.

The Andean Amazon is one of the areas of greatest biodiversity in the world and an essential part of the hydrological cycle in Peru. As such, the Amazon is often the location of the upper basin through which water flows to the Atlantic Ocean, as well as the location of many water diversion projects from the Atlantic to the Pacific watershed. Basins such as Madre de Dios and Inambari contain a wide diversity of Andean and Amazonian wetlands, which influence the hydrology of the Amazon basin (Barthem et al., 2016[36]). Some of the greatest threats affecting biodiversity in Peru are overfishing (with a large increase in the Amazon), the significant pollution of water in the Pacific watershed, invasive species, oil and mercury spills in the Amazonian rivers in the Atlantic watershed due quite often to illegal mining activities, climate change and the creation of hydroelectric plants (MINAM, 2019[37]). Inadequate water quality interferes with the provision of aquatic ecosystem services, including the economic use of water resources, such as crop irrigation, aquaculture, fishery, landscaping, recreational and navigation services and ecosystem services. Integrated water resources management and good environmental quality of water bodies are thus essential to the conservation of rainforest and biodiversity as well as to the health of the hydrological cycle.

Managing water under uncertainties

Wider governance failures in Peru challenge policy effectiveness and implementation in the water sector. In recent years, Peru has been undergoing political and social turmoil, which jeopardises the policy continuity and leadership required for public policies, including water and sanitation, to deliver intended outcomes. The democratic transition that started in late 2001 coincided with an economic boom, fuelled by high international commodity prices, a strong mining sector and expanding private consumption. However, this remarkable macroeconomic performance did not deliver on political, social and environmental grounds. In recent years, Peru ran into political challenges that can largely be traced to the 2016 Odebrecht affair.[3] Between 2018 and 2021, the Peruvian presidency changed four times. Despite recent instability, Peru has set water issues high on the political agenda. Since the presidency of Pedro Pablo Kuczynski (2016-18), ensuring universal and continuous access to water and sanitation[4] to the whole Peruvian population and across urban and rural areas has been seen as a major priority. Nevertheless, shifting from impact remedial approaches (mostly ad hoc, unplanned and reactive) to long-term risk management requires effective, efficient and inclusive governance, which is intrinsically a reflection of a country's culture, legal regime, legacy issues, political setup and territorial development patterns.

In the context of climate change, governance challenges come about with an unprecedented level of uncertainty. Between 2000 and 2020, floods in Peru affected an estimated 4.43 million people, of which 57 025 were made homeless, 1 666 were injured and 787 died (Guha-Sapir, 2021[38]). The flood that affected the most people (1.8 million) caused USD 3.1 billion in economic damages spread across 6 departments, including Lima, in 2017. The 2017 El Niño Costero was one of the country's worst meteorological events of the 21st century (MINAM, 2016[39]). In the Amazon, excess rainfall mainly comes from La Niña events. An increase in flooding also brings about *huaicos,* highly destructive mudslides occurring in upper altitude areas and accounting for up to 4% of total emergency events between 2003 and 2014 (MINAM, 2016[39]). *Huaicos* displace large volumes of land, impacting human settlements and infrastructure, and causing strife and loss of life. The *huaicos* carry sediments and do not allow adequate water capture by the treatment plant. Between 2000 and 2020, landslides affected 1 140 people, of which 307 died. El Niño is also at the origin of drought events in the southernmost areas of Peru. According to a SENAMHI analysis (2019[40]) of 20 Peruvian departments, excluding the arid areas of coastal departments (as they receive less than 2% of Peruvian rainfall annually), 10 moderate to extreme drought events occurred in Peru between 1981 and 2018. Managing water in the face of uncertainty demands: the acknowledgement of conflicts between the flows of services and the conservation of water assets (stocks); the challenging trade-offs implied in the joint provision of private and public goods from aquatic ecosystems; the critical importance of water use for economic growth but the essential role of water conservation for sustained progress and sustainable development; the pervasive externalities derived from the interconnected nature of the hydrological cycle; the relevance of long-term water security and the increasing uncertainty about future supplies that make extreme precautionary options a sensible policy attitude, and the high fixed (capital) cost of water infrastructures and the still unsolved problem of how to design effective and efficient cost- and benefit-sharing schemes.

References

ANA (2020), *Cuentas ambientales y económicas del agua en el Perú: Documento técnico 2018*, Autoridad Nacional del Agua, http://repositorio.ana.gob.pe/handle/20.500.12543/4705 (accessed on 10 February 2021). [41]

ANA (2019), *ANA REGISTRO*, http://snirh.ana.gob.pe/snirh/ConsultarRegistros.aspx. [6]

ANA (2015), *Calidad de agua en cuencas hidrográficas a nivel nacional*, http://repositorio.ana.gob.pe/handle/20.500.12543/2673 (accessed on 12 March 2021). [25]

ANA (2015), *Conflictos sociales y recursos hídricos*, Autoridad Nacional del Agua, https://repositorio.ana.gob.pe/handle/20.500.12543/2807. [21]

ANA (2013), *Plan Nacional de Recursos Hídricos del Perú: Memoria*, Autoridad Nacional del Agua, http://www.ana.gob.pe/sites/default/files/plannacionalrecursoshidricos2013.pdf. [2]

Barthem, R. et al. (2016), *INAMBARI Hacia un enfoque integrado de la gestión de cuencas hidrográficas, available at: https://programs.wcs.org/beta/R*, https://programs.wcs.org/beta/Resources/Publications/Publications-Search-II/ctl/view/mid/13340/pubid/DMX3216900000.aspx. [36]

CADE (2018), *CADE Ejecutivos 2018*, https://www.ipae.pe/cade-ejecutivos-2018/ (accessed on 12 March 2021). [26]

FAO (2015), *Perfil de País – Perú, AQUASTAT Informes*, Food and Agriculture Organization, United Nations, http://www.fao.org/3/ca0447es/CA0447ES.pdf. [4]

Guha-Sapir, D. (2021), *EM-DAT, the International Disaster Database*, CRED/UCLouvain, Brussels, http://www.emdat.be (accessed on 18 February 2021). [38]

ILO (2020), "Impact on the labour market and income in Latin America and the Caribbean, Second edition, Technical note", International Labour Organization, https://www.ilo.org/wcmsp5/groups/public/---americas/---ro-lima/documents/publication/wcms_756697.pdf. [9]

INEI (2021), *Medio Ambiente*, Instituto Nacional de Estadística de Informática, https://www.inei.gob.pe/estadisticas/indice-tematico/medio-ambiente/. [23]

INEI (2020), *Perú: Formas de Acceso al Agua y Saneamiento Básico - Nro 09*, Instituto Nacional de Estadística e Informática. [19]

INEI (2018), *Resultados Definitivos de los Censos Nacionales 2017*, Instituto Nacional de Estadística e Informática, https://www.inei.gob.pe/media/MenuRecursivo/publicaciones_digitales/Est/Lib1544/. [1]

INEI (2017), *III Censo De Comunidades Nativas 2017: Resultados Definitivos, Tomo 1: Lima*, Instituto Nacional de Estadística e Informática, https://www.inei.gob.pe/media/MenuRecursivo/publicaciones_digitales/Est/Lib1598/TOMO_01.pdf. [16]

INEI (2015), *Anuario de Estadísticas Ambientales 2015, Agua, available at:*, Instituto Nacional de Estadística e Informática, https://www.inei.gob.pe/media/MenuRecursivo/publicaciones_digitales/Est/Lib1342/cap03.pdf. [5]

INEI (2009), *Censos Nacionales 2007: XI de Población y VI de Vivienda. Resultados de Población y Vivineda en las Comunidades Indígenas.* [18]

INEI/UNFPA (2020), *Estado de la Población Peruana 2020*, https://www.inei.gob.pe/media/MenuRecursivo/publicaciones_digitales/Est/Lib1743/Libro.pdf. [3]

INRENA (2005), *Mapa de Deforestación de la Amazonía Peruana, Memoria Descriptiva*, https://sinia.minam.gob.pe/documentos/mapa-deforestacion-amazonia-peruana-memoria-descriptiva. [31]

MEF (2020), *Marco Macroeconómico Multianual 2021-2024.* [8]

MINAGRI (2019), *Boletín Estadístico de Comercio Exterior Agrario*, https://www.midagri.gob.pe/portal/boletin-estadistico-de-comercio-exterior-agrario. [12]

MINAGRI (2017), *Programa Presupuestal Multisectorial 0089: "Reducción De La Degradación De Los Suelos Agrarios" Anexo 2*, https://www.minagri.gob.pe/portal/download/programas-presupuestales/inf-programa/anexo2-pp89-2017.pdf. [32]

MINAM (2019), *Sexto Informe Nacional sobre Diversidad Biológica: La Biodiversidad en Cifras*, https://cdn.www.gob.pe/uploads/document/file/360831/La_Biodiversidad_en_Cifras_final.pdf. [37]

MINAM (2016), *Estrategia Nacional de Lucha Contra la Desertificación y la Sequía 2016-2030.* [30]

MINAM (2016), *La Conservación de Bosques en el Perú: Conservando los bosques en un contexto de cambio climático como aporte al crecimiento verde (2011-2016)*, http://www.minam.gob.pe/informessectoriales/wp-content/uploads/sites/112/2016/02/11-La-conservaci%C3%B3n-de-bosques-en-el-Per%C3%BA.pdf. [35]

MINAM (2016), *Tercera Comunicación Nacional del Perú a la Convención de Cambio Marco de las Naciones Unidas sobre el Cambio Climático*, http://www.minam.gob.pe/wp-content/uploads/2016/05/Tercera-Comunicaci%C3%B3n.pdf. [39]

MVCS (2019), *Programa Nacional de Saneamiento Rural*, http://pnsr.vivienda.gob.pe/portal/ (accessed on 12 March 2021). [28]

MVCS (2012), *Manual de operaciones del programa de saneamiento.* [29]

OECD (2020), "COVID-19 in Latin America and the Caribbean: Regional socio-economic implications and policy priorities", *OECD Policy Responses to Coronavirus (COVID-19)*, OECD, Paris, https://www.oecd.org/coronavirus/policy-responses/covid-19-in-latin-america-and-the-caribbean-regional-socio-economic-implications-and-policy-priorities-93a64fde/. [10]

OECD (2019), *Linking Indigenous Communities with Regional Development*, OECD Rural Policy Reviews, OECD Publishing, Paris, https://doi.org/10.1787/3203c082-en. [20]

OECD (2017), "Mining regions and their cities: Scoping paper", OECD, Paris, http://www.oecd.org/cfe/regional-policy/Mining%20discussion%20paper%20FINAL_CM.pdf. [13]

Ombudsman's Office (2015), "Social conflicts and water resources", Defensoría del Pueblo. [15]

PCM (2020), *Willaqniki N° 12-2019: Monthly Report December 2019.* [22]

SENAMHI (2019), *Caracterización espacio-temporal de la sequía en los departamentos altoandinos del Perú*, https://www.senamhi.gob.pe/load/file/01401SENA-78.pdf. [40]

SUNASS (2020), *Benchmarking regulatorio 2020 de las Empresas Prestadoras (EP)*, https://cdn.www.gob.pe/uploads/document/file/1467031/Benchmarking%20regulatorio%202020%20de%20las%20Empresas%20Prestadoras%20%28EP%29.pdf. [27]

UN (2017), *Country (or area) | SDG 6 Data*, https://www.sdg6data.org/country-or-area/Peru (accessed on 12 March 2021). [24]

World Bank (2021), *Agriculture, forestry, and fishing, value added (% of GDP)*, https://data.worldbank.org/indicator/NV.AGR.TOTL.ZS (accessed on 12 March 2021). [11]

World Bank (2021), *Peru Overview*, https://www.worldbank.org/en/country/peru/overview (accessed on 17 March 2021). [7]

World Bank (2015), *Latinoamérica Indígena en el Siglo XXI.* [17]

World Bank (2013), *El Futuro del Riego en el Perú: Desafíos y Recomendaciones*, http://www.worldbank.org (accessed on 18 March 2021). [33]

WWF (2019), *El bioma amazónico frente a la contaminación por mercurio.* [14]

WWF (2015), *La Deforestación en el Perú: Cómo las comunidades indígenas, agencias gubernamentales, organizaciones sin fines de lucro y negocios trabajan juntos para detener la tala de los bosques*, World Wide Fund for Nature, https://d2ouvy59p0dg6k.cloudfront.net/downloads/la_deforestacion_en_el_peru.pdf. [34]

Notes

[1] Departments with the lowest coverage are Tumbes (78.9%), Huánuco and Ucayali (76%), Puno (69.7%) and Loreto (56.8%). The highest coverage areas (higher than 95%) can be found in the departments of Áncash, Apurímac, Arequipa, Ayacucho, Callao, Lima, Moquegua and Tacna.

[2] World Food Programme in Peru, Peru's 2018 Annual Executive Conference (CADE).

[3] The Odebrecht Affair is an ongoing corruption case involving the Brazilian construction company Odebrecht and political figures, including heads of state, mainly in Latin America. In Peru, four former heads of state are accused of being involved in this corruption scandal.

[4] "*Saneamiento*" in most Latin American countries, including Peru, includes (drinking/potable) water supply and sanitation (collection of wastewater effluents), but also other services in the urban water cycle such as water reuse. Article 1 of Decreto Legislativo 1280 is even more relevant for the purposes of definition. Sanitation services are defined as follows: potable water, sewerage, wastewater treatment, effluent discharge or reclaimed water reuse, and final disposal of waste, both in urban and rural areas.

2 Multi-level water governance in Peru

This chapter argues that despite the existence of a consolidated legal framework on water in Peru and the progress made in terms of integrated water resources management, co-ordination across levels of government should be strengthened towards an effective multi-sectoral approach to water. The chapter emphasises multi-level governance gaps and suggests policy recommendations to bridge them, building on international experience.

The legal framework for water resources management

There is a consolidated legal framework in relation to water management in Peru. The relevant legislation for water resources management and the protection of aquatic ecosystems stems from the 1993 Political Constitution of Peru, affirming the promotion of the sustainable use of natural resources and the right to the protection of health (Articles 7, 66 and 67). The National Environmental Policy (Supreme Decree No. 012-2009-MINAM) is the reference framework for sustainable development, taking into account international treaties, commitments and declarations endorsed by Peru in environmental matters. Peru has been endowed with specific water-related legislation since 2009. The Water Resources Law (No. 29338/2009) and its implementing regulation (Supreme Decree No. 001-2010-AG) set the legal and institutional framework for water resources management. It also established the National Water Resources Management System (SNGRH) and its planning instruments (see below). State Policy No. 33/2012 on Water Resources (Acuerdo Nacional, 2012[1])[1] is the political and technical instrument that acknowledges water as part of the public domain and recognises the human right to water and sanitation, following the United Nations (UN) Assembly Declarations in 2010 and 2015. It also highlights the relevance of implementing integrated water resources management (IWRM) in order to guarantee the equitable and sustainable use of water nationwide.

The IWRM in Peru is implemented through the National Water Resources Management System (*Sistema Nacional de Gestión de los Recursos Hídricos*, SNGRH) (Figure 2.1). The SNGRH is the set of institutions, principles and norms allowing for the articulation and co-ordination across public and private entities to meet water demands, avoid conflicts, carry out projects, etc. It is embodied in the National System of Environmental Management (*Sistema Nacional de Gestión Ambiental,* SNGA). The SNGA comprises the SNGRH but also the National System of Natural Protected Areas, the National System of Environmental Assessment and Control, the System of Environmental Impact Assessment, and the National System of Environmental Information. In principle, the SNGRH ensures the integrated, participatory and multi-sectoral management of water to promote its sustainable use, conservation and quality. It also implements, oversees and evaluates compliance with key planning initiatives, such as the National Water Resources Policy and Strategy (*Política y Estrategia Nacional de Recursos Hídricos*, PENRH) and the National Water Resources Plan (*Plan Nacional de los Recursos Hídricos*, PNRH) at all levels of government, fostering stakeholder engagement and co-ordination across all members.

The SNGRH is formed by different ministries, regional and local authorities, water user organisations and civil society groups. The National Water Authority (ANA) is the governing body of the SNGRH, which is composed of: the Ministry of the Environment (MINAM); the Ministry of Agricultural Development and Irrigation (MIDAGRI); the Ministry of Housing, Construction and Sanitation (MVCS); the Ministry of Energy and Mining (MINEM); the Ministry of Production (PRODUCE); the Ministry of Health (MINSA); regional governments; local governments; water user organisations; water and sanitation service providers (*Empresas Prestadoras de Servicios de Saneamiento*, EPs), municipal operators [*Unidades de Gestión Municipal*], specialised operators [*Operadores especializados*] and community-based organisations [*Organizaciones comunales*]); organisations representing farmers, peasant communities and native communities; and other public entities linked to water resources management and water services delivery such as the National Superintendence of Sanitation Services, the economic regulator of sanitation services (*Superintendencia Nacional de Servicios de Saneamiento,* SUNASS), the Peruvian National Service for Meteorology and Hydrology (SENAMHI), the Supervisory Body for Investment in Energy and Mining (OSINERGMIN), the Agency for Environmental Assessment and Enforcement (OEFA), the National Service of Environmental Certification for Sustainable Investments (SENACE), the Directorate-General for Captaincy and Coast Guard of Peru (DICAPI) and sectoral environmental authorities.

Figure 2.1. Composition of the National Water Resources Management System in Peru

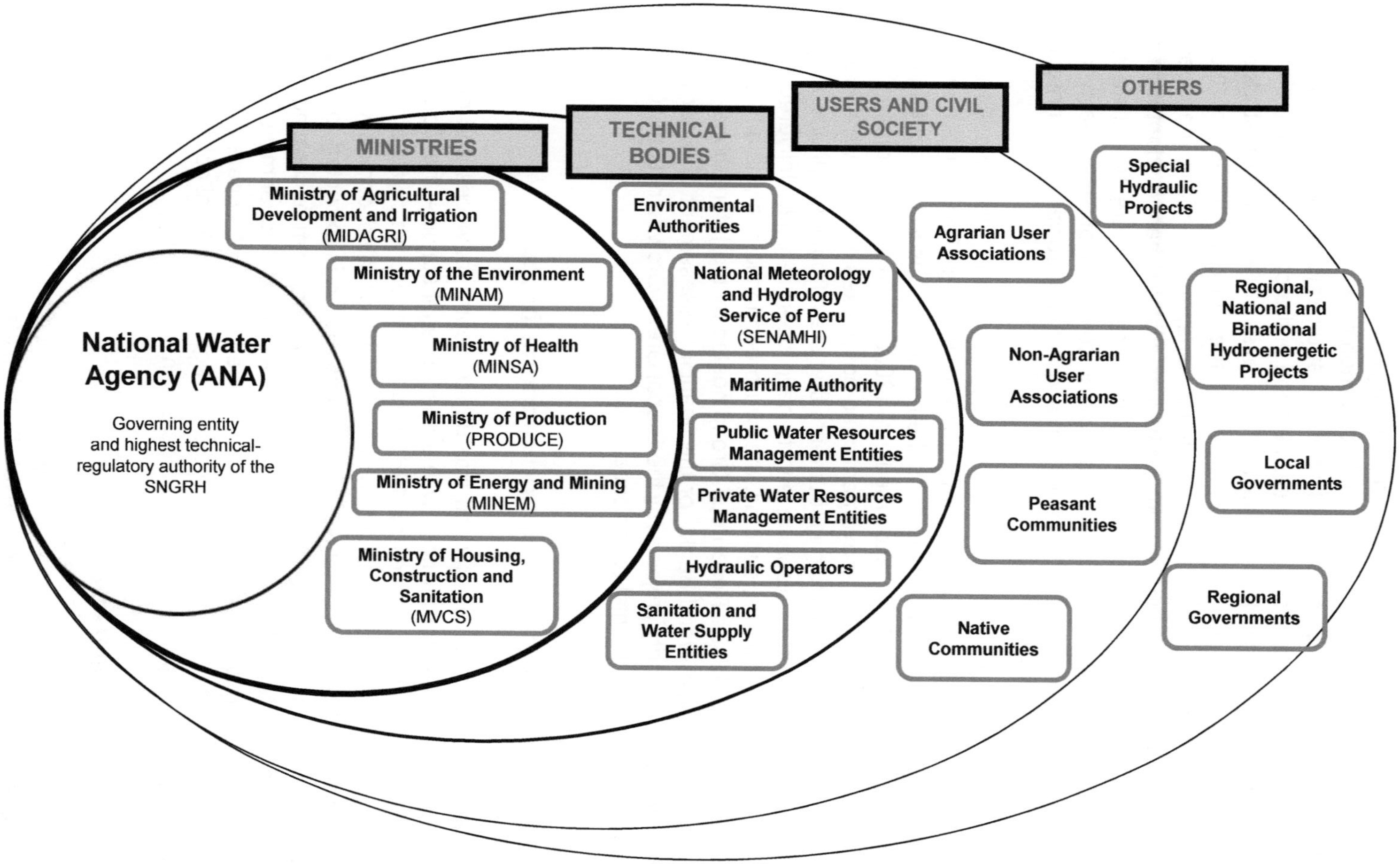

Source: Author's elaboration based on ANA (2017[2]), *Marco de Gestión Ambiental y Social del Proyecto de Gestión Integrada de los Recursos Hídricos en Diez Cuencas Hidrográficas (Código SNIP N° 302961)*, https://www.ana.gob.pe/proyectos-ana/pgirh.

Two main tools are part of the SNGRH: the National Policy and Strategy on Water Resources and the National Water Resources Plan.

- State Policy No. 33/2012 on Water Resources is the benchmark to develop the water resources management instruments that complement the scope of the Water Resources Law. On this basis, the National Water Resources Policy and Strategy (PENRH) (Supreme Decree No. 06-2015-MINAGRI) is one of the main planning tools considered in the SNGRH. The PENRH comprises "principles, guidance, strategies and public policy instruments guiding actions to be taken both by the public and private sectors to meet water demand of the country in the short, medium and long term". The 2015 PENRH includes 5 policy pillars or axes, 18 intervention strategies and 85 action lines formulated on the basis of the analysis of the current situation of the country's water resources.[1] The five water policy axes are quantity management, quality management, opportunity management, water culture management, as well as climate change adaptation and weather and climate extreme events. The main objective of each axis is to ensure the satisfaction of current and future water demands, as well as to ensure water conservation, the quality of available water resources and its efficient and sustainable use, according to social, environmental and economic criteria (ANA and MINAGRI, 2016[3]) .
- The 2015 National Water Resources Plan (PNRH, Supreme Decree No. 013-2015-MINAGRI) is the strategic planning instrument for the implementation of the PENRH. It is formulated on the basis of diagnosis at the basin level and contains the financing gaps to be bridged so as to meet water demands in the short (2021) and medium (2035) terms. Investments are grouped into 30 programmes aligned with the abovementioned policy axes and intervention strategies set up in the PENRH. Beyond those planning instruments that stem from legal provisions (i.e. Art. 99 of the Water Resources Law), other planning efforts have been recently delivered with the support of multilateral and bilateral donors, such as: the hydro-economic analysis and prioritisation of water resources (by the 2030 Water Resources Group hosted by the International Finance Corporation-IFC and currently by the World Bank); or the financial assessment of water projects in Peru and the implementation of priority projects (by the Global Green Growth Institute, GGGI, a treaty-based, international, inter-governmental organisation).

Institutional mapping of water roles and responsibilities

The territory of Peru is administratively divided into departments, provinces and districts. It is currently composed of 24 departments and 2 provinces with a special legal status – the Constitutional Province of Callao and the Province of Lima – as well as 196 other provinces, which as of mid-2016 were further divided into 1 874 districts. A process of regionalisation, which also comes with relevant levels of decentralisation and devolution, is underway. This process, which is expected to be confirmed through binding referenda, is mainly supported by fiscal incentives, with the aim of creating new regional entities through merging departments (OECD/ECLAC, 2017[4]). As such, the administrative decentralisation process has fiscal and economic consequences, such as the transfer of a share of the revenues collected via the so-called mining exports excise (*canon minero*) to regional and local governments. This has led to an increase in municipal and regional fiscal resources and investments.

Who does what at the national level?

The section below will describe in-depth who does what at different levels of government in the water sector (Figures 2.2 and 2.3). At the highest level, the Presidency of the Council of Ministers, beyond co-ordinating national and sectoral policies, deals with social conflicts that relate to the water sector, amongst others. The Ministry of Economy and Finance, in particular through the Agency for Private Investment Promotion, promotes public infrastructure works in water resources management and sanitation services. Regarding water resources management, the National Water Authority (ANA) is the governing body, while the Ministry of the Environment and the Ministry of Agricultural Development and Irrigation, where ANA is located, are key institutions for water resources management. The Ministry of Housing, Construction and Sanitation is the governing body for sanitation, while SUNASS is the decentralised public regulatory body responsible for regulating, supervising and assessing the provision of urban and rural water and sanitation services. The Ministry of Health and the Ministry of Development and Social Inclusion also contribute to the national policies in relation to safe drinking water and sanitation.

*The Presidency of the Council of Ministers (*Presidencia del Consejo de Ministros*, PCM) or Cabinet Office*

The PCM or Cabinet Office is the body responsible for the co-ordination of national and sectoral policies that are the responsibility of the country's executive power and for the co-ordination with other state powers (legislative and judicial), constitutional bodies, regional and local governments and civil society.[2] The PCM has legal powers for the modernisation of administration, territorial development, decentralisation, spatial demarcation, public dialogue and social consultation, digital government, communication of the policy actions of the central government and other powers assigned by law.[3] Through its Secretariat of Social Management and Dialogue (SGSD), it collects information, classifies and addresses a range of selected social conflicts dealt with by the cabinet itself, including on water use. Beyond the PCM, other institutions in the country (such as ANA, the Ministry of Mining and Energy, a Special Attorney for Environmental Crimes and the Ombudsman Office) also gather information systematically on social conflicts around water use.

*The Ministry of Economy and Finance (*Ministerio de Economía y Finanzas*, MEF)*

The MEF is the governing body in terms of economic and financial policy at the national and sectoral levels and different government scales. It is in charge of the administrative systems of the public budget, the Treasury, public debt, national accounting and public investment. The MEF is at the core of decisions on public financing, as it allocates fiscal budget, promotes private engagement in the sanitation sector, through the Private Investment Promotion Agency (*Agencia de Promoción de la Inversión Privada*, PROINVERSION). It administers the consolidated system for the registration, evaluation and monitoring of public investment (*Invierte.pe,* former National System of Public Investment or *Sistema Nacional de Inversión Pública*, SNIP), the debt of public companies with the National Housing Fund (*Fondo Nacional de Vivienda*, FONAVI) and the National Superintendence of Customs and Tax Administration (*Superintendencia Nacional de Aduanas y de Administración Tributaria*, SUNAT).[4] The Ministry of Economy and Finance set up a programme of incentives to improve the municipal management of public services. The incentives are released upon the achievement of results (*Presupuesto por Resultado*: Outcome-oriented Budget). While this mechanism is not linked to the National Sanitation Plan, it is worth noting that the Ministry of Housing, Construction and Sanitation (MVCS) awards incentives based on results in relation to the implementation of the National Urban Sanitation Programme and the National Rural Sanitation Programme.

The Agency for Private Investment Promotion, PROINVERSION, is responsible for implementing national private investment promotion policies. PROINVERSION mainly promotes private investments in public services and public infrastructure through public-private partnerships (PPPs), either led by public or private initiatives. It also provides assistance to subnational public entities, upon request, and information services to investors, and helps create an attractive environment for private investments. Beyond PPPs and similar contractual arrangements, PROINVERSION also promotes the participation of private companies in the development of public infrastructure works (in different sectors, including water resources management and sanitation services) which are performed by subnational levels of government through a mechanism called Works for Taxes. This is a unique mechanism in Peru and its adoption is currently being explored by other countries in the region such as Colombia.

Figure 2.2. Institutional mapping for water resources management in Peru

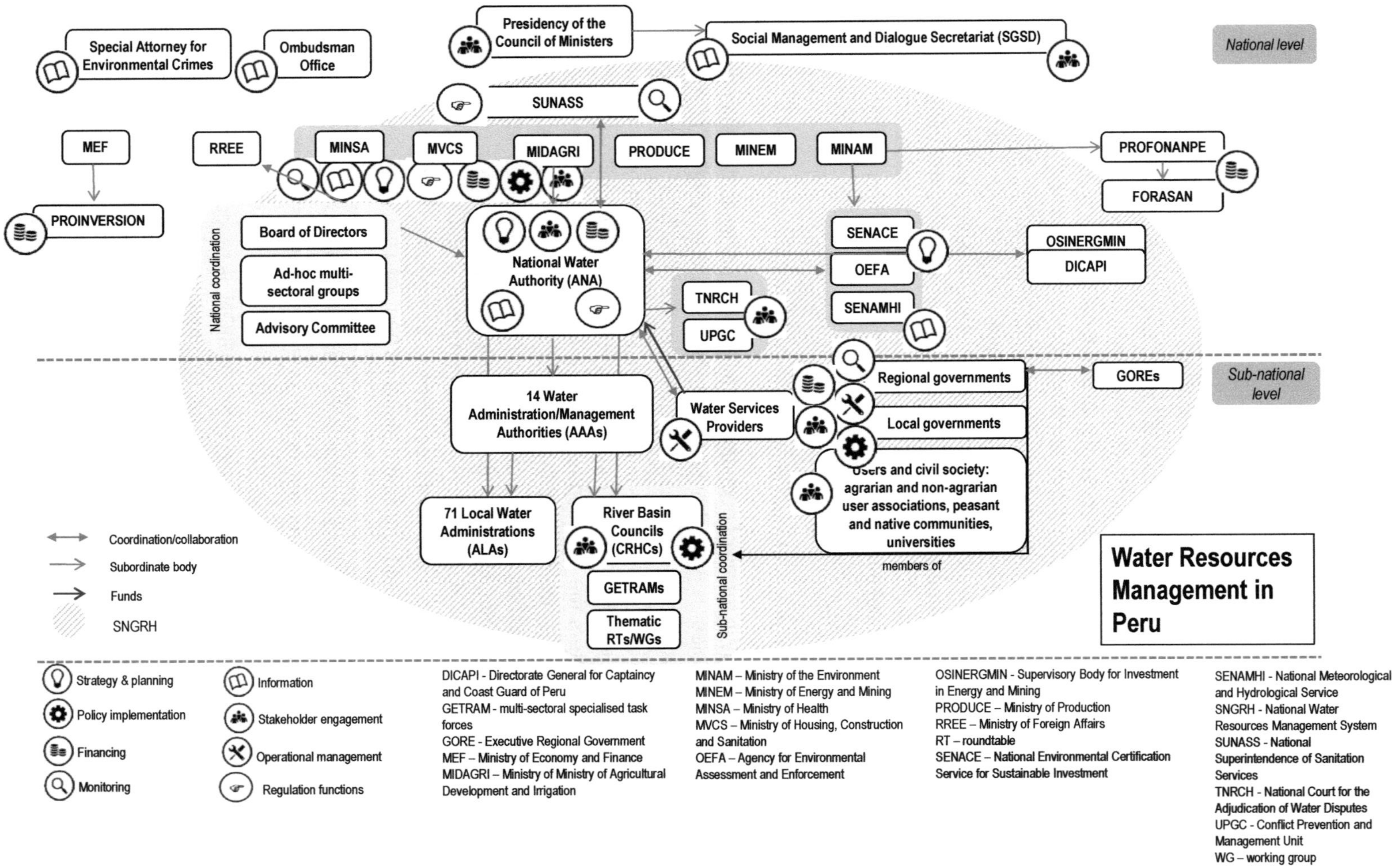

Water resources management

The National Water Authority (*Autoridad Nacional del Agua*, ANA)

ANA is the governing body for integrated water resources management (IWRM) policy. It is a specialised technical and regulatory body with its own budget and legal status. It was created in March 2008 by Legislative Decree No. 997. ANA is the governing body of the SNGRH and is as such responsible for its operation and co-ordination across its members. It elaborates, manages, executes and supervises the National Water Resources Policy and Strategy, devises regulations and establishes procedures for integrated and multi-sectoral management of water resources (both surface and groundwater). Its decision is binding for approval of Environmental Management Instruments (*Instrumento de Gestión Ambiental*, IGA) related to water resources.[1] A significant number of public entities related to water resources management co-ordinate their actions with ANA:[2] the National Superintendence of Sanitation Services (SUNASS), the National Meteorology and Hydrology Service (SENAMHI), the Supervisory Body for Investment in Energy and Mining (OSINERGMIN), the Agency for Environmental Assessment and Enforcement (OEFA), the Directorate-General of Captaincy and Coast Guard of Peru (DICAPI), and other sectoral, environmental authorities and water and sanitation service providers (EPs).

ANA is a deconcentrated body, providing coverage to the 159 river basins in Peru (ANA, 2014[5]). It does so by means of a central headquarters in Lima and 14 regional offices or Administrative Water Authorities (*Autoridades Administrativas del Agua*, AAAs),[3] responsible for 14 wide hydrographic regions, 71 Local Administrative Water Authorities (*Administraciones Locales del Agua*, ALAs) and 13 River Basin Councils (*Consejos de Recursos Hídricos de Cuenca*, CRHC). The Ministry of Foreign Affairs participates in and co-ordinates with ANA on the management of the 34 transboundary watersheds (OECD/ECLAC, 2017[4]) and the necessary work in international conventions and other agreements.[4]

ANA leads the Nationally Determined Contribution (NDC) on Water. The NDC Water aligns with the UN Sustainable Development Goals (SDGs) and identifies specific objectives and indicators that will be reported to the United Nations Framework Convention on Climate Change (UNFCCC) by 2025 and 2030. It also identifies the enabling conditions that are required (financing, information, capabilities, regulations), the roles and functions of the different actors involved in promoting and informing adaptation measures that include actions in each of the four specific subcomponents to increase water supply, achieve greater efficiency of use and better water management in a context of climate change. The NDC Water is carried out under the leadership of ANA and the technical support of MINAM, along with the participation of MIDAGRI, MINEM, the MVCS, the National Civil Defense System (*Instituto Nacional de Defensa Civil*, INDECI), SERNANP INAIGEM.

The Ministry of the Environment (*Ministerio del Ambiente*, MINAM)

MINAM is involved in water resources management (both surface runoff and groundwater) and multi-purpose water infrastructure. MINAM has responsibilitiesin protecting headwaters, issuingissues opinions on environmentally vulnerable areas,[5] promoting watershed protection and preservation,[6] and developing strategies and plans for the prevention and adaptation to the effects of climate change on water availability at the local, regional and national scales.[7] The ministry develops, conducts, supervises and executes the National Environmental Policy.[8,9] It is the governing body of the National Environmental Management System (SNGA), within which both the National Water Resources Policy and its strategy and the National Water Resources Plan are elaborated.[10] MINAM is responsible for approving and overseeing the application of environmental prevention, control and restoration instruments related to control of the reclamation and reuse of wastewater effluents, amongst others.[11] MINAM is the governing body in ecosystem services.[12] It is responsible for designing, regulating and furthering policies, legal standards and procedures for the development, implementation and supervision of the Ecosystem Services Compensation Mechanism (*Mecanismo de Retribución por Servicios Ecosistémicos*, MERESE). Along these lines, according to the regulation of Law No. 30215 (Supreme Decree No. 009-2016-MINAM), "water regulation" and "natural risk regulation" are ecosystem services liable to participation in MERESE. In some cases, while legal powers are with ANA, there are overlapping competencies between ANA and MINAM on site.

SENAMHI, SENACE and OEFA are bodies attached to MINAM. SENAMHI is the National Meteorological and Hydrological Service, which is in charge of generating and providing meteorological, hydrological and climatic information and knowledge in a reliable, timely and accessible manner. SENACE is in charge of environmental impact assessment studies, regulated in Law No. 27446,[13] of public, private or mixed capital investment projects that involve activities, constructions, works and other commercial and service activities that may cause significant environmental impact, also in terms of use of water resources. The Agency for Environmental Assessment and Enforcement (OEFA) and the ANA evaluate Environmental Quality Standards (ECA) for natural water bodies. More precisely the OEFA determines the quality of natural bodies, coordinating it supervision with the ANA. The Directorate-General for Environmental Health and Food Safety (*Dirección General de Salud Ambiental e Inocuidad Alimentaria*, DIGESA) evaluates the quality parameters of water for human consumption. MINAM chairs the National Wetlands Committee, a multi-sectoral commission that promotes the sound management of wetlands[14] in addition to the implementation of the commitments of the Ramsar Convention. MINAM provides technical assistance and support for the development of a number of relevant regional or co-operation planning tools (Box 2.1).

The Ministry of Agricultural Development and Irrigation (*Ministerio de Desarrollo Agrario y Riego*, MIDAGRI)

MIDAGRI, through ANA, is the governing body and the highest technical-legal authority of the SNGRH and more specifically in terms of water resources management.[15] MIDAGRI is thus the entity to which ANA is attached. MIDAGRI issues the supreme decrees proposed by ANA in order to regulate the integrated and multi-sectoral management of water resources.[16]

MIDAGRI implements a number of financing mechanisms for water management projects. These include the Sierra Azul Fund Implementing Unit, which aims to increase irrigation water security through the natural retention and harvesting of water from the high Andean agricultural and highland areas, favouring primarily those farmers with lower levels of income, in a situation of poverty and extreme poverty. This fund finances infrastructure and irrigation investment projects, irrigation modernisation and water retention and harvesting interventions, within the framework of the National Multi-year Programming and Investment Management System (Invierte.pe). This fund is intended to contribute to closing gaps established by the sector in Ministerial Resolution No. 493-2019-MINAGRI.

Box 2.1. Regional and co-operation planning tools for water management in Peru

The Regional Water Fund (FORASAN) is designed to capture, manage and channel investment resources to guarantee the quantity and quality of water resources in the Chira-Piura basin). FORASAN is a regional fund created by the resolution of a watershed council that received contributions from international development aid. FORASAN is administered by PROFONANPE and therefore could receive public funds; however, local entities have mostly decided not to use this financial facility to channel funds toward desired projects. Since private funds cannot receive public resources, they require a large amount of capital (if it is a trust fund operating off of returns) or large, consistent contributions by private sector entities, in order to effectively carry out natural infrastructure investments. In Peru, neither currently exists. Funding for natural infrastructure investments is currently available from regional and local governments through one-off public investment projects; the only assured flow exclusively for natural infrastructure investments are allocated in water tariffs from water utilities. These tariffs do not contribute money to a fund; rather, the tariff funds are kept in a separate account within the utility, for use exclusively in MERESE projects. The same applies to resources that the rate assigns to disaster risk reduction and climate change adaptation.

PROFONANPE, a private non-profit and public interest entity authorised by law to manage and administer public funds, affiliated with MINAM, is, in turn, a fund for the promotion of protected natural areas in Peru. It has proved a useful (if limited) tool for biodiversity conservation and climate change adaptation. In 2020, the merger by absorption of Profonanpe FONAM was approved, becoming the only environmental fund in Peru (Sixth Provision of URGENCY DECREE No. 022-2020) and expanding its competence to areas such as remediation of environmental liabilities.

AQUAFONDO is a private non-profit entity that works to conserve and protect natural water sources that supply the population of Greater Lima and Callao: it is not authorised to manage or administer public funds. Hence, it acts as a project developer and implementer that receives funds through grants, donations and contracts, primarily from philanthropic sources and private companies. Aquafondo is not the only entity that plays the role of project developer and implementer for the conservation of the watersheds of the Metropolitan Area of Lima (Peru): a number of non-governmental organisations (NGOs) also work on these issues, including for example Alternativa, Caritas Peru, The Mountain Institute and Global Water Partnership. A critical role is also played by the Natural Infrastructure for Water Security (NIWS) project, funded by the United States Agency for International Development (USAID) and the Government of Canada, which aims to scale up investments in natural infrastructure in Peru to safeguard natural water supply sources and increase climate resilience.

Source: MINAM (2011[6]), *Conversatorio internacional: Mecanismos de financiamiento para la conservación de los ecosistemas y la biodiversidad*, repositorio.ana.gob.pe/bitstream/handle/20.500.12543/4433/ANA0002933.pdf?sequence=1&isAllowed=y ; Albán Contreras, L. E. (2017[7]), *El Fondo del Agua Quiroz-Chira: Un mecanismo de gestión para los ecosistemas de montaña de Piura, Perú - Sistematización de la experiencia*, https://cooperacionsuiza.pe/wp-content/uploads/2017/02/faqch-final-web.pdf.

Drinking water and sanitation

The Ministry of Housing, Construction and Sanitation (*Ministerio de Vivienda, Construcción y Saneamiento*, MVCS)

The MVCS is the governing body for sanitation,[17] but also housing, construction, spatial development and urban development. It has exclusive power over the development, planning, co-ordination, implementation and overseeing of national specific and related policies in relation to sanitation services as public service (Figure 2.3). In particular, it fosters efficient management and delivery of services by providers through the Sanitation Sector Capacity-building System (SFCS) and related mechanisms, determines through norms and plans how to close the gaps in infrastructure and promotes quality and sustainability in the delivery of sanitation services, including wastewater treatment.

The MVCS leads, manages and administers the Water and Sanitation Information System (SIAS),[18] which contains sectoral information on the infrastructure and management indicators of sanitation services in urban and rural areas. The Rural Water, Sanitation and Hygiene (WASH) Information System (DATASS), which started in 2014, is led by the MVCS with the collaboration of the MEF and Ministry of Development and Social Inclusion (MIDIS). Prior to its implementation, there was very poor information on rural WASH. Currently, a virtual platform with 9 000 users provides information on sanitation services in around 100 000 population centres. Regional and local governments are responsible for information collecting, entering and upgrading (under Legislative Decree No. 1280). The objective was to promote the use of information decision-support systems in the rural sanitation sector, hence paving the way for the identification of coverage gaps (MVCS, 2018[8]). DATASS Geographic Information Systems (GIS) includes information from MINAM, MIDAGRI, DIGESA, SUNASS, the Technical Agency for the Administration of Sanitation Services (OTASS) and the MVCS (MVCS, 2019[9]).

The National Sanitation Plan is the main instrument for the implementation of the sectoral public policy to achieve universal coverage of sanitation services. It contains, among others, information from the Regional Sanitation Plans on the existing gaps, establishing the programming investment. The plan is prepared for a time span of five years and is updated annually. Its compliance is mandatory by the sanitation service providers (EPs). The 2017 National Sanitation Plan[19] establishes that SUNASS is responsible for making the necessary provisions aimed at promoting, designing and implementing MERESE. A mid-term evaluation of the 2017-21 National Sanitation Plan has been carried out, which mostly shows that targets for 2019 were not met and also points to a failure in achieving targets for 2020 and the bicentennial of the Independence of Peru (2021). Emergency Decree No. 011-2020 aims at closing gaps in the water and sanitation sector, whilst delivering a sustainable and quality level of service, and managing services in an efficient way.

Together with the Ministry of Health (MINSA), the MVCS works for the implementation of the strategy to increase the share of rural households with access to chlorinated water in the rural areas of Peru.[20] The Water for All programme, created in 2007,[21] had the objective to provide low-income households with adequate sanitation services, potable water and sewerage. The National Rural Sanitation Programme (*Programa Nacional de Saneamiento Rural*, PNSR), created in 2012,[22] aims to serve the neediest rural populations with comprehensive, quality and sustainable water and sanitation services. Within the framework of the PNSR, the MVCS co-ordinates with the Ministry of Economy and Finance (MEF) by means of the Incentive Programme for Municipal Management Improvement and Modernisation (PI) (see section below on co-ordination mechanisms).

The Technical Agency for the Administration of Sanitation Services (*Organismo Técnico de la Administración de los Servicios de Saneamiento*, OTASS)

OTASS, attached to the MVCS,[23] promotes and implements the policy of the MVCS regarding the management, administration and provision of sanitation services. It was created in 2013, though it became operational in 2015 as a consequence of weaknesses detected in the management and administration of public water and sanitation service providers (EPs), many of them being insolvent by then. OTASS is also mandated and empowered to take control on public EPs under municipal ownership in case of financial and operational insolvency, so as to improve their performance. OTASS is funded through transfers from the central government (Treasury), donations from international development aid, external debt, directly collected revenues, and occasionally from the private sector (through Works for Taxes and PPPs).

In 2017, OTASS assumed new powers, providing technical assistance and transferring resources to water utilities, in order to recover their operational capacity.[24] In this context, 19 companies joined a Transitional Support Scheme (*Régimen de Apoyo Transitorio*, RAT), due to the deterioration of their financial status, and are undergoing bailout by OTASS. There seem to be some positive outcomes, since water supply was available on average by 2.1 hours/day more. Yet, financial profitability has gone from -5% (2017) to + 1% (June 2019). Nevertheless, OTASS has detected that water utilities in areas of higher water stress and facing frequent water shortages are often obliged to carry out outlawed initiatives to secure water availability. Under these conditions, water utilities have even had to incur additional costs.

The National Superintendence of Sanitation Services (*Superintendencia Nacional de Servicios de Saneamiento*, SUNASS)

SUNASS is the decentralised public regulatory body responsible for regulating, supervising and assessing the provision of urban and rural sanitation services. It was created in 1992[25] as an attached body to the PCM with the legal status of internal public law and administrative, functional, technical, economic and financial autonomy.[26] Its main duties are to guarantee a quality level of service for urban and rural water supply and sanitation users. SUNASS regulatory functions were substantially enlarged both spatially and in terms of duties.[27] Up to 2016, SUNASS was responsible for supervising urban water utilities in cities with more 15 000 inhabitants; after 2016, small cities and and rural sanitation services providers were also included. In terms of duties, SUNASS is now covering also the demarcation of the boundaries of the areas for the provision of services[28] the evaluation of service providers, as well as the supervision and auditing of compliance with their legal and technical obligations (see Chapter 4).

The Ministry of Health (*Ministerio de Salud*, MINSA)

MINSA, through the Directorate-General for Environmental Health and Food Safety (DIGESA), regulates and monitors the compliance in terms of quality parameters of water for human consumption.[29] In fact, DIGESA is the technical and regulatory body on the quality of water for human consumption but monitoring and surveillance are carried out by the regional governments (Supreme Decree No. 031-2010-SA approving the regulation of water quality for human consumption). MINSA also oversees and monitors water quality for human consumption in water supply through different quality indicators (microbiological, parasitological, physical and chemical ones).

The Ministry of Development and Social Inclusion (*Ministerio de Desarrollo e Inclusión Social*, MIDIS)

The MIDIS is the governing body of national policies that promote development and social inclusion and is responsible for interventions in terms of investments in sanitation services in rural areas and for the maintenance and rehabilitation of water and sanitation systems, as per Supreme Decree No. 18-2017-VIVIENDA.

Who does what at the subnational level?

River Basin Councils (CRHCs)

CRHCs are ANA bodies created at the initiative of regional governments. They are created in order to achieve meaningful and permanent participation of stakeholders in the planning, co-ordination and agreement for the sustainable use of water resources in their respective areas.[30] The CRHCs are comprised of representatives from ANA, regional and local governments, water users (agricultural/non-agricultural), professional associations, universities, farmers and indigenous communities and operators of special projects of water infrastructure. Additionally, as appropriate, it includes a representative of the water transfer areas (giving and receiving basins), a representative of peasant communities, a representative of Indigenous communities, a representative of special projects that operate public water infrastructure and a representative of the Ministry of Foreign Affairs. Ordinary and extraordinary sessions of CRHCs are convened by the Technical Secretary in co-ordination with the Chairperson of the Council. In areas where there are no CRHCs, ANA's deconcentrated bodies may create specialised multi-sectoral task forces (*Grupo Especializado de Trabajo Multisectorial*, GETRAM), which offer spaces for co-ordination of analysis and planning of actions that address the water issues in the basin. Seven such task forces (four in the Pacific hydrographic region – Ancash-Pacífico, Chao-Virú, Chaparra-Acarí and Ica) and three in the Amazon hydrographic region – Alto Amazonas, San Martín and Ucayali) have been set up.

ANA plans to create 28 councils overall, of which 12 have already been created and 3 were ongoing[31] before the COVID-19 pandemic (ANA, 2018[10]) . The CRHCs already created are located in Caplina–Locumba, Chancay-Huaral, Chancay-Lambayeque, Chillón-Rímac-Lurín, Chira-Piura, Jequetepeque-Zaña, Mantaro, CRHC Pampas, Quilca-Chili, Tambo-Santiago-Ica, Tumbes and Vilcanota-Urubamba. In turn, CRHCs under creation are located in Mala-Omas-Cañete, Tambo-Moquegua and Titicaca. Further, a hydrographic sub-unit in the Amazon has been created within the scope of Rio Mayo (Figure 2.4).

Figure 2.3. Institutional mapping for water Supply and Sanitation in Peru

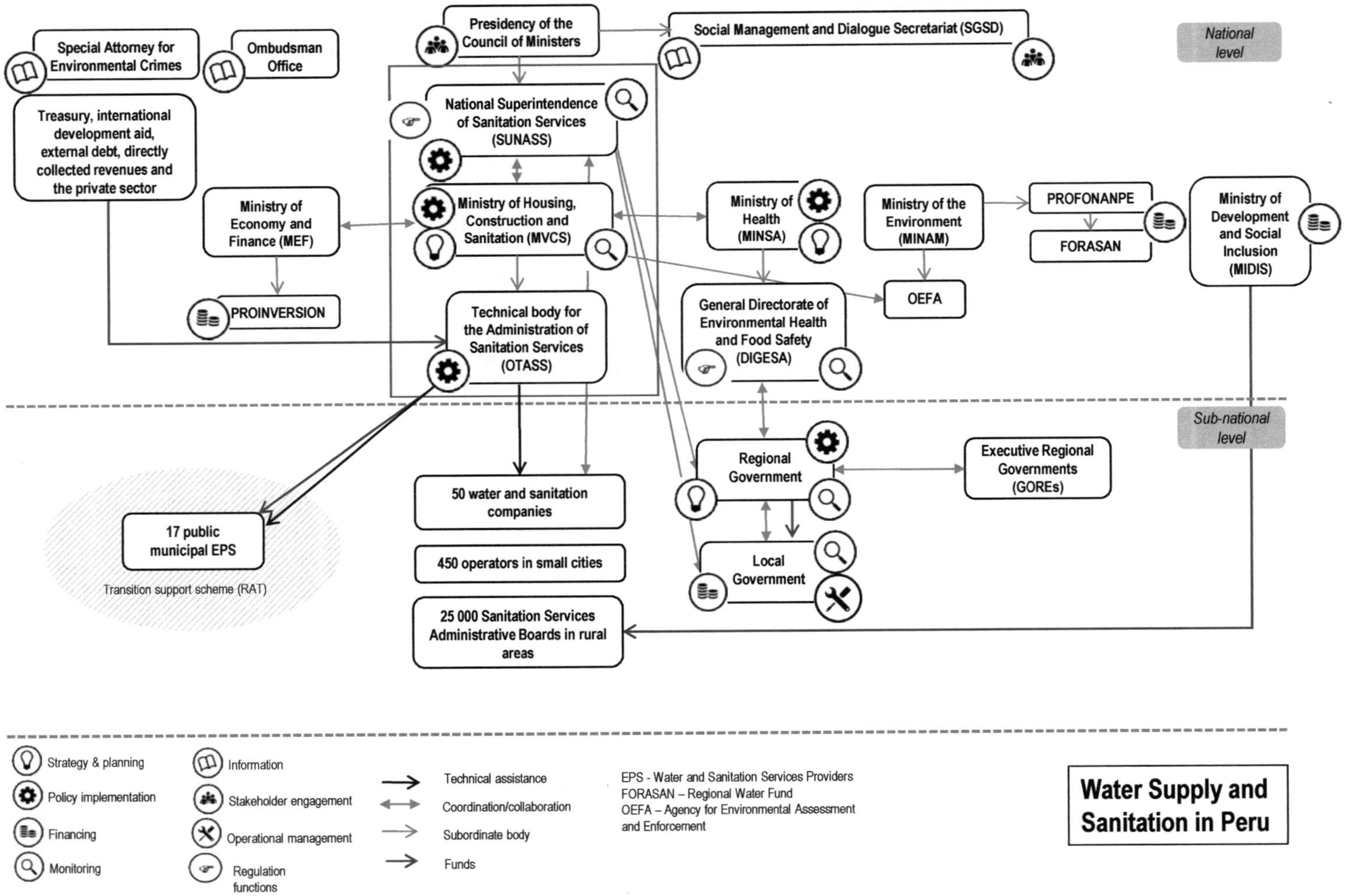

The main management tool of the CRHC is the Water Resources Management Plan (*Plan de Gestión de Recursos Hídricos de Cuencas*, PGRHC, the Spanish acronym for RBMP). It is drafted with the active engagement of the members of the council, within the frame of the PENRH and the National Plan for Water Resources. Likewise, the water resources management plans, in aspects of water resources conservation, must be consistent with the objectives of creation and conservation objects of protected natural areas, as well as with the Master Plan for Protected Natural Areas. River Basin Management Plans build on a commonly accepted principle in international water policy: that the river basin should be considered as the basic territorial unit for water management planning.[1] From 2010 to 2015, RBMPs were implemented in six selected pilot river basins in the Pacific watershed within the framework of the Water Resources Management Modernisation Project (WRMMP) funded by the World Bank and the Inter-American Development Bank (IDB): Chancay-Huaral, Chancay-Lambayeque, Chira-Piura, Locumba-Sama-Caplina, Quilca-Chili and Tumbes. Annually, the CRHC elaborates a Water Use Plan (*Plan de Aprovechamiento de Disponibilidades Hídricas*, PADH), on the basis of the assessment of the availability of water resources. To this end, a task force is formed by the Technical Secretary of the Council of Water Resources of Cuenca (Chair), local water administrators (ALA representatives), a representative from the operators of each major and minor water infrastructure, a representative of SENAMHI in the area and the Regional Director of Agriculture.

Regional and local governments

Regional and local governments participate in the management of water resources and are represented both on the Board of Directors of ANA and in the River Basin Councils.[2] In terms of irrigation, regional governments carry out control and surveillance of water use, by monitoring water conveyance by users' organisations or other operators under the regulations issued by MIDAGRI. They also promote and implement projects and works dealing with irrigation and its improvement and soil and water resources management and conservation. According to the Article 141 of Law No. 27972, local governments have competencies in the sustainable management of water resources, in order to tackle environmental degradation, as well as poverty and social issues.

In terms of water services, regional and local governments[3] are responsible for ensuring the efficient provision of water and sanitation services.[4] By law, regional governments hold responsibilities in: drawing up, approving and evaluating regional sanitation plans and policies; promoting technical assistance; providing technical and financial support to local governments for services delivery; collecting data and upgrading water supply and sewerage infrastructure and services management indicators. In turn, local governments should: manage public domain assets for service provision; set up Municipal Technical Areas (*Área* Técnica *Municipal*, ATM) in charge of monitoring, supervising and providing technical assistance and training to sanitation services providers; allocate financial resources for investments in sanitation infrastructure in the Concerted Municipal Development Plans (PDMC) and local participatory budget as set up in the National Sanitation Plan (*Plan Nacional de Saneamiento*, PNS); finance and co-finance investments for the maintenance and replacement of sanitation infrastructure in rural areas; collect data and input them into SIAS.

*Executive Regional Government (*Gobierno Regional-Ejecutivo*, GORE)*

GORE are structures for implementing the decentralisation policy reform agenda between national and regional governments and decentralising and monitoring reform efforts (PCM, 2017[11]). GORE seem to have been useful to speed up sanitation projects (170 projects by 2017) and for strengthening the implementation of MERESE (Government of Peru, 2016[12]). Currently, Peru is in the process of implementing Regional Development Agencies (*Agencias Regionales de Desarrollo*, ARD), starting with Tacna.

Figure 2.4. Progress in the creation of River Basin Councils

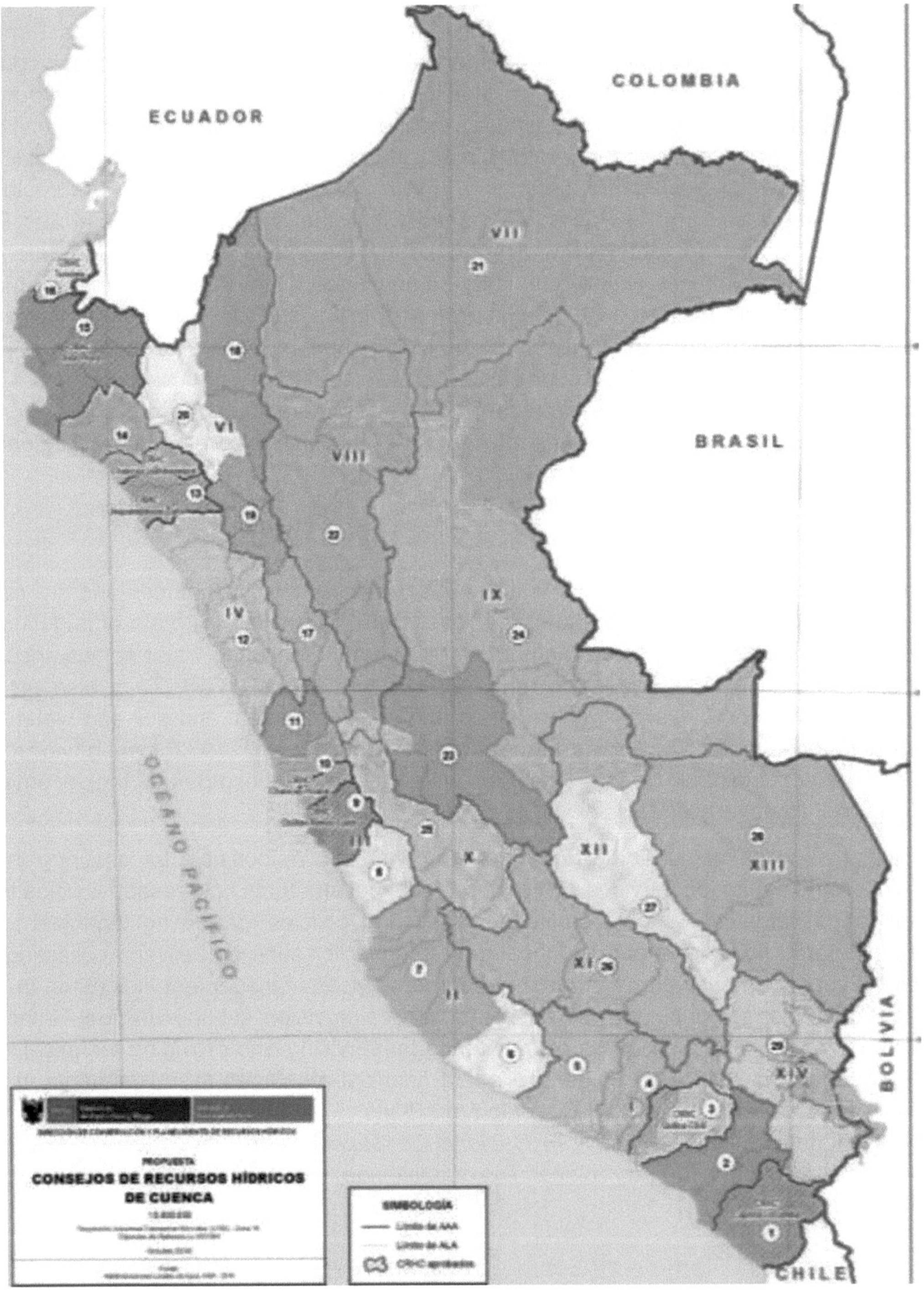

Source: ANA (2020[13]), *Consejos de Recursos Hídricos de Cuenca*, https://www.ana.gob.pe/nosotros/planificacion-hidrica/plan-gestion-cuencas.

Water users' organisations

Water user organisations are non-profit organisations of natural or legal persons, which channel the participation of water users in the multi-sectoral management and sustainable use of water resources. The purpose of water user organisations is to channel the participation of water users in the multi-sectoral management of water resources, representing and defending their rights and interests. They promote the efficient and sustainable use of water resources (Article 13 paragraph 13.1 and Article 14 of Supreme Decree No. 005-2015-MIANGRI).

Water operators

Water operators are public or private entities that provide the surface water supply service or the groundwater monitoring and management service, through the operation and maintenance of the hydraulic infrastructure. They are responsible for responding in a timely manner to the requests and claims submitted by the users of the service (Article 3 paragraph 3.1 of Chief Resolution No. 327-2018-ANA). They also collect water charge revenues (*retribuciones económicas por el uso del agua*) and transfer them to ANA. It is their duty to preserve and protect water resources linked to water infrastructure.

Small farmers and native communities

Small farmers and Indigenous peoples are both represented in the Board of Directors of ANA and on the CRHC. They participate in the elaboration of River Basin Management Plans (PGRHC), as established by Art. 18 of the Regulation of the Water Resources Law.

Assessment of multi-level water governance

The OECD Principles on Water Governance provide a reading template through which assess the water governance system at various levels of government (OECD, 2015[14]) (Box 2.2). Using this guiding framework, some of the key challenges in water governance in Peru are analysed below.

Box 2.2. The OECD Principles on Water Governance

The OECD Principles on Water Governance aim to enhance water governance systems that help manage "too much", "too little" and "too polluted" water and foster universal access to drinking water and sanitation, in a sustainable, integrated and inclusive way, at an acceptable cost and in a reasonable timeframe. The principles acknowledge that good governance is a means to an end to master complexity and managing trade-offs in a policy domain that is highly sensitive to fragmentation, silos, scale mismatch, negative externalities, monopolies and large capital-intensive investment. The principles consider that governance is good if it can help to solve key water challenges, using a combination of bottom-up and top-down processes while fostering constructive state-society relations. It is bad if it generates undue transaction costs and does not respond to place-based needs. The principles support the achievement of effective, efficient and inclusive water governance systems:

1. Effectiveness relates to the contribution of governance to define clear sustainable water policy goals and targets at all levels of government, to implement those policy goals, and to meet expected targets.
2. Efficiency relates to the contribution of governance to maximise the benefits of sustainable water management and welfare at the least cost to society.
3. Trust and engagement relate to the contribution of governance to building public confidence and ensuring the inclusiveness of stakeholders through democratic legitimacy and fairness for society at large.

Figure 2.5. OECD Principles on Water Governance

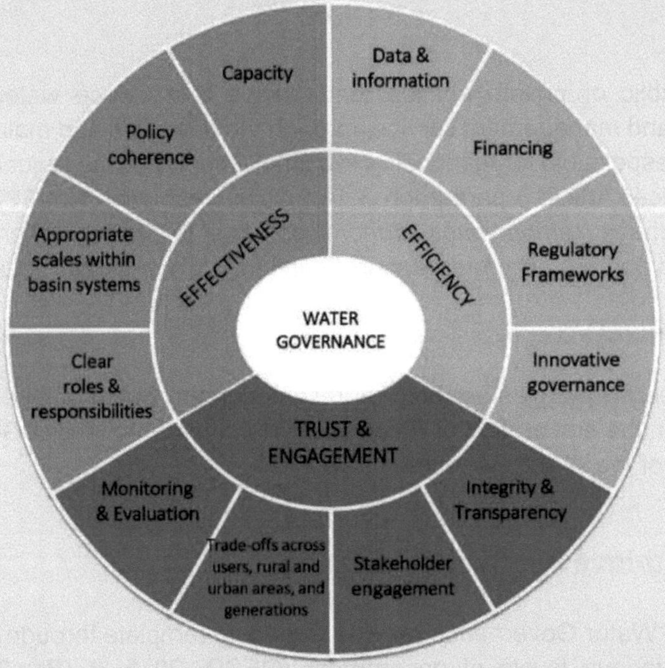

Source: OECD (2015[14]), *OECD Principles on Water Governance*, http://www.oecd.org/cfe/regional-policy/OECD-Principles-on-Water-Governance.pdf.

The 12 principles are the following:

- Principle 1. Clearly allocate and distinguish roles and responsibilities for water policymaking, policy implementation, operational management and regulation, and foster co-ordination across these responsible authorities.
- Principle 2. Manage water at the appropriate scale(s) within integrated basin governance systems to reflect local conditions, and foster co-ordination between the different scales.
- Principle 3. Encourage policy coherence through effective cross-sectoral co-ordination, especially between policies for water and the environment, health, energy, agriculture, industry, spatial planning and land use.
- Principle 4. Adapt the level of capacity of responsible authorities to the complexity of water challenges to be met, and to the set of competencies required to carry out their duties.
- Principle 5. Produce, update and share timely, consistent, comparable and policy-relevant water and water-related data and information, and use it to guide, assess and improve water policy.
- Principle 6. Ensure that governance arrangements help mobilise water finance and allocate financial resources in an efficient, transparent and timely manner.
- Principle 7. Ensure that sound water management regulatory frameworks are effectively implemented and enforced in pursuit of the public interest.
- Principle 8. Promote the adoption and implementation of innovative water governance practices across responsible authorities, levels of government and relevant stakeholders.

- Principle 9. Mainstream integrity and transparency practices across water policies, water institutions and water governance frameworks for greater accountability and trust in decision-making.
- Principle 10. Promote stakeholder engagement for informed and outcome-oriented contributions to water policy design and implementation.
- Principle 11. Encourage water governance frameworks that help manage trade-offs across water users, rural and urban areas, and generations.
- Principle 12. Promote regular monitoring and evaluation of water policy and governance where appropriate, share the results with the public and make adjustments when needed.

Source: OECD (OECD, 2015[14]), *OECD Principles on Water Governance*, http://www.oecd.org/cfe/regional-policy/OECD-Principles-on-Water-Governance.pdf.

Effectiveness

Roles and responsibilities

Peru has a complex institutional setup for water management. The institutional framework is linked to quite a solid legal framework, especially after the passing of the Water Resources Law and its regulation in 2009. Most challenges remain as to the implementation of that legal framework to improve integrated water resources management (IWRM). These challenges are described below.

The role of water resources management from a multi-sectoral perspective could be refined and clarified in practice, beyond the legal dimension of the allocation of legal powers. The effectiveness of the SNGRH, as a multi-sectoral platform and as co-ordination mechanism between different actors of the integrated water management system, is in question. Strengthening the management of SNGRH entities and capacities, both technical and human, could help to drive forward-looking policy development, planning and implementation, to ensure effective, equitable and sustainable management of water resources in a multi-sectoral fashion. Currently, the lack of regular meetings and unbalanced participation of water users in the SNGRH, beyond the agricultural sector, hinder such goals and reveal a weak leadership and convening power of ANA governing board.

The place of ANA as a governing body is undisputed but a number of doubts emerge as per its actual delivery. The year 2008 was a tipping point in water resources management in Peru with the passing of the Water Resources Law and the creation of ANA to oversee its implementation and become the regulator of water resources management. On paper, ANA responds to international best practice in the sense that it is a multi-sectoral body (thus overcoming sectoral biases), fosters the participation of stakeholders, deepens the decentralised management of natural resources and acknowledges water as a social and economic good. Several doubts remain, though, regarding the integration of sectoral policies. But in practice, there are two main considerations regarding ANA's activity. The first is related to deconcentration at the territorial level: while that process is aimed at enhancing the subsidiarity principle, it generated multiple overlaps and redundancy across accountable authorities and a situation with inadequate capacities and resources in deconcentrated entities with subsequent dysfunctionalities of water management and implementation deficits at the regional and local levels. An additional consideration is that ANA operates under the line of the Ministry of Agricultural Development and Irrigation, something that is increasingly questioned by a number of stakeholders due to the cross-cutting nature of water resources management and related difficulties to manage trade-offs among competing water uses given the large share of water for irrigation in Peru, as in many other countries. The cornerstone of any effort to strengthen water management and policy lies in the redefinition and empowerment of ANA, which includes either obtaining higher levels of autonomy from MIDAGRI or being institutionally reassigned, working on the factual autonomy of river basin organisations, securing financial resources for the cost-effective implementation of their mandate and ensuring adequate co-ordination with ministries and other relevant public bodies.

Overlaps, duplications and grey areas in regulations and implementation are the consequences of complex relationships across national institutions and levels of governments. In rural sanitation, for example, water and sanitation services are the responsibility of local authorities. As the governing body of the sector, the MVCS finances projects presented by subnational governments, as well as formulates and implements them in urban and rural areas. The MVCS implements a national programme for rural sanitation services since 2012 to provide sanitation services to rural populations. Previously, activities related to rural areas were led by the National Rural Water Supply and Sanitation Project (PRONASAR). MINSA, in turn, has an overseeing function. It monitors the quality of drinking water from a public health perspective but is not accountable for the planning and execution of sanitation policies. In fact, MINSA, through DIGESA, monitors the quality of water for human consumption but that competency is shared with regional governments. This already sophisticated framework is reinforced by the activity of multilateral development banks (mostly the IDB, in what concerns rural sanitation) and, above all, a bilateral development agency (Swiss Agency for Development and Cooperation, SDC) that developed long ago a full-fledged framework for interventions on rural sanitation, in co-ordination with infrastructural investments via the National Rural Sanitation Programme (PNSR). Despite this level of complexity, remarkable gaps remain in rural areas in terms of the coverage and sustainability of services. Rural areas are lagging. The creation of OTASS was an important innovation included in the 2013 Sanitation Services Modernisation Law. In 2017, the framework law transferred most of its functions to SUNASS, creating questioning from OTASS about the legitimacy and efficiency of SUNASS to fulfil some of the functions.

Appropriate scale(s)

In many countries, a significant mismatch has been observed between administrative boundaries (regions, municipalities, other sub-national divisions) and hydrological units. This feature, which can also be observed in Peru, precludes the adequate implementation of water and other public policies and becomes a source of conflict between elected representatives. The latter is the case in Ica and Huancavelica, where there is an imbalance in water resources between the upper and lower basin and dissention between departments (Annex A). Conflicts can also rise across water management authorities or a wide range of water users, such as between the concessionaire companies in Project Olmos and small farmers in the Olmos Valley or the headwaters, or between farmers and citizens and mining companies in a number of examples (Annex B). Identifying and addressing gaps, trade-offs and conflicts of interest is of chief importance since these obstacles to vertical policy co-ordination are especially relevant when the level of autonomy of river basin authorities is still limited, at best (unlike in France with water agencies or in Spain with hydrological confederations, Box 2.3).

Box 2.3. River basin organisations: Experiences from France and Spain

Spain has one of the longest histories in developing formal governmental authorities at the river basin scale. Since 1926, the country has established 13 hydraulic confederations (HCs), 9 of which are inter-regional (across several autonomous communities) and 4 intra-regional (within one autonomous community). In their early years, HCs were hydro-technical agencies devoted to building dams, reservoirs and water conveyance facilities, while water law administration and management of water uses were handled by a separate agency before the central government merged these functions into one basin-wide authority.

Since 1985, HCs have had combined responsibilities for: i) physical management (monitoring of water resources conditions, water transfers); ii) infrastructural management (waterworks); and iii) water use management (water licensing, water planning and enforcement of national and European Union (EU) regulations). Two separate boards, *Junta de Gobierno* and *Junta de Explotacion*, govern HCs. The boards are composed of government representatives and water users (public and private water supply companies, irrigation associations, hydroelectric companies and industrial users) to ensure broad participation by various stakeholders in its decision-making process. In addition, the Water Users Assembly makes recommendations concerning HC policies for the co-ordinated management of hydraulic works and water resources, while the Basin Water Council (*Consejo del agua de Cuenca*) approves the basin hydrological plan. HC administration and operations are funded by a combination of revenues from the central government and revenues generated by the HC, mainly by tariffs (on water users and basin residents) and taxes (discharge fees, severance taxes on sand and gravel, and tax on hydroelectric power).

In 1964, France established six water agencies (*agences de l'eau*) for each of the main river basins (Water Law – 16 December 1964 updated in 1992 and 2006) which aim to facilitate the co-ordination of actions of common interest to the basin.

Dialogue and the organisation of needed data and information production and management are institutionalised at the national, basin and local levels. At the national level, the National Water Committee is consulted on the trends of the national water policy and drafts of legislative and regulatory texts. At the level of each of the six large river basins, the water agencies levy pollution and water intake charges, grant subsidies for reducing pollution and formulate the basin management plan called SDAGE (*Schéma directeur d'aménagement et de gestion de l'eau*). The SDAGE contains the principles for "balanced water resources management", encompasses the principal plans and programmes, and defines the principal objectives with respect to quantitative and qualitative aspects of water as well as the instruments to reach these objectives. At the sub-basin level, a local water commission (*Commission locale de l'eau*) designs and ensures implementation of the sub-basin management plans (called SAGE – *Schéma d'aménagement et de gestion de l'eau*) within the framework of the SDAGE. These consist of 50% of local government representatives, 25% of national government representatives and 25% of user group representatives.

Source: OECD (2011[15]), *Water Governance in OECD Countries: A Multi-level Approach*, https://doi.org/10.1787/9789264119284-en; OECD (2015[16]), "OECD Studies on Water, Country profile, Spain", https://www.oecd.org/spain/Water-Resources-Allocation-Spain.pdf.

Basins have been identified as the relevant management units in Peru; yet, some challenges remain, mostly as to the delineation of those basin districts (especially in the headwaters) or the actual use of planning instruments (not just from a hydrological viewpoint). The delineation of headwaters has become a relevant challenge, with consequences on investments in natural infrastructures. Law No. 30640 from 2017 establishes technical criteria for the identification and demarcation of basin headwaters. ANA is currently developing a methodological framework setting technical criteria for the identification, demarcation and zoning of headwaters of the Pacific, Atlantic and Lake Titicaca watersheds. Several stakeholders have suggested that ANA should clearly define the technical criteria to qualify the levels of environmental vulnerability of headwaters, and based on this, establish the most appropriate protection measures according *ad hoc*. As of June 2019, 42% of the basins had been identified and delineated within the framework of Law No. 30640 (ANA, 2019[17]). Although this effort is widely considered as a promising one, some doubts have been expressed in relation to the lack of expertise and experience of ANA to tackle some of the challenges as to the demarcation of headwaters and the need to factor a very wide diversity of aquatic and terrestrial ecosystems in the assessment framework (Chirinos, 2018[18]).

The creation of CRHCs in Peru is a positive, yet insufficient step. The River Basin Councils (CRHCs) were created initially on a pilot basis, with the support of the WRMMP, co-funded by the IDB and the World

Bank. Despite their consultative nature and substantial deficits in terms of financial sufficiency and capacity, this type of concertation of stakeholders, as an embryo of multi-stakeholder platforms that could give rise in due course to river basin authorities, is essentially of an unprecedented nature in Latin America. Although it is early for a comprehensive assessment of their effectiveness, some issues deserve attention:

- Where they exist, river basin management plans are overall poorly implemented and enforced.
- Although legal amendments ensure the presence of the urban water and sanitation sector, there tends to be an over-representation of agricultural users within the councils. Also, there might be a risk of political capture due to the fact that the regional government is the presiding body.
- The financial capacity of CRHCs is acknowledged to be insufficient and leading to a lack of capacity development, both in terms of technical knowledge and human resources. The Technical Secretaries that provide technical support to the CRHCs are funded against ANA's budget. A methodology for setting charges for water use and treated wastewater discharge was also defined. The collection of these charges currently accounts for a large share of ANA's revenues, which includes the administrative costs of ANA headquarters in Lima, its decentralised offices (ALAs and AAAs) and the basin councils. For the implementation of the Water Resources Management Plans in each basin, CRHCs receive funding from regional governments, local governments and relevant sectoral bodies of the central government, as well as, occasionally, from private parties, as part of a number of PPP arrangements (i.e. works for taxes, PPP contractual arrangements, etc.).
- CRHCs lack staff and personnel. Technical Secretariats, designated via public tender by ANA, fulfil the functions of technical support to CRHC members but they have limited human resources. This is not the case for the councils in Chancay-Lambayeque, Chira-Piura or Quilca-Chili, which seem to be performing at reasonable levels.

Policy coherence

A common failure in water policy is that of confusing means and ends, in other words, policy instruments and policy goals. In such cases, water policy ends up being an impact remedial effort rather than a proactive and pre-emptive policy that anticipates risks and opportunities. The case of Peru testifies the implications of an inadequate insertion of sustainable water resources management in the overall social and economic development strategy of the country. Nevertheless, Peru has made progress in defining concrete goals to address the effects of climate change on water resources within the framework of the Paris Agreement, which led Peru to establish 31 climate change adaptation measures with the objective of increasing the availability of current and future water for multi-sectoral uses of water.

The country shows evidence of a very high number of intense trade-offs between sectoral policies, across territorial development, urban development, mining and energy, agriculture, biodiversity conservation, forestry, etc. In particular, there is no national land use policy (although there are legal provisions on territorial development) and the lack of co-ordination with the economic sectors is a serious hindrance to effective water resources management. Generally, manufacturing industries, including agro-food companies, have not been showing meaningful efficiency in water use. For example, in Pisco (Ica Region), every year during the dry season, water stress affects the provision of drinking water for the population. However, despite such a deficit, most farmers continue to use flood irrigation techniques. Thus, regulatory requirements regarding the efficiency of water use are prevailing only in the supply of drinking water for the population (as regulated by SUNASS), rather than for other productive sectors that, as is the case of agriculture, consume the largest volume of water. However, agro-exporting companies are subject to strict international certifications on the efficient use of water

Water resources and water services plans are neither adequately implemented, nor connected to one another although some recent progress was observed, for instance as a result of Supreme Decree No. 029-2018-PCM by the National Centre for Strategic Planning (*Centro Nacional de Planeamiento Estratégico*, CEPLAN), which approves the National Policies Regulation, seeking to strengthen the implementation of national policies. Along these lines, all national entities must identify and update policies within the framework of their legal powers, seeking, among others the articulation with other sectoral or multi-sectoral policy frameworks, in order to enhance the efficiency of intervention models, promote synergies and avoid significant overlaps. There is also a need to align a number of planning instruments including the following: the National Sanitation Plan, the National Water Resources Plan, plans related to anaemia and chronic malnutrition, as well as plans against parasites.

The lack of policy coherence across water and related domains leads to unintended outcomes. Measures leading to strong incentives to increase water consumption in certain sectors, in an unintended way, contrast with the use of water charges to incentivise water savings in those same sectors. For example, this relates to the impacts of environmentally harmful subsidies at different levels as well as deficiencies in bulk water pricing (i.e. water abstraction and pollution fees by ANA) and other water pricing instruments (tariffs for major and minor infrastructure use, household water tariffs, etc.). Another example is the existing link between treated (and untreated) wastewater effluents and the agriculture sector. Although Legislative Decree No. 1280 establishes that EPs may trade treated (and untreated) wastewater effluents under (non-regulated) market criteria, so that there is technical and economic efficiency as a country in the reclamation and reuse of regenerated water, this requires linking it to water use regulations for irrigation purposes.

Capacity

ANA faces important capacity gaps from a financial, human and technical standpoint. Although engineering profiles are relatively abundant, planning and policymaking ones are not. Furthermore, the institutional capacity to deal with problems and needs is developed through deconcentrated bodies (14 AAAs and 71 ALAs) for the 159 hydrographic units of the nation. Financial constraints explain part of the deficit in such deconcentrated units (see below on funding gap). Deficits in capacity are even more evident when it comes down to River Basin Councils, although this may also be explained by the low level of commitment of some regional governments and local authorities in the implementation of the national plan and the adequate fulfilment of the functions of River Basin Councils. Over the years, ANA has been gradually implementing capacity building programmes for all SNGRH actors. ANA, through the civil service programme SERVIR promotes merit-based hiring among its public officers. The ANA Area of Water Culture (one of the strategic axes of the national plan) also supports training for high-level officers in decision-making.

Capacity gaps also exist in MINAM and across authorities in relation to the implementation of the Ecosystem Services Compensation Mechanism (MERESE). Whilst ANA was created out of the former National Institute on Natural Resources (INRENA), MINAM emerged as Peru's first ministry of the environment more than ten years ago. Both administrations can therefore be considered to be very young institutions, thus, to a large extent, at the beginning of a learning curve. Regarding the implementation of MERESE, there are several capacity gaps. On one side, there are institutional lock-ins linked to the capacities of organisations and institutions involved, such as instability and high rotation of policymakers in some regional and local governments and in the organisations and institutions that participate in the development of MERESE (Boards of Directors of EPs, or the Boards of Directors of Sanitation Services Administrative Boards [*Juntas Administradoras de Servicios de Saneamiento,* JASS], etc.). On the other hand, there are technical lock-ins in terms of knowledge gaps, in particular regarding the operation and/or management of a MERESE project due to the lack of or incomplete information and the design of natural infrastructure projects. As an illustration, part of those deficits adds to constraints in the Lima Water and Sewerage Service (*Servicio de Agua Potable y Alcantarillado de Lima*, SEDAPAL), for instance, for the lack of delivery of projects against the revenues collected from MERESE for Greater Lima. In order to provide tools that facilitate the design and implementation process of the MERESE, the MINAM recently approved "Guidelines for the Design and Implementation of Remuneration Mechanisms for Ecosystem Services" (R.M. No. 014-2021-MINAM).

Other national institutions would also benefit from further investment in capacity building, especially for the implementation of plans at the subnational level. The Directorate of Sanitation at the MVCS, for example, does also require a larger number of human and financial resources in its different areas, to carry out adequate monitoring and to design and implement encompassing measures under the National Sanitation Policy. Assistance would be required for the implementation of the 24 Regional Sanitation Plans, containing the investments in the three levels of government for closing infrastructure gaps linked to sanitation. However, various strategies have been applied for better compliance with actions, such as remote technical assistance, a limited number of trips to the field, articulation with other MVCS programmes or the creation of work teams with related entities.

In terms of water and sanitation services, capacity deficits in service operators are also critical. Performance evaluations of water utilities (EPs) carried out by OTASS and SUNASS reveal that the performance of those companies is unsatisfactory and not necessarily sustainable. Poor coverage levels come along with concerns over services quality and sustainability, especially in rural areas, which adds to the critical financial situation of a large share of EPs. To a greater extent, problems mainly arise in the segment that serves small cities, which also face problems of economies of scale and scope. Water distributed to the population in small cities may not always be safe since disinfection is not applied on a permanent basis. In addition, service operators show serious deficiencies in commercial, operational and administrative management, since they lack a commercial cadastre. There is no continuity in the management and preservation of commercial information of services, nor supply cuts due to non-payment, which generates high non-revenue water rates.

Likewise, the economic and financial situation of the majority of EPs does not allow them to set up the necessary investments to achieve universal coverage. The assessment carried out by OTASS shows that 25 EPs recorded net losses in 2016 and 8 companies had profits that did not exceed PEN 60 000 (approximately USD 18 000). Additionally, it should be noted that a group of EPs are currently in the Transitory Support Regime of OTASS, providing technical assistance and transferring resources to water utilities, in order to recover their operational capacity. Most providers lack the institutional, operational and financial capacity to take care of the delivery of sanitation services by themselves. Cost-recovery rates are very low. SUNASS drafts and approves a Tariff Review study that integrates an operational and investment plan and a financial plan for EPs. EPs have an Optimised Master Plan (PMO), which is a long-term planning tool with a 30-year horizon that contains the programming of investments in conditions of efficiency and the financial and economic projections of the efficient development of operations. The PMO include a diagnosis of long-term availability and demand leading to an investment plan for bridging gaps and ensuring the sustainability of services. The abovementioned financial plan, currently not in place, was structured around the objective of complying with one of the key principles of economic regulation: that of financial viability. According to this principle of financial feasibility, the regulator establishes a certain rate that guarantees that revenues for EPs allow for the recovery of the economic and financial costs required for its efficient and sustainable operation, based on the quality and service levels set by SUNASS, as well as for the replacement of assets (mostly infrastructures) at the end of their useful life, an aspect that proves challenging in Peru and other countries. This has not prevented many EPs from suffering from cashflow and solvency constraints. Within the context of its new mandate and through a resolution of its board (028-2018-SUNASS-CD), SUNASS approved, in July 2018, the methodology to fix a household payment (*cuota familiar*) for the delivery of water and sanitation services in rural areas.

Inadequate technical solutions are observed for certain geographical areas, in particular in rural areas. Technical records of investments in water and sanitation do not follow a uniform criterion for urban and rural areas, due to the absence of standardised investment instruments that, based on technical and least-cost criteria cost, allow for efficient investment decisions for the sector. As a result, the investments made do not have the expected economic and social return since they are oversized and, in some cases, developed without any sustainability criteria. Therefore, these investments become idle and the operator does not have the ability to operate and/or properly maintain ageing infrastructures. In rural areas, the

MVCS has established a technical design standard with technological options for sanitation systems in rural areas, with the objective to define the final designs of sanitation technological options, criteria for choice, design and delivery mechanism (Ministerial Resolution No. 192-2018-VIVIENDA). Yet, further dissemination and training actions in the use of this standard are necessary in order to ensure that project designs for rural livelihoods are effective and sustainable. Another difficulty is that of the capacity of communal water supply organisations, where the personnel is voluntary and endowed with very low administration, operation and maintenance capacity.

Efficiency

Data and information

Information is scattered and fragmented in different institutional silos, which hinders its effective use for policy and decision-making. Water Resources Law No. 29338 created the National Information System of Water Resources, partly to address fragmentation issues in data collection and encourage the interoperability of data of specialised entities in the field of water resources. In terms of environmental enforcement, the Interactive Portal for Environmental Enforcement (PIFA) and the Agency for Environmental Assessment and Enforcement (*Organismo de Evaluación y Fiscalización Ambiental*, OEFA) contain and publish information related to water evaluation and monitoring.[5]

The significant lack of models of robust climatological forecasts at the basin level prevents the development of river flows forecast, which would, for example, improve flood warning systems in the main basins of the country. Information on vulnerability to hazards associated with climate change has been developed at the sectoral level (e.g. agriculture, industry), which clearly prevents an integrated approach. Flood events and landslides have become more frequent and intense events, which happen in the absence of adequate early warning systems, a problem that is also being observed in a number of cases of eutrophication and proliferation of cyanobacteria. The nationally determined contribution (NDC) on Water will progressively increase co-ordination through its 4 components and the focus on 31 adaptation measures to be implemented in a shared responsibility with regional and local governments. This includes, for example, the modernisation of the granting of water use rights in basins especially vulnerable to climate change, incorporating climatic scenarios as well as the implementation of early warning systems for floods, droughts, landslides and dangers of glacial origin.

Despite recent progress, water databases are incomplete, hydro-meteorological data are still in analogical format and digital information needs to be reviewed for consistency and quality assurance (World Bank, 2017[19]). Data collection on volumes of water withdrawn (delivered and used) is often quite opaque. Reporting by water users and infrastructure operators, as established by law, is not carried out in a timely manner or information is not exhaustive for data collection and management (metering, quality monitoring systems, etc.). The Water Resources Management Modernisation Project in Peru, set by the World Bank in support of ANA, has made a crucial contribution to improving the knowledge and information base on water management in the country. It mainly applies to the six pilot basins in the Pacific watershed, where river basin management plans were designed. Even in those basins, though, some doubts remain as to hydrological balances or prioritisation of investments. Outside those basins, available water resources information is still weak. The lack of reliable information jeopardises attempts to diversify water supply sources, as in the case of the reclamation and reuse of regenerated wastewaters. Generally, mechanisms to enforce water rights show much leeway for improvement. ANA's ability to control and reallocate resources is thus compromised.

Information on rural water and sanitation services have been increasingly collected but challenges remain. The Rural WASH Information System (DATASS) presents some overlaps with other information systems such as the Water and Sanitation Information System (SIAS). In some cases, there are also some conflicting criteria and methods across systems (including classification typologies). DATASS does not provide the same completeness of data throughout the country: while some regions have managed to bridge information gaps; others are still in process. This information asymmetry has an impact on the quality of the sector diagnoses and consequently on the quality of the policy responses. The Ministry of Health leads the information system on water quality for human consumption (though DIGESA) and the health status of the drinking water infrastructure. The DIGESA information system provides real-time information on all regional micro-networks and health networks, thus contributing to decision-making for prioritising investment on drinking water.

The lack of information on groundwater resources is quite a challenge in some cases, which translates into problems in the enforcement of groundwater use rights, with illegal wells springing up. This is not only relevant for the adequate management of this back-up resource but also for compliance with the groundwater management and monitoring service tariff established by SUNASS in Greater Lima (SEDAPAL) and, in the near future, in La Libertad (SEDALIB), Ica and Tacna, for instance, which primarily rely on groundwater to sustain agricultural activities. The Ica Valley, Villacurí and Yarada are among the most overexploited aquifers in Peru, in productive areas that contribute to a large extent to Peru's agricultural gross domestic product (GDP) and exports.

Financing

There is a diversity of funding gaps in Peru, some relating to the ability to ensure the necessary investments (in terms of upfront capital investment) or to sustain programmes and projects in terms of operational expenses; and others relating to how cost-recovery is conceived and ensured, following the principle that water should fund water. In Peru, it is also of paramount importance to strike the balance between resources made available at the central level and revenues and expenditures at the subnational levels. Peru has rules for the promotion of investment, such as the Law for the Promotion of Investments for Economic Growth and Sustainable Development, No. 30327, which includes provisions for the simplification and integration of permits and procedures, as well as investment promotion measures.

Funding constraints can actually be observed at the level of two of the regulating entities: ANA and SUNASS (OECD, 2016[20]). As per ANA, three funding sources are available: central government's regular budgetary sources, revenue collection from water abstraction and pollution fees (following the rates approved every year for surface and groundwater and for agricultural and non-agricultural users) and funds or donations being made by third parties (multilateral and bilateral development organisations and others). According to the Water Resources Law, payments should cover the costs of IWRM to be implemented by ANA. However, this is hardly ever the case. To determine the value of those fees,[6] which are paid to ANA as a result of using a public-domain resource, there is a methodology to be approved by ANA through a resolution (RJ 457-2012-ANA). These fees are levied per cubic meter of water used whatever the form of the user right granted. Beyond collecting fees for water abstraction and pollution, by the Water Resources Law (Art. 15.4), ANA approves the tariffs for the use of water infrastructures. Revenues are mainly used mainly to cover the costs of operation and maintenance.. Regulation of the referred law[7] stipulates that water infrastructure operators present their proposals for rates in accordance with the technical and economic guidelines established by ANA.[8]

Some improvements have been made recently to achieve water quantity and quality objectives. Payments for groundwater are gradually being implemented, with some environmental criteria being factored in (e.g. water availability to somehow reflect scarcity, level of pressures and aquifer status). Besides, surface water use also entails specific coefficients to reflect water availability and type of use. Groundwater uses are regulated through different coefficients on the basis of the specific aquifer status (underexploited, in equilibrium, overexploited). Every year's supreme decree also sets up "flat rates" for certain uses and sources, provided that the abstraction volume is lower than a certain threshold. Treated wastewater discharges are also set up for domestic and industrial discharges (sanitation and others, including from purification plants and brines from desalination of brackish and saltwater; energy; mining; agro-food;

industry; fishing) and according to the environmental quality standards of the receiving water body (ECA-Water 1, 2, 3 or 4). Flat rates are also set up for specific cases (e.g. rural areas).

According to ANA, revenues collected from the abstraction and treated wastewater discharge fees in 2017 amounted to roughly USD 50 million, out of which 23% corresponds to discharges of wastewater effluents and 77% to withdrawals, 23% to groundwater use and 77% to surface water use, 15% to agricultural uses, 85% to non-agricultural ones (ANA, 2019[21])). Under the provisions of Article 95 of the Water Resources Law, these payments should cover the cost of IWRM for which ANA is responsible, along with the recovery and the remediation of environmental damage caused by whatever discharges or abstraction beyond sustainable rates. The OECD (OECD/ECLAC, 2017[4]) had already observed that in previous years those revenues had proved insufficient to cover its regular operational costs. ANA's Strategic Plan 2018-21 considers the need to increase the fees rates, although the impact of this measure might be limited unless more provisions on the monitoring of payments are made, especially from agricultural users (ANA, 2017[22]). There is a need to disclose how the revenues are being used in order to determine if the objectives included in the Regulation on the Water Law are being fulfilled, in terms of improvements in the availability and quality of water resources.

The National Water Resources Plan established an investment programme, demanding an investment of PEN 53 909 million (USD 46 640 million) towards 2035 (ANA, 2013[23]). Funding gaps prevent the securitisation of water use rights for agriculture of 1 632 076 hectares in 36 835 irrigation blocks, requiring an investment of approximately PEN 93 million to legalise water use rights for public water supply purposes of 89 777 population centres (with 5 000 inhabitants) and the same number of licenses with an investment of PEN 180 million, among others.

With regards to SUNASS, the main sources of financing for its regulating functions are revenues from collecting drinking water rates (see Chapter 4). This incorporates the costs of conservation and recovery of ecosystem services provided by ecosystems, which integrates wastewater treatment costs to protect receiving bodies such as rivers, lakes, oceans, etc. In addition, SUNASS is funded from revenues collected through the service tariff for monitoring and management of groundwater, by non-agricultural users with their own wells (which should allow for the conservation of aquifers in order to guarantee the provision of the drinking water service especially in cases of extreme events). Finally, SUNASS is funded from transfers made by the central government through the Ministry of Economy and Finance (MEF). Since 2017 and because of the new functions of SUNASS concerning small cities and rural areas, the MEF has been transferred funds for the progressive implementation of the new role of SUNASS and the compliance with national policy. SUNASS does not receive funds from the National Rural Sanitation Programme, whose objective is to bridge gaps in rural areas.

Long terms investments in the drinking water and sanitation sector have sometimes downplayed the need to ensure the financial sustainability of infrastructure investments. The National Sanitation Policy includes Policy Axis 2 on Financial Sustainability, which aims to ensure the generation of financial resources and their efficient use by EPs. Provisions are made for planning long-term water, sewerage, wastewater treatment services investments from the national, regional and local levels. Furthermore, financial resources are allocated according to a multi-annual investment plan and national goals. National resources are made compatible with resources available at the regional and local levels. Over the last few years, these investments have been driven by the policy priority of closing water and sanitation services gaps but this has sometimes downplayed the need to ensure the financial sustainability of infrastructure investments. Part of those self-sufficiency concerns are explained by low levels of tariff rates. It has proved difficult to convey the idea that a progressive structure of tariffs would largely help ensure a sustainable collection of revenues to meet cost-recovery targets and to enable cross-subsidies schemes for low-income households.

Many water utilities are not able to cover operational costs. According to the National Sanitation Plan 2017-21, among all EPs in the country, SEDAPAL had registered a positive operational margin in 4 consecutive years (19.92% in 2015, 23.75% in 2014 and 16.86% in 2013 and 3.69% in 2012). This situation reveals that rates are not covering costs systematically. In some other cases, rate increases, if any, are absorbed by costs that rise at a faster rate. Regional sanitation plans also contain an ad hoc chapter with a financial plan; this shows the main sources of financing. Each of the regional governments should have a regional sanitation plan with a lifespan of three years. This plan is prepared based on the multi-year investment programming by the MVCS. The plan must be updated periodically.

There is a lack of adjustment between the average time of approvals and the temporal scale of needs once projects have been included in the public investment system. This has been pointed out by PROINVERSION as one of the weaknesses in the investment framework in Peru (former SNIP, current Invierte.pe) is the 7-year average time of approval and the temporal scale of needs. Furthermore, a significant degree of fragmentation of projects in the assessment procedure has been observed. It has also been suggested that co-ordination should be strengthened between FED (Outcome-oriented Fund for the Stimulus of Performance at the social level), FONAVI (National Housing Fund) and PROINVERSION.

Regulation

Overall institutional capacity in the water management sector is still developing. Fundamentally, there appears to be a mismatch between the sophisticated legal framework and the capacity of Peru's institutions to implement it. The lack of capacity contributes to and is compounded by a lack of clarity around roles and responsibilities, undermining the road to the achievement of Peru's ambitious water supply and sanitation (WSS) goals. For example, both the Ministry of Housing, Building and Sanitation (MVCS) and the Ministry of Development and Social Inclusion (MIDIS) have roles in rural sanitation: while the MVCS leads on policy setting and investment in the sector, the MIDIS works through its International Co-operation Fund for Social Development (*Fondo de Cooperación para el Desarrollo Social*, FONCODES) to channel development assistance funds to programmes targeting poor rural populations, including supporting local governments with basic WSS services (MIDIS, 2019[24]). A detailed analysis of the regulatory obstacles is available in Chapter 4.

Trust and engagement

Progress in terms of IWRM at a river basin scale is needed to prevent, mitigate and manage social conflicts. There are currently two main approaches to dealing with social conflicts, which follow different conceptualisation, methodologies and typologies. On the one hand, the Ombudsman (*Defensoría del Pueblo*) classifies social conflicts according to areas and features (socio-environmental, national government issues, regional government issues, local government issues, community, territorial demarcation, labour, illicit coca cultivation, electoral disputes). Some doubts remain as per the availability of an updated and upgraded methodological approach to social conflict identification and management. On the other hand, the National Office for Dialogue and Sustainability (*Oficina Nacional de Diálogo y Sostenibilidad* ONDS (linked to the PCM) identifies eight types of conflicts related to the following activities/sectors: mining; energy; hydrocarbon; hydrological; informal/illicit mining; territorial demarcation; agriculture, forestry and coca cultivation; and labour. Further, the Ministry of Mining and Energy also has a specialised unit to address conflicts linked to mining activities.

The representation of various categories of stakeholders in River Basin Councils should be improved for greater citizen trust and government accountability. The creation of CRHCs has made some space for wider stakeholder engagement, including in the negotiation and definition of their priorities or demands. Ad hoc working groups on water availability, water quality, financing, research, water culture and risk management also add value in terms of inclusiveness and accountability. The participation of critical stakeholders, such as small peasant communities, needs to be improved, as they are clearly under-represented despite their critical role in the conservation of headwaters (ANA, 2017[25]; 2017[26]). Further, technical secretariats within the River Basin Councils need to improve co-ordination with ANA's decentralised bodies (AAAs and ALAs). Not all entities with representatives in the working groups are formal members of CRHCs.

The implementation of MERESE provides a good illustration of the potential leeway for improvement in terms of accountability. By definition, success in the implementation of MERESE is highly dependent on political decisions at different levels (across sectors and levels of government). Critical decisions can happen in state institutions and grassroots organisations, such as the boards of irrigation districts, the peasant communities or the boards of directors of water utilities (as the signing of the agreement depends on the social acceptance of MERESE interventions). Nationwide, there is a clear lack of installed capacity in terms of human resources in EPs to deliver MERESE. Due to a lack of will between parties and the absence of seamless channels of communication and dialogue, some of these schemes for payment of ecosystem services tend to be compromised. Further to improving the actual implementation of MERESE, unlocking some of the prevailing obstacles, it seems imperative to develop communication mechanisms that allow those paying to know where and how their contributions would be invested. For instance, there is significant distrust between the drinking water users, actually paying MERESE in their water bill with the relevant EPs, and the EPs themselves in terms of the use of the funds raised. There is also a mistrust from farming communities and agricultural users to accept projects supported by public or private funds, which creates delays or in some cases prevents the implementation of the project itself.

Ways forward to strengthen multi-level water governance

Water governance as a means to an end

Water governance plays a critical role in enhancing water security in Peru. Water is a valuable economic asset and a driver for social development, among many other things. Water security directly contributes to fostering the establishment of a competitive export-oriented agricultural sector, increasingly inserted in the global economy, the potential expansion of a modern mining and energy industry, or the rapid urbanisation process. Likewise, water security also drives growth as it is of chief importance for the entire production system to the induced demand of services associated with economic activities and the delivery of linked commodities and services.

Peru's challenge is very much one of progressing from approaches driven by crisis management to water resources management rather than driven by risk and opportunity management within a context of increased uncertainties and the need for climate change adaptation. The current economic downturn and the associated fiscal consolidation effort, in a context of global pandemic and health crisis, both contribute to reducing public funds availability to supporting new grey infrastructural development, ad hoc responses to droughts and floods as well as water conflict management through additional subsidies or other short-term expansionary fiscal policy measures.

Enhanced water governance, is a means to an end. It is not important in itself but only as a result of the benefits it delivers and not only in terms of improved environmental quality but ultimately of social well-being. In Peru, the challenge in terms of water governance is very much one of improving social responses to water scarcity and wider water-borne risk mitigation whilst increasing the resilience of social and economic development.

Ways forward

Based on the specific characteristics of the legal and institutional framework of Peru, on existing approaches to water management, both as a resource and as a service, and on international best practices, the section below suggests ways forward to:

- Progress towards a **holistic and integrated approach** to water security.

- Ensure **sufficient capacity** in terms of numbers of staff and qualification profiles at the national, regional and local levels.
- Strengthen the **information and knowledge base** about current and future risks of pollution, droughts and floods.
- Enhance **strategic planning** for more effective public investment.
- Redesign economic and financial **incentives**.
- Engage **stakeholders** in defining the acceptable levels of water risk.

Progress towards a holistic and integrated approach to water security

Peru should ensure that forms (e.g. governance structures such as ministries etc.) follow functions (e.g. water as a driver to sustainable development and economic growth). This implies that regardless of its institutional attachment, ANA should strengthen its multi-sectoral character. This would entail the following actions:

- Raise the profile of water policy both at an executive (i.e. Cabinet Office, Vice-presidency, etc.) and legislative level, avoiding restructuring legal powers across public agencies and ministries' portfolios as a mere administrative change (e.g. the overall ministerial attachment of ANA). Regardless of its location and belonging in the Cabinet, ANA should have direct, effective and high-level access to inter-ministerial policymaking at the national level and should be strengthened in different ways to be recognised by all water users and all policymakers as *the* reference for water policy, as it is the case of the National Water Agency in Brazil, for instance (Box 2.4). ANA should perceived by all interested parties as an independent "honest broker" and that the attachment and status of ANA in the overall governmental setup should support this.
- Clearly distinguish between those legal powers in ANA that have to do with water for irrigation and those that clearly demand a strong multi-sectoral approach.
- Improve representation of connected policy areas within different institutions (in particular ANA, DIGESA, water utilities and the CRHC, as well as in similar bodies in other policy areas and in local and regional governments). Potential indicators to evaluate progress could be the number of effective meetings of the National Water Resources Council a year and the seats for non-agricultural users in the National Water Resources Council.
- Set up formal mechanisms for sectoral co-ordination, for example through the operationalisation of a memorandum of agreement with ANA. For example, in Australia, the National Water Initiative (NWI) was developed in 2004 as an inter-governmental agreement whereby commitments to reach targets related to the efficient and sustainable management of water are made across levels of government and closely monitored.

Box 2.4. The National Water Agency of Brazil (ANA)

The National Water Agency of Brazil (*Agência Nacional de Águas*, ANA) was created in 2000 by federal law, with the status of a regulatory agency and definition of its structure by decree. It is a special autarchy, with administrative and financial autonomy, linked to the Ministry of the Environment. Its main purpose is to implement the national water resources policy. The agency serves as the meeting point between top-down and bottom-up trends and policies, as well as the overarching link between subsidiarity-based (states and municipalities) and solidarity-based (river basins) decentralisation.

ANA was created as the "meeting point" of two distinct needs and, to some extent, contradictory dynamics. On one hand, it is the driver of the reform process to help states create their own agencies and to provide incentives and support to the creation of basin committees. In short, ANA should help drive forward decentralisation. On the other, it is the "mastermind" at the central level with very good technical capabilities and political independence, able to provide answers to the many needs of the nation.

The combination of a high standard and hierarchical position of a regulator at the federal level and the capacity to keep its "feet on the ground" as a national executive agency for matters related to federal rivers (e.g. licensing water uses, collecting water charges) gives ANA some flexibility, credibility and national presence.

Source: OECD (2015[27]), *Water Resources Governance in Brazil*, https://dx.doi.org/10.1787/9789264238121-en.

A second way forward is to further integrate policies related to all the water realms (glaciers, river ecosystems, coastal areas and marine ecosystems), under the umbrella of climate change adaptation (CCA) and disaster risk reduction (DRR) policies, with a clearer approach to social-ecological resilience. A National Strategy or Blueprint for Long-term Water Security within the context of climate change could provide additional (internal and external) consistency to current policies and planning efforts, as well as connecting water policy in a much more explicit way to other sectoral policies and climate change mitigation and adaptation efforts. For example, the Delta Programme is a national programme to ensure water security in the Netherlands in the long term, for the next 100 years, and to make sure it keeps being a safe and attractive place to live and work for present and future generations (Box 2.5).

Box 2.5. The National Delta Programme in the Netherlands

The Delta Programme (DP) is a national programme implemented in the Netherlands since 2010 which consists of strategies to protect the Netherlands against high water and flooding, to ensure a sufficient supply of fresh water and to contribute to rendering the Netherlands climate-proof and water-resilient. The programme aims at advancing an adaptive governance approach and relies on updated standards for flood protection, a policy framework regarding flood-proof urban (re)development and efforts to improve disaster management.

As part of this programme, district water boards, municipalities, provinces, ministries and the Rijkswaterstaat (the executive branch of the Ministry of Infrastructure and Water Management) are represented in the Delta Programme Steering Committee as well as in the thematic and regional board. They jointly prepare key decisions, develop strategies and implement measures, in close co-operation with private stakeholders including NGOs as well as knowledge institutions. The Delta Commissioner directs this multigovernmental process, monitors progress, reports to parliament every year and takes the necessary steps when problems arise.

The DP resulted in a new Delta Law providing the legal framework for the independent Delta Commissioner to formulate, actualise and execute the DP, and the setup of the Delta Fund to secure continuity in finance for the cost of maintenance and development of new infrastructure. In addition, the formulated Delta Decisions have been embedded in the National Water Plan as policy decisions by the Dutch government in 2014; the Delta Programme Agreement was signed in 2014 by the provinces, water boards, municipalities and the Minister of Infrastructure and the Environment to anchor the Delta Decisions and preference strategies in their own plans; and a National Water and Climate Knowledge and Innovation Programme to stimulate innovations, joint-programming and connecting clients with contractors was set up.

The DP is one of the five elements of this long-term investment plan; the other four are the Delta Decisions, the Delta Commissioner, the Delta Fund and the Delta Act.

Along with continuity in policy, the success of the DP is to be explained by the effective combination of bottom-up and top-down processes in this development; which ensure ownership and long-term commitment for successful implementation while ensuring timely progress and rational decision-making.

Some measures of the DP are entirely or partially funded from the Delta Fund, containing financial resources which the central government has earmarked to fund investments in flood risk management, freshwater supply and water quality. In the period 2021-34, a sum of approximately EUR 18.6 billion will be available in the Delta Fund, which brings the annual budget to an average of EUR 1.3 billion.

Source: OECD (2013[28]), *Water and Climate Change Adaptation: Policies to Navigate Uncharted Waters*, https://doi.org/10.1787/9789264200449-en; OECD (2014[29]), *Water Governance in the Netherlands: Fit for the Future?*, https://doi.org/10.1787/9789264102637-en; OECD (n.d.[30]), *Country Profile: The Netherlands*, OECD, Paris; EC (2018[31]), "Mission-oriented R&I policies: In-depth case studies", Case Study Report Delta Plan/ Delta Programme (The Netherlands), European Commission; Government of the Netherlands (n.d.[32]), "National Delta Programme 2021, Staying on track in climate-proofing the Netherlands".

Third, to progressively move away from crisis management towards risk and opportunity management, exploring complex linkages between sectoral policies (with emphasis on the nexus water-energy-mining-food-climate-biodiversity), through:

- Enhancing water demand management, from a nexus approach, measuring the number of intersectoral links identified and the high-level initiatives to promote dialogue across crosscutting issues. MIDAGRI, the MVCS, MINEM, MINSA, and PRODUCE could co-ordinate sectoral policies and mainstreaming water policies. The MINAM could take responsibilities to make this happen.
- Considering the inclusion of tariffs in other sectors that are dependent on water resources for sustainability (power generation, agriculture) to effectively recover the costs associated with (consumptive and non-consumptive) water uses.
- Strengthening an integrated approach for relevant public health issues, such as child anaemia and illegal mining through joint initiatives from the public sector (MINEM, MIDIS, MINSA, MINAM, etc.).

Complementing traditional supply augmentation projects with major water use efficiency improvements and nature-based solutions is also much needed. There is more to be done in contemporary water policy rather than working with long-term availability in mind, with a bias towards supply augmentation or traditional flood management. The timely development of natural or conventional infrastructure, or a hybrid approach, might in principle avoid critical situations due to lack (or excess) of water. Indeed, considering hybrid and adaptive approaches to infrastructure development (combining grey and natural-based solutions) could be achieved through:

- Ensuring that reconstruction plans with changes include the obligation to execute a percentage of nature-based actions within the grey infrastructure projects under the responsibility of the MVCS and the PGRHC.
- Including the obligation to consider a natural infrastructure component that is integrated into the grey infrastructure components in the PGRHC and the grey infrastructure projects in charge of the competent sanitation authorities.
- Developing the analysis of water risks at the basin scale for the effective use of MERESE funds and that allow making decisions on prioritised basins for the design and implementation of natural infrastructure.
- Initiating a process of evaluation and documentation on the results and performance of the natural infrastructure interventions in terms of the desired hydrological result.

Peru's water resources management strives to diversify water supply sources (via water reuse and saltwater and brackish water desalination), in addition to considering surface runoff and groundwater (including joint management of these). Additional supplies to cope with temporary shortages should be considered, whilst also promoting the substitution of the most vulnerable water supply sources in order to reduce overexploitation. The latter should be done through the diversification of water supply sources but also water demand management schemes. For both, refining pricing schemes to redesign incentives is critical. It would also be helpful to engage more closely with the academia and research institutions for fostering research and technological development on alternative water supply sources for different purposes (e.g. seawater could be useful for coastal areas from Tacna to Tumbes, lacking water but not quality soils).

Another priority is to strengthen the link between water resources management and water supply and sanitation services to avoid a decoupled policy approach. Examples of suggested actions in this area could be:

- For ANA to build or upgrade a national water resources plan based on long-term scenarios (including climate change ones) and risk assessments (30+ years) and developing, together with SUNASS, a national inventory of water resources that are suitable for drinking water production. The strategic plan could take the form of a thorough review of the PNRH and put in place a more concerted action towards improved resilience and long-term water security within the context of CCA efforts, building on the opportunity provided by the Intended Nationally Determined Contributions (INDC) process to strengthen co-ordination, which has ben set in place since the Paris Agreement in 2016. The strategic plan could take the form of a thorough review of the prevailing PNRH and could put in place a more concerted action towards improved resilience and long-term water security within the context of CCA efforts, building on current INDC by MINAM, a process that is intended to strengthen co-ordination, also benefitting from the approval of the Framework Law for Climate Change (LMCC). For example, the California Water Plan Update (2018) is the most recent of the state's strategic plan for sustainably managing and developing water resources for current and future generations. The water plan is much more than a planning or guidance document as it provides a policy forum for elected officials, agencies, California Native American Tribes, resource managers, businesses, academia, stakeholders and the public to collaboratively develop findings and recommendations that inform decisions about water policies, actions and investments. The plan is a key tool for strengthening these partnerships.
- For the ministries active in rural areas (e.g. the Ministry of Social Development and Social Inclusion), with whom SUNASS had little to no contact when its functions were limited to utilities in urban areas, to establish effective co-ordination between water management and access to quality water services. There are many co-ordination mechanisms in Peru (Box 2.6); however, it would be key to improve the representation of connected policy areas within different institutions (in particular ANA, DIGESA, water utilities and CRHCs as well as in similar bodies in other policy areas and local and regional governments). An enduring mechanism for incentivising inter-governmental co-operation is needed to improve planning and strategic investment, basin management and regulation of water services amongst others.

Box 2.6. Co-ordination mechanisms across levels of government in Peru

In Peru, there are several co-ordination mechanisms at the horizontal and vertical levels of government:

- The National Water Resources Management System can be considered a multi-sectoral co-ordination mechanism across several institutions at the national and subnational levels and a variety of stakeholders. At the national scale, co-ordination takes place through the Board of

Directors, ad hoc multi-sectoral groups (e.g. multi-sectoral committees, thematic roundtable) and advisory committees.

- At the subnational scale, through River Basin Councils, multi-sectoral specialised task forces (*Grupo Especializado de Trabajo Multisectorial*, *GETRAM*) and thematic roundtables or working groups. Regional governments and local authorities co-ordinate with each other and with ANA, in order to: harmonise their policies and sectoral objectives; avoid conflicts of competency; and contribute with coherence and efficiency in achieving the objectives and purposes of the SNGRH. Significant improvement at this level would be expected though.
- A platform for dialogue across levels of government is the Muni-Executive. It promotes, develops and strengthens the joint and co-ordinated action of the municipal governments and the national government, reinforcing decentralisation and improving the conditions for municipal governments to develop the management of their initiatives, projects and policies.
- According to the law, public entities linked to water management should co-ordinate their actions with ANA. These entities are SUNASS, SENAMHI, OSINERGMIN, OEFA, DICAPI, sectoral competent environmental authorities and water and sanitation services providers (EPs). The MVCS with SUNASS and OTASS co-ordinate their actions to provide technical assistance to the EPs for the application of maximum wastewater discharge thresholds for industrial users. Besides, the MVCS co-ordinates with the MEF within the framework of the National Programme on Rural Sanitation (PNSR) by means of the PI (Incentive Programme for Municipal Management Improvement and Modernisation), which is implemented by the MEF and includes specific objectives for housing; funded actions are aimed at capacity building for guaranteeing the sustainability of sanitation projects in rural areas. The MVCS also works together with MINSA for the implementation of a strategy to increase the percentage of rural households with access to chlorinated water in rural areas of Peru.
- In terms of social conflict management, several bodies are co-ordinating their activities: the Social Management and Dialogue Secretariat, dependent of the PCM; the Conflict Prevention and Management Unit (UPGC), dependent of ANA and the Social Management Unit at MINAM. Further, the National Court for the Adjudication of Water Disputes (*Tribunal Nacional de Resolución de Controversias Hídricas*) is a body attached to ANA with functional autonomy. It is an administrative court of last resort that adjudicates administrative complaints and appeals issued against the administrative resolution of the Water Administrative Authorities and ANA.
- The National Centre for Strategic Planning (CEPLAN) is an entity attached to the Presidency of the Council of Ministers that promotes articulation between sectoral and regional instruments, especially those that are linked to national policies. CEPLAN contributes to co-ordinate national policies, in the absence of incentive mechanisms towards the implementation of the PENRH and PNRH that currently are subject to the availability of each SNGRH member to consider the policies and strategies as part of their own toolboxes and policy mixes.

Ensure sufficient capacity in terms of numbers of staff and qualification profiles at the national, regional and local levels

The country would benefit from strengthening capacity and institutional memory by providing staff who have relevant competencies with strong incentives to remain in their positions and thus reduce staff turnover at both the central government and local levels (CRHCs, WSOs and AAAs). Within capacity building initiatives, a multidisciplinary approach should be taken so as to strengthen the understanding of the complexity of water resources management. Capacity building is also needed to make the existing river basin management plans fully operational. A stronger regional or local political leadership in the CRHCs should be coupled with adequate human and technical resources, as well as access to government finance and subsidies conditional on effective design and implementation of PGRHCs and sanitation plans.

It would be advised to carry out a review of resource needs for water resources management across all involved authorities, including an assessment of the scope for rationalisation and elimination of overlapping tasks, and to consider how these needs can be financed, either through user charging or public funds.

Practical steps could be the following:

- Continue the process of creation of the 29 CRHCs.
- Enhance the level of autonomy of river basin authorities.
- Improve (quantity and quality) of the personnel and their skills. For example, a change in the training of engineers and professionals is needed to make possible a quicker, well-informed assessment that also allows for decision-making based on expert knowledge when data is missing, etc.
- Focus on communal organisations (e.g. JASS), where the personnel are voluntary, unpaid and with very low administration, operation and maintenance capacity.
- Promote professional management preventing political capture of public utilities.
- Reduce instability and high rotation of policymakers in local and regional governments

Box 2.7. Brazil's National Water Management Pact

The Programme for the National Pact for Water Management instituted in 2011 in Brazil (Progestão) is a voluntary-based multi-level governance contract aiming to support the implementation of an integrated, decentralised and participative water management model. Recognising that improving water management requires better integration of the federal- and state-level water management systems, the National Pact for Water Management was designed to improve capacity and strengthen water resources management at the state level, to foster convergence between states and increase flexibility and adaptability to address the diverse situations and levels of ability ranging between states. Its overarching goals consist in:

- Establishing commitments among federative units to overcome common challenges and lack of harmonisation.
- Encouraging multiple and sustainable use of water resources, especially in shared river basins.
- Promoting an effective articulation between water resources management and regulation processes at the national and state levels.
- Empowering states towards greater capacity and awareness in dealing with water risks.

Through the pact, ANA builds capacity at the state and municipal levels by providing target- and results-based financing through the Consolidation Programme of the Pact, Progestão, which makes BRL 100 million (approximately USD 40 million) available over a 5-year period to states reaching their goals. Funding is proportional and contingent on the successful implementation of what states themselves have committed to undertaking. Progestão also interacts with other ANA programmes, such as INTERAGUAS, which contributes to strengthening planning and governance. ANA also provides technical support, instruments and resources to shed light on the weaknesses and needs of states.

The first cycle of the project, which involved 27 participating states, started in 2013 and ended in 2017. The second cycle which started in 2018 will last until 2022 and involves 24 states – the difference in the number of participating states is due to the lack of compliance by some states to administrative requirements.

The evaluation conducted at the end of the first cycle resulted in some modifications including changes in the criteria related to resource management, the creation of a new target relating to federative co-operation, an emphasis on training in water resources, etc.

Source: OECD (2015[27]), *Water Resources Governance in Brazil*, http://dx.doi.org/10.1787/9789264238121-en; P.A.C. Libanio (P.A.C. Libanio, 2017[33]), "Promoting and assessing water governance at subnational level: the experience of Brazil's National Water Management Pact", https://doi.org/10.1080/02508060.2017.1328638; BCG Foundation (2016[34]), "The Brazilian Progestão, a national agreement for managing freshwater resources", https://www.centreforpublicimpact.org/case-study/brazils-national-pact-for-water-management/.

Strengthen the information and knowledge base about current and future risks of pollution, droughts and floods

To support the development of river basin plans, the AAAs should build long-term scenarios at the level of river basins and their sub-basins based on water balances and taking account of possible or expected developments in land use, economic activity, climate and demography in the basin. Since 2014, hydrological measurement networks have been modernised, automating the registration and data transmission processes. With projected increases in drought and flood risks, investment in policy-relevant indicators will become even more important. However, national water indicators may be less meaningful in the case of a large country like Peru, characterised by a high diversity of bioclimatic zones, hydrological regimes and water demands. Hence, national averages may hide serious water-stress conditions at the regional, basin-level scale. Accurate water balances at the basin level should therefore become a priority. Having reliable and quality assured water data and measuring water stress at the water basin scale and aggregating at the national level on this basis would constitute an improvement in this regard. MINAM, ANA and SUNASS could collaborate to:

- Continue promoting measurement networks to get accurate water balances at the basin level.
- Have reliable and quality assured water data, especially for groundwater resources.
- Increase the granularity of data at the subnational level: a country-scale indicator may mask serious water-stress conditions at the regional, basin-level scale.
- Reduce asymmetry or lack of information due to institutional silos or malfunctions in the allocation of legal powers and administrative co-ordination mechanisms.
- Provide mechanisms to monitor payments, especially from agricultural uses.

Enhance strategic planning for more effective public investment

Strategic planning can be a significant lever to simplify and accelerate public investment procedures and align them better with decision-making schemes. It is particularly key to streamline investment evaluation procedures within the National Multi-year Programming and Investment Management System (Invierte.pe) to minimise obstacles, as compared to conventional infrastructure projects. While several schemes are in place for the conservation of biodiversity and ecosystem services, ranging from legally protecting headwaters to MERESE, natural infrastructure would allow for synergies between sectoral policies: forest, spatial development, water. As such, specific regulatory measures could be applied to allow streamlining investments in natural infrastructure by approving alternative routes to the public investment system.

For sanitation, financial incentives could also be considered for local governments to comply and adhere with department sanitation plans, for instance by modulating access to governmental grant finance accordingly. An example of an effective capacity-building programme across levels of government is the National Water Management Pact in Brazil (Box 2.7). The EU supports the implementation of policies and legislation by providing financial incentives to member states, applying *ex ante* conditionality that each country must fulfil in order to qualify for financial support. In particular, the following should be considered:

- Increasing municipal and regional fiscal resources and investments, for instance by transferring a share of the revenues collected via the so-called mining exports excise (*canon minero*) to regional and local governments.
- Simplifying and accelerating public investment procedures and align with decision-making schemes to maximise timelines and co-ordination. An example of such an approach could involve matching the Optimised City Masterplan, which includes investment projects, with the municipal sector plan, which includes urban development projects. It is critical to note that Resolution No. 004-2019-EF/63.01, which approved the General Guidance for the Identification, Formulation and Evaluation of Investment projects, establishes that all investment projects need to follow the same investment assessment cycle. It is also important to establish that, in solidarity with other stakeholders in the basins, the EPs maintain the responsibility of investment in addressing water risks for the provision of the public service they provide and that the optimised masterplan be co-ordinated with instruments and public management plans in the watersheds to ensure the financing of interventions in natural infrastructure based on needs.
- Creating strong financial incentives for local governments to comply with and adhere to department sanitation plans, e.g. by modulating access to governmental grant finance accordingly.
- Following uniform criteria for investments in water and sanitation for urban and rural areas, that is standardised investment instruments that, based on technical and least-cost criteria cost, allow for efficient investment decisions for the sector.

Further engagement with the private sector is also needed, through strengthened public regulation towards guaranteeing the public interest and improving the connection of research, technological development and, above all, innovation in the water sector, which has become a priority. There has been significant progress in co-operating with the private sector through shared value initiatives promoted by multilateral donors and national organisations. However, the most proactive private partners seem to be facing a number of constraints in terms of investment procedures, risk management facilities, project appraisal and procurement. Insights from multi-stakeholder platforms should be accounted for to ensure more beneficial inputs from the private sector, beyond prevailing mechanisms (i.e. PPPs, works for taxes, etc.). The following actions can be considered by the MEF, MIDAGRI, MINEM and the MVCS:

- Create fiscal incentives or expand Works for Taxes schemes.
- Remove harmful subsidies.
- Promote private investments in public services and public infrastructure through PPPs, led either by public or private initiatives.
- Provide information services to investors and help to create a conducive environment, attractive for private investments, improving information sharing across public policies.
- Improve the temporal scale of project evaluations in the public investment system (Invierte.pe).
- Avoid fragmentation of investment projects.
- Strengthen co-ordination between FED (Outcome-oriented Fund for the Stimulus of Performance at the social level), FONAVI (National Housing Fund) and PROINVERSION.
- Promote a framework for PPPs for water and resilience projects – while developing a new asset class (e.g. natural infrastructure).

Redesign economic and financial incentives

Economic and financial incentives should not only strive to raise revenue but also consider water quantity and quality objectives while taking into account distributional effects. As such, improving pricing schemes, with emphasis on bulk water pricing (ANA's water abstraction and treated wastewater discharge fees) would contribute to adapting water availability and demand, especially in the most water-stressed basins. In turn, this would guarantee additional supplies to cope with temporary shortages, whilst promoting the substitution of the most vulnerable water supply sources in order to reduce overexploitation. More specifically, this improvement should contribute to pricing access to non-conventional water sources in a way that induces farmers to signal their responsible use of groundwater resources under their control. This would lead to an increase in resilience through increasing water security for urban uses by reducing shortages of water for irrigation, via relaxing surface water abstraction. A likely outcome would also be the increase of buffer stocks in the medium term (by an excess supply of non-conventional sources in normal periods) and in the longer term (by allowing better conservation levels in aquifers).

Setting an opportunity cost for groundwater overexploitation would allow to regain control of groundwater resources**.** The prevailing groundwater management and monitoring tariff is a relevant milestone. These include considering incentives for more efficient abstraction and consumption of groundwater use, more ambitious monitoring initiatives, analysis of behavioural patterns of groundwater users, expanding the micro-metering of groundwater use, controlling informal users, fostering reclaimed wastewater reuse or connecting the groundwater tariff to the MERESE, as in the case of the Lima region. However, without making more information available about current trends of groundwater resources (both in terms of availability and quality), the tariff is likely to have limited impact. Furthermore, this tariff is not currently levied on agricultural users. Aquifers are being used de facto as an insurance policy with no role whatsoever for the financial sector as yet. In the future, if such an opportunity cost on groundwater use is foreseen nationwide, there would be an opportunity to stabilise farmers' income in dry periods through reducing incentives to extract from already depleted aquifers and providing incentives to signal a responsible use of aquifers. This would ensure collective control of aquifers, as compensation in dry periods might be contingent on the proof that no overdraft occured in a particular irrigation district.

While redesigning economic and financial incentives, no one should be left behind and distributional effects should be considered. Protection of consumers and low-income farmers is an essential part of IWRM that is lagging. Peru does not yet have enough tools to protect consumers or rural livelihoods in general, even though there is legislation available. New tools to protect low-income households and small-scale subsistence farmers should be created, mostly through focused subsidies on demand and measures beyond water policy that address the actual societal challenge, namely poverty and social exclusion. For example, the following could be considered:

- Reinforce the role of CEPLAN.
- Promote coverage and sustainability of services in rural areas.
- Explore a progressive structure of tariffs as the best way to ensure a sustainable collection of revenues to meet cost-recovery targets and to establish cross-subsidies schemes for low-income households.
- Define operational mechanisms for the fair compensation of benefits to those who are directly linked to the fulfilment of the objectives and results of the projects in the basins.

The OECD Guidelines on Corporate Governance of State-Owned Enterprises give concrete advice to make state-owned enterprises more competitive, efficient and transparent (OECD, 2015[35]). Examples of consultation bodies can be found in the Essential Services Commission of South Australia, the Customer Forum in Scotland, the Local Public Services Consultation Commission in France.

Engage stakeholders in defining acceptable levels of water risk

Bringing stakeholders together to agree on acceptable levels of water risks for the community would give ANA an extremely powerful "entry point" on the ground and allow it to play its full role as a water authority. Important investments (e.g. mining investments) for the Peruvian economy have been missed for lack of prior agreement on such acceptable levels of risks. The risk-based approach would also mitigate the risk of having to resort to the Water Conflict Adjudication Court to resolve appeals against administrative decisions emanating from ANA. CRHCs, despite their consultative nature and significant deficits in terms of financial and technical capacity, have experience in engaging stakeholders. However, the representation of various users and their voice in the planning and management of water resources should be carefully considered to avoid the risk of capture by some categories (i.e. agricultural users). As such, it would be important to:

- Strengthen the engagement of regional and local authorities and their commitment to the implementation of the national plan and the adequate fulfilment of the functions of River Basin Councils.
- Improve co-ordination between technical secretariats and AAAs and ALAs in working groups.
- Improve the social legitimacy of charges (develop communication mechanisms that allow those paying to know where and how their contributions would be invested).
- Convene a national summit gathering national, provincial and local governments and policymakers.
- Complete the process of setting up multisector working groups (GETRAM) with the inclusion of regional governments.

An example of stakeholder engagement for water policy is the EU Better Regulation Guidelines. Following the adoption of the 2015 Better Regulation Guidelines, the European Commission has extended its range of stakeholder engagement methods to enable stakeholders to express their view of the entire lifecycle of a policy, including water policy (fitness check of the Water Framework Directive -WFD and Flood Directive-FD).

References

Acuerdo Nacional (2012), *Política de Estado sobre Recursos Hídricos, Secretaría Ejecutiva del Acuerdo Nacional, Perú*, https://www.ana.gob.pe/sites/default/files/politica_de_recursos_hidricos_33_documento.pdf. [1]

Albán Contreras, L. (2017), *El Fondo del Agua Quiroz-Chira: Un mecanismo de gestión para los ecosistemas de montaña de Piura, Perú - Sistematización de la experiencia*, Naturaleza y Cultura Internacional and Andean Forests programme of the Swiss Agency for Development and Cooperation (COSUDE), https://cooperacionsuiza.pe/wp-content/uploads/2017/02/faqch-final-web.pdf. [7]

ANA (2020), *Consejos de Recursos Hídricos de Cuenca*, https://www.ana.gob.pe/nosotros/planificacion-hidrica/plan-gestion-cuencas (accessed on 18 March 2021). [13]

ANA (2019), "Autoridad Nacional del Agua informa sobre proceso de zonificación de cabeceras de cuenca, noticia (11 junio 2019)", Autoridad Nacional del Agua, https://www.ana.gob.pe/noticia/autoridad-nacional-del-agua-informa-sobre-proceso-de-zonificacion-de-cabeceras-de-cuenca. [17]

ANA (2019), *Compendio nacional de estadísticas de recursos hídricos 2017 (SNIRH)*, Autoridad Nacional del Agua, https://www.ana.gob.pe/publicaciones/compendio-nacional-de-estadisticas-de-recursos-hidricos-2017. [21]

ANA (2018), *Memoria Anual 2017*, https://repositorio.ana.gob.pe/handle/20.500.12543/2442 (accessed on 12 March 2021). [10]

ANA (2017), *Gestión integrada de recursos hídricos en el Perú: Consejos de Recursos Hídricos de Cuenca, avances y retos para la gobernanza hídrica*, Autoridad Nacional del Agua, http://repositorio.ana.gob.pe/handle/20.500.12543/681. [25]

ANA (2017), *Marco de Gestión Ambiental y Social del Proyecto de Gestión Integrada de los Recursos Hídricos en Diez Cuencas Hidrográficas (Código SNIP N° 302961)*, Autoridad Nacional del Agua, https://www.ana.gob.pe/proyectos-ana/pgirh. [2]

ANA (2017), *Plan Estratégico Institucional–PEI 2018-2021*, Autoridad Nacional del Agua, https://www.ana.gob.pe/sites/default/files/archivos/manager/2018-10/PEI%202018%20-%202021_FINAL.pdf. [22]

ANA (2017), "Representatividad y poder de decisión en Consejos de Recursos Hídricos de Cuenca Perú", Autoridad Nacional del Agua, https://www.riob.org/sites/default/files/IMG/pdf/JAVER_-_PRESENTACION_BRASILIA_JRP.pdf. [26]

ANA (2014), "Protocolo para la prevención y gestión de conflictos sociales vinculados con los recursos hídricos", Autoridad Nacional del Agua, http://repositorio.ana.gob.pe/handle/20.500.12543/216. [5]

ANA (2013), *Plan Nacional de Recursos Hídricos del Perú: Memoria*, Autoridad Nacional del Agua, http://www.ana.gob.pe/sites/default/files/plannacionalrecursoshidricos2013.pdf. [23]

ANA and MINAGRI (2016), *Priorización de cuencas para la gestión de los recursos hídricos*. [3]

BCG Foundation (2016), "The Brazilian Progestão, a national agreement for managing freshwater resources", https://www.centreforpublicimpact.org/case-study/brazils-national-pact-for-water-management/. [34]

Chirinos, K. (2018), "Implicancias de establecer un Marco Metodológico para identificar, delimitar y zonificar las cabeceras de cuenca en el Perú. Análisis de la modificación del artículo 75º de la Ley de Recursos Hídricos", PUCP, Facultad de Derecho, Perú, http://tesis.pucp.edu.pe/repositorio/bitstream/handle/20.500.12404/13733/Chirinos_Espinoza_Implicancias_establecer_marco1.pdf?sequence=1&isAllowed=y. [18]

EC (2018), "Mission-oriented R&I policies: In-depth case studies", Case Study Report Delta Plan/ Delta Programme (The Netherlands), European Commission. [31]

Government of Peru (2016), *Se destrabaron 170 obras de agua potable y alcantarillado en beneficio de un millón de Peruanos*, https://www.gob.pe/institucion/presidencia/noticias/9416-se-destrabaron-170-obras-de-agua-potable-y-alcantarillado-en-beneficio-de-un-millon-de-peruanos (accessed on 15 March 2021). [12]

Government of the Netherlands (n.d.), "National Delta Programme 2021, Staying on track in climate-proofing the Netherlands". [32]

MIDIS (2019), *Quiénes Somos?*, http://www.foncodes.gob.pe/portal/index.php/nosotros/quienessomos3. [24]

MINAM (2011), *Conversatorio internacional: Mecanismos de financiamiento para la conservación de los ecosistemas y la biodiversidad*, http://repositorio.ana.gob.pe/bitstream/handle/20.500.12543/4433/ANA0002933.pdf?sequence=1&isAllowed=y. [6]

MVCS (2019), *DATASS - Modelo para la toma de decisiones en saneamiento*, https://datass.vivienda.gob.pe/ (accessed on 15 March 2021). [9]

MVCS (2018), *DATASS: Modelo para la toma de decisiones en Saneamiento. Sistema de Diagnóstico sobre Abastecimiento de Agua y Saneamiento en el Ámbito Rural*, Ministerio de Vivienda, Construcción y Saneamiento, https://cooperacionsuiza.pe/wp-content/uploads/2018/11/DATASS-Modelo-para-la-toma-de-decisiones-web.pdf. [8]

OECD (2016), *Regulatory Policy in Peru: Assembling the Framework for Regulatory Quality*, OECD Reviews of Regulatory Reform, OECD Publishing, Paris, https://doi.org/10.1787/9789264260054-en. [20]

OECD (2015), *OECD Guidelines on Corporate Governance of State-Owned Enterprises, 2015 Edition*, OECD Publishing, Paris, https://dx.doi.org/10.1787/9789264244160-en. [35]

OECD (2015), *OECD Principles on Water Governance*, OECD, Paris, http://www.oecd.org/cfe/regional-policy/OECD-Principles-on-Water-Governance.pdf. [14]

OECD (2015), "OECD Studies on Water, Country profile, Spain", OECD, Paris, https://www.oecd.org/spain/Water-Resources-Allocation-Spain.pdf. [16]

OECD (2015), *OECD Water Governance Principles (brochure)*, OECD, Paris, https://www.oecd.org/gov/regional-policy/OECD-Principles-on-Water-Governance-brochure.pdf. [36]

OECD (2015), *Water Resources Governance in Brazil*, OECD Studies on Water, OECD Publishing, Paris, https://dx.doi.org/10.1787/9789264238121-en. [27]

OECD (2014), *Water Governance in the Netherlands: Fit for the Future?*, OECD Studies on Water, OECD Publishing, Paris, https://doi.org/10.1787/9789264102637-en. [29]

OECD (2013), *Water and Climate Change Adaptation: Policies to Navigate Uncharted Waters*, OECD Studies on Water, OECD Publishing, Paris, https://doi.org/10.1787/9789264200449-en. [28]

OECD (2011), *Water Governance in OECD Countries: A Multi-level Approach*, OECD Studies on Water, OECD Publishing, Paris, https://doi.org/10.1787/9789264119284-en. [15]

OECD (n.d.), *Country Profile: The Netherlands*, OECD, Paris. [30]

OECD/ECLAC (2017), *OECD Environmental Performance Reviews: Peru 2017*, OECD Environmental Performance Reviews, OECD Publishing, Paris, https://doi.org/10.1787/9789264283138-en. [4]

P.A.C. Libanio (2017), "Promoting and assessing water governance at subnational level: The experience of Brazil's National Water Management Pact", *Water International*, Vol. 42/4, pp. 385-399, https://doi.org/10.1080/02508060.2017.1328638. [33]

PCM (2017), *Peru: A Reliable Partner for the OECD*, Gobierno de Perú/GIZ/World Bank, https://sgp.pcm.gob.pe/wp-content/uploads/2017/05/brochure-PERU-OECD.pdf. [11]

World Bank (2017), *Project Appraisal Document on a Proposed Loan in the Amount of us$ 40 Million to the Republic of Peru for a Peru Integrated Water Resources Management in Ten Basins Project (April 05, 2017)*, Report No: PAD2104, World Bank, Washington, DC, http://documents.worldbank.org/curated/en/634181493604098313/pdf/Peru-Integrated-Water-Resources-Mngt-in-Ten-Basins-P151851-PAD-04112017.pdf. [19]

Additional references

ANA (2017), *Plan Estratégico Institucional–PEI 2018-2021*, Autoridad Nacional del Agua, https://www.ana.gob.pe/sites/default/files/archivos/manager/2018-10/PEI%202018%20-%202021_FINAL.pdf.

ANA (2018), *Memoria Anual 2017*, Autoridad Nacional del Agua, https://hdl.handle.net/20.500.12543/00.12543/2442.

ANA/MINAGRI (2016), *Priorización de Cuencas para la Gestión de los Recursos Hídricos*, https://www.ana.gob.pe/sites/default/files/publication/files/priorizacion_de_cuencas_para_la_gestion_de_los_recursos_hidricos_ana.pdf.

OECD (2011), *Water Governance in OECD Countries: A Multi-level Approach*, OECD Studies on Water, OECD Publishing, Paris , https://doi.org/10.1787/9789264119284-en.

Notes

[1] The national agreement was signed in 2002 by all the political forces represented in Congress, civil society members and the government, to build consensus on state policies and contribute to a shared vision of the country.

[1] It is based upon a previous draft from 2009 (R.J. No. 0250-2009-ANA) and a series of subsequent validated versions (2011, 2012 and 2013).

[2] Art. 17, Law No. 29158: Organic Law of the Executive Power, LOPE.

[3] PCM ROF, Supreme Decree No. 022-2017-PCM.

[4] Supreme Decree No. 18-2017-VIVIENDA

[1] Within the framework of the National System of Environmental Impact Assessment (SEIA) and in accordance with the provisions of Article 53 of the Regulation of the SEIA Law, as well as the provisions Article 81 of Law No. 29338 on Water Resources.

[2] Article 19, Regulation of the Water Resources Law.

[3] Created by ANA's Resolution No. 546-2009-ANA on the basis of MINAGRI-ANA, 2009.

[4] Articles 11, 87 and 90 of the General Environmental Law, No. 28611, regulate the integrated management of transboundary natural resources and inland waters, noting that the state promotes and controls its sustainable use and creates strategic alliances for this purpose, considering compliance with national environmental norms.

[5] The protection of headwaters is promoted by ANA, MINAM, the MEF, MIDAGRI and MINAM through a working party for the preparation of a Methodological Framework for Technical Criteria for the Identification, Delimitation and Zoning of Headwaters of Basins, as established in Law No. 30640, highlighting, among the contributions of MINAM, the insertion of the ecosystem approach in environmental vulnerability and the zoning of the headwaters of the basin, supported by the National Ecosystem Map, which will allow reaching a consensus for the good of the country.

[6] Art. 84, Water Resources Law.

[7] This is done in co-ordination with ANA and with the scientific support of the National Institute for Glacier and Mountain Ecosystem Research (INAIGEM), the Research Institute of the Peruvian Amazon (IIAP) and the Geophysical Institute of Peru (IEP), all of them under the institutional umbrella of MINAM.

[8] Supreme Decree No. 002-2017-MINAM.

[9] The MINAM is responsible for proposing environmental targets and ensuring the protection of the environment and the conservation of natural resources within the framework of the National Environmental Policy. This is done through its main directorates-general, DG Policies and Regulation on Building and Sanitation (DGPRCS), and the attached Directorate of Sanitation, DG Programmes and Building and Sanitation Projects (DGPPC) and DG Environmental Issues (DGA). The Directorate- General for Environmental Issues (*Dirección General de Asuntos Ambientales*, DGAA) is the body responsible for setting environmental objectives, drafting guidance and strategies for the development of the MINAM's legal powers, ensuring the protection of the environment and the conservation of natural resources within the framework of the National Environmental Policy.

[10] Art. 12, Regulation of the Water Resources Law.

[11] Supreme Decree No. 18-2017-VIVIENDA.

[12] Art. 12 Law No. 30215.

[13] Amended by Legislative Decree No. 1078 (Article 2).

[14] For the preparation of the National Inventory of Wetlands, a working group has been created. It is composed of the Ministry of the Environment, the National Water Authority, the Forest and Wildlife Service, the Research Institute of the Peruvian Amazon and the Institute of the Sea of Peru, and is chaired by ANA, with the task of defining the "General Guidelines for the preparation of the National Inventory of Wetlands". The purpose of this process is to generate information on the distribution of wetlands in the country, which, together with the inventory of water sources, will allow adequate decisions to be made for the management of these strategic ecosystems. To date, a number of pilots of the methodology have been implemented in different basins of the country, pending the definition and approval of the guidelines to steer the realisation of this important planning and management instrument at the national level.

[15] Law No. 31075, Law on the organisation and functions of MIDAGRI (23 November 2020).

[16] Article 13, Regulation of the Water Resources Law.

[17] As set up in the Legislative Decree No. 1280 (Framework Law for the Management and Provision of Sanitation Services – hereinafter Framework Law), sanitation services include the following: drinking water supply, sewerage, wastewater treatment and sanitary disposal of excreta).

[18] Legislative Decree No. 1280.

[19] Numeral 3, sub-section 7.1 of Article 7 of Supreme Decree 019-2017-VIVIENDA on the regulation of the Framework Law of Management and Delivery of Sanitation Services.

[20] Ministerial Resolution No. 078-2019-VIVIENDA.

[21] Supreme Decree No. 006-2007-VIVIENDA.

[22] Supreme Decree No. 002-2012-VIVIENDA.

[23] Supreme Decree No. 006-2019-VIVIENDA.

[24] Enactment of the new Framework Law for the Management and Provision of Sanitation Services, via Legislative Decree No. 1280 in 2016 and its regulation (Supreme Decree 019-2017-VIVIENDA) Art. 8, Regulation of the Framework Law for the Management and Provision of Sanitation Services, Supreme Decree No. 019-2017-VIVIENDA.

[25] Legislative Decree No. 25965.

[26] Law No. 27332, Framework Law of Regulatory Agencies of Private Investment in Public Services, Supreme Decree No. 042-2005-PCM.

[27] With the enactment in 2016 of the new legal framework of sanitation services (Framework Law for the Management and Provision of Sanitation Services, Legislative Decree No. 1280 and its Regulation: Supreme Decree No. 019-2017-VIVIENDA) derogated the 1994 General Law of Sanitation Services and the 2013 Law of Sanitation Services Modernisation).

[28] Service area: "the zone under the responsibility of a provider for supply sanitation services. It also includes the potential area in which efficient services could be provided efficiently" (methodology for establishing the areas for provision of services, Resolution No. 13-2020-SUNASS-CD).

[29] Supreme Decree No. 031-2010-SA.

[30] Article 20, Regulation of the Water Resources Law, Supreme Decree No. 001-2010-AG, with competencies clearly defined in its Part II, Chapter IV.

[31] Resolution No. 575-2010-ANA, following the General Guidelines for the Creation of River Basin Councils as well specific guidelines for their internal regulation, as established in Resolution No. 290-2012-ANA.

[1] Art. 194.1 of the implementing regulation of the Water Resources Law: Supreme Decree No. 001-2010-MINAGRI.

[2] In accordance with their organic laws, the Water Resources Law and its Regulation, as in Art. 15.

[3] In accordance with Article 141 of Law No. 27972, Organic Law of Municipalities, municipalities located in rural areas, in addition to basic competencies, are in charge of those related to the promotion of sustainable management of natural resources: soil, water, flora, fauna, biodiversity, in order to integrate the fight

against environmental degradation with the fight against poverty and the generation of employment, within the framework of concerted development plans.

[4] Framework Law for the Management and Provision of Sanitation Services (Legislative Decree No. 1280) following the Organic Law of Regional Governments No. 27867 and the Organic Law of Municipalities No. 27972.

[5] Within the framework of the National Water Resources Information System, specific agreements were signed with the data producers, such as: the National Service of Hydrometrics and Meteorology (SENAMHI); the Chira Special Project – Piura; the Tacna Special Project; the Olmos Special Project – Tinajones; the Pasto Grande Special Project; the SEDAPAL National Geographic Institute (IGN); the Geological, Mining and Metallurgical Institute (INGEMMET); the National Centre for Estimation, Prevention and Reduction of Disaster Risk (CENEPRED); and the National Commission of Aerospace Research and Development (CONIDA). Information is available and freely accessible at http://www.ana.gob.pe/portal/snirh.

[6] Art. 15.4 of the Water Resources Law.

[7] Approved by Supreme Decree No. 001-2010-AG (Art. 191).

[8] These guidelines were approved by Resolution RJ No. 307-2015-ANA and amended by Resolution No. RJ 337-2016-ANA.

3 Economic instruments for water risk management

This chapter discusses the state of the art and ways forward for setting and using economic instruments for water resources management, with a focus on payments for ecosystem services and environmental charges. It examines how public financial support could be considered for the rehabilitation of Peruvian rivers. Finally, the chapter underlines the need for coherence between economic instruments for water resources management and sectoral policies.

Policy instruments of extremely varied design and practical application can be used to manage water risks such as water shortage, water pollution, flooding and the risk of undermining the resilience of freshwater systems. Based on the classification provided by the (OECD, 2008[1]), such instruments may be placed into seven categories: environmental taxes/charges and tradeable permit systems (pricing instruments), public financial support and payments for ecosystem services (financial support instruments), information measures and voluntary schemes. Discussing the effectiveness, cost -efficiency and feasibility of all of these instruments, and their combinations, is beyond the scope of this chapter.

Instead, the chapter discusses in depth two key instruments in water risk management in Peru, the payments for ecosystem services and the environmental charges, evaluating their implementation and proposing ways forward. The chapter also assesses the merits of mobilising public financial support to implement a river rehabilitation policy in Peru. Finally, the chapter underlines the need for these water policy instruments to be consistent with sectoral policies and environmental policies.

Payments for ecosystem services

A conceptual framework

Various definitions of payments for ecosystem services (PES) exist, with no agreed single definition (Schomers and Matzdorf, 2016[2]). However, PES may be broadly defined as a voluntary transaction where ecosystem managers (e.g. landowners) are compensated through conditional payments by ecosystem beneficiaries (often governments, with the public being the general beneficiary), for the additional cost of maintaining ecosystem services above legally required levels. PES assessment involves criteria of effectiveness and cost efficiency. PES that are both effective and cost-efficient can be said to be cost-effective. Another criterion is the feasibility of PES implementation, which is obviously essential if a PES is actually to be introduced and function cost-effectively.[1]

Effectiveness

To be effective, PES instruments employ the "beneficiary pays" principle. Beneficiaries (or buyers of ecosystem services) make conditional payments to ecosystem service managers (or sellers of ecosystem services – typically landowners) to maintain a level of ecosystem services that would otherwise not be in the private economic interest of (or regulatory obligation for) the ecosystem service manager to pursue. The payments to the landowner (which may be either cash or benefits in kind) (Asquith, Vargas and Wunder, 2008[3]) are intended to make forest conservation, the most common target of PES, particularly in developing countries (Engel, Pagiola and Wunder, 2008[4]), at least as economically attractive to the landowner as conversion to pasture. This maintains water and, with it, biodiversity and carbon sequestration services. The buyers may be either private or public sector actors, depending on the nature of the ecosystem service targeted (Figure 3.1). For instance, the buyer may be a private hydropower generator, paying upstream landowners to conserve water management-related ecosystem services (e.g. via forest conservation) for private economic benefit (a user-funded system). The buyer in this scenario may also be a government or other public sector organisations, paying to maintain forest-related ecosystem services that are public goods, such as biodiversity preservation (a government-funded system).

Figure 3.1. The logics of a PES Instrument

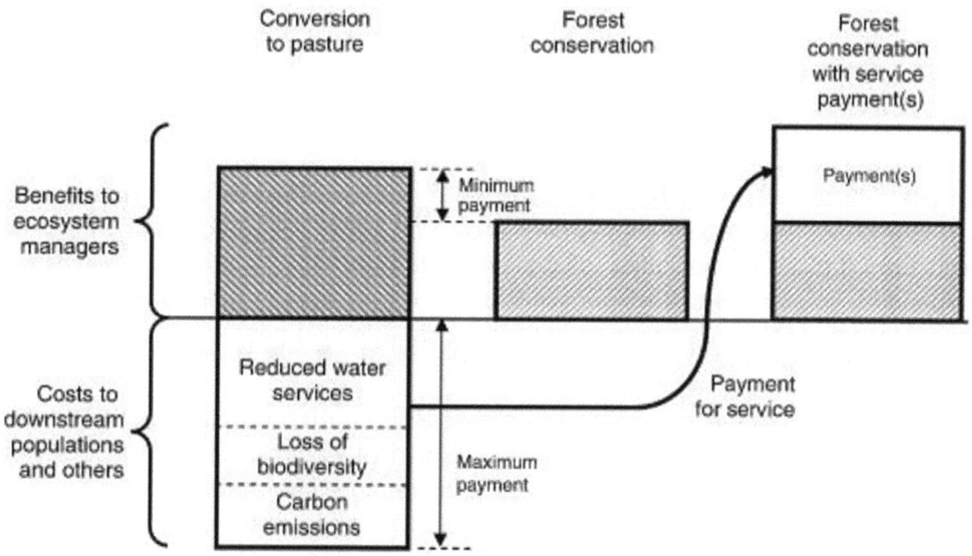

Source: Engel, S., S. Pagiola and S. Wunder (2008[4]), "Designing payments for environmental services in theory and practice: An overview of the issues", https://doi.org/10.1016/j.ecolecon.2008.03.011.

In order to provide sufficient incentive for sellers to accept PES, and therefore allow the instrument to operate, the minimum level of payment should be the differential between the private economic value gained from the presence of the ecosystem services (e.g. forest conservation) and the most profitable use of the land for the owner authorised by law (e.g. conversion to pasture), thus compensating for income loss. The maximum level of payment for cost-effective instrument operation is discussed in the cost efficiency section below.

The point of application should be impact-based and made directly on the basis of ecosystem services provided. However, measuring the provision of "additional units" of ecosystem services delivered against a pre-defined baseline requires a detailed understanding of causal pathways (recognising spatial extent and distribution) (Tomich, Thomas and Noordwijk, 2004[5]), that are often either not fully understood or are impractical to monitor. In such cases, proxies or indicators may be used, such as additional extent or density of forest cover, against which payments can be made. Monitoring such land use related proxies is common (Pagiola and Platais, 2007[6]).

Thus far, despite their growing use around the world, relatively few PES systems have been subject to rigorous *ex post* analysis in either high- or low-income countries (Engel, Pagiola and Wunder, 2008[4]; Pattanayak, Wunder and Ferraro, 2010[7]). However, Pattanayak, Wunder and Ferraro (2010[7]), using an available sample of such studies, found generally positive but limited effectiveness in producing additional ecosystem services. However, such analyses suffer from particular difficulties in determining counterfactual conditions (especially concerning "additionality") and therefore induced change.

As with "polluter pays" instruments, PES systems retain the possibility of inducing the pollution haven effect, with the original ecosystem service-degenerating activity simply shifting ("leaking") to another location. Wunder, Engel and Pagiola (2008[8]) conclude that although little is known about leakage from PES systems due to observation difficulties, some studies cite anecdotal evidence of local leakage (i.e. simply converting another plot of land nearby to substitute for another under a PES contract). Whilst the opportunity for leakage of localised ecosystem services decreases with the increasing scope of the instrument (e.g. proportion of coverage in a watershed for water-related services), the likelihood for the leaking of activities that degenerate global public goods services (e.g. deforestation and biodiversity preservation), the focus of government-funded systems, increases (Wunder, Engel and Pagiola, 2008[8]).

Leakage may also occur across time, with an upcoming PES system creating a perverse incentive for landowners to further degenerate their ecosystem services to receive additional payments in future for restoring them (e.g. deforestation to allow future reforestation). This may be overcome by, for example, setting the baseline against historical circumstances.

Cost efficiency

As with other market-based instruments, PES instruments are cost-efficient when addressing the correct market failure. Additionally, the maximum payment should be either the marginal private benefit or social benefit received from the "additional units" of the ecosystem service in question (as also illustrated in Figure 3.1), depending on whether the instrument is user- or government-funded respectively. The use of reverse auctions may be useful in determining the most cost-effective price point within these parameters and across actors (OECD, 2010[9]).

Pagiola and Platais (2007[6]) argue that user-funded systems are theoretically likely to be the most cost-efficient and Wunder, Engel and Pagiola (2008[8]) find empirical evidence to support this view. Actors in user-financed systems (particularly buyers) are likely to have more information on the marginal benefit of the provision of an ecosystem service and therefore the maximum payment level, whereas calculating the marginal social benefit of public goods' ecosystem services is an extremely difficult task. In addition, actors in user-financed systems have clearer incentives to ensure the instrument operates effectively, are able to more specifically target and observe directly whether the required service is being delivered, and have the ability to rapidly respond and renegotiate the terms of (or terminate) the agreement. Government-funded instruments that purchase public goods services generally suffer from a reduced ability to monitor whether additional services are being provided and a reduced incentive to ensure the instrument is working effectively. Other objectives in government-funded systems, such as poverty alleviation, may also impact cost efficiency in delivering the environmental objective (Pagiola and Platais, 2007[6]). Government-funded instruments may also constitute a subsidy to some actors in the private sector if not applied directly to a pure public good (i.e. non-excludable and non-rival in consumption), such as biodiversity preservation. Many water services are, for example, club goods (i.e. excludable) (Engel, Pagiola and Wunder, 2008[4]).

Can we pay the same land for different ecosystem services? Whilst a given PES system may target a single ecosystem service, separating such services is often not possible (as also illustrated in Figure 3.1). As such, PES may produce both positive and negative side effects (improving one ecosystem service may degenerate or reinforce another). For example, the provision of water management services may change the local habitat, reducing or increasing biodiversity services. Where synergies are identified, ecosystem services may be "bundled" together, allowing the potential for additional benefits and reduced transaction costs (OECD, 2010[9]).[2]

Feasibility

PES instruments may be applied to address a variety of ecosystem services provided by a range of environments managed by different types of entities. When an impact-based approach is infeasible – as is commonly the case with PES instruments, the use of proxies or indicators in an output-based approach may be tailored to the local environment (and other constraints). Conditionality requirements may also be tailored to account for events beyond the control of ecosystem managers (such as vegetation disease or forest fire). For example, as long as indicator thresholds are achieved every four in five years, full payments may still be received (Schwarz et al., 2008[10]).

For a PES instrument (particularly government-funded) to be effective, well-defined criteria for who is entitled to receive payments, along with agreed definitions for the baseline, "units" of additionality and performance metrics, must be clear. Whilst PES instruments do not necessarily require a specific legal framework beyond basic contract law, clear definition and attribution of property rights is a precondition for a feasible system (Greiber, 2009[11]). Construction of the instrument and potentially substantial monitoring and enforcement requirements may produce high transaction costs and require significant administrative capacity. Such issues may reduce the feasibility of PES instruments in low-income countries, particularly for government-funded systems. Further legal complications may also impact the feasibility of a PES instrument. For example, World Trade Organization (WTO) rules may prevent the use of government-funded PES (or other support) systems where private commercial actors (such as farmers) receive payments that effectively subsidise their output. For an instrument to fall within the WTO's "Green Box", [3] payments to a production industry (e.g. agriculture) may only compensate for extra cost or loss of income from maintaining or increasing the provision of environmental services (FAO, 2007[12]).

As a financial support instrument, PES instruments are generally preferred by recipients to "polluter pays" instruments and are similarly subject to deadweight costs when actors are paid to provide services they would have provided anyway. Although the difficulties of monitoring PES systems have been discussed, it tends to be easier to secure co-operation from ecosystem service managers (e.g. landowners) when "offering them carrots than when threatening them with a stick" (Engel, Pagiola and Wunder, 2008[4]). In high-income countries, large agricultural producers have been able to steer the direction of policy towards financial support for environmental goods, rather than taxation on environmental bads. In low-income countries, the providers of environmental services are generally thought to be poorer than service users (or buyers), creating an equity preference for PES (Pagiola and Platais, 2007[6]). Although poverty alleviation is a common secondary (or parallel) objective of many government-financed PES systems (often introduced to increase public acceptability), there is little empirical verification surrounding distributional impacts (Engel, Pagiola and Wunder, 2008[4]).

The requirement for a continued funding stream with no direct economic return may substantially reduce the political feasibility of government-financed systems. Although government-funded systems are the only option when considering the protection of ecosystem services that are pure public goods (such as biodiversity preservation), national governments are disincentivised to implement such instruments unilaterally when they produce global public benefits. This is particularly likely to be the case in lower-income countries. In such cases, the provision of other incentives is likely to be required such as seeking biodiversity co-benefits for measures aimed at other environmental objectives, such as carbon sequestration.

The state of play in Peru

Peru has introduced a legal framework for PES. In 2015, Peru's Ministry of the Environment (*Ministerio del Ambiente*, MINAM) introduced an innovative PES mechanism, called Ecosystem Services Compensation Mechanism (*Mecanismo de Retribución por Servicios Ecosistémicos*, MERESE). The MERESE Act No. 30215 of 2014 and its regulation (Supreme Decree No. 009-2016-MINAM) aim to channel financial resources towards the conservation, recovery and sustainable use of sources of ecosystem services through agreements between parties. It encourages the involvement of the public and private sectors in conserving sources of ecosystem services and stipulates that the actions of those who retain these services can be remunerated. Implemented by MINAM, the law aims to ensure the permanence of the benefits generated by ecosystems.

Prior to that, the Sanitation Services Modernisation Act No. 30045 of 2013 already required each water and sanitation service company (*Empresa Prestadora del Servicio de Saneamiento*, EP) to establish environmental compensation and watershed management mechanisms in their Optimised Master Plan (*Plan Maestro Optimizado*, PMO). The PMO provides for investments (over the next 30 years) as well as tariff increases (for the next 5 years). It is subject to the approval of Peruvian water regulator SUNASS (*Superintendencia Nacional de Servicios de Saneamiento*). SUNASS approves the tariff structure of each EP (by resolution), including the share of tariff revenue allocated to MERESE. Many EPs have thus created specific MERESE funds financed by the water bill, representing up to 11% of their turnover. The funds will compensate communities that commit to providing hydrological services, such as protecting high mountain lake watersheds through reforestation (USD 44 million has been raised nationwide through 2020) (SUNASS, 2020[13]).

The MERESE Regulation of 2016 takes up the obligation for EPs to participate in MERESE. At the end of 2020, 40 of the 50 EPs had a resolution approved by SUNASS for the creation of a MERESE reserve fund according to their PMO. The MERESE Regulation also opens the possibility for board of users of the hydraulic sector (*Junta de Usuarios del Sector Hidráulico,* JUSH) to participate in the financing of MERESE, within the framework of their Operation, Maintenance and Development Plan of the Hydraulic Infrastructure (POMDIH), on a voluntary basis. The MERESE Regulation specifies that the JUSH and hydraulic infrastructure operators can sign MERESE agreements as long as they include actions for the conservation, enhancement and sustainable use of POMDIH water sources. Chief Resolution No. 230-2019-ANA provides guidance for the preparation and implementation of POMDIH by small operators of hydraulic infrastructure. In addition to being voluntary, the process of JUSH participation in MERESE (the decision to participate in the financing of water source conservation) is more complex than that of the EPs in that it must be approved by the assembly of irrigators, which implies a broad awareness-raising process to reach an agreement.

Table 3.1 details the share of EPS revenues allocated to the MERESE reserve fund at the end of 2018 (i.e. in 34 cities in 19 departments across Peru). During the five-year water tariff period, SUNASS can approve an increase in the amount of the reserve fund if the "viable" MERESE projects exceed the amount originally estimated in the PMO. This may lead to an increase in the water tariff subject to approval by SUNASS at the request of the EPs. A similar mechanism was put in place in 2011 to create funds for disaster risk management (*Gestión de Riesgo de Desastres*, GRD) and adaptation to climate change (*Adaptación al Cambio Climático*, ACC) in accordance with Law No. 29664 of 2011 establishing the National System of Disaster Risk Management (SINAGERD)[4] (Table 3.1). In June 2015, SUNASS helped develop and approved the PMO of the Lima water company (*Servicio de Agua Potable y Alcantarillado de Lima*, SEDAPAL) which plans to allocate 1% of the company's turnover to a MERESE fund and 3.8% to 3.5% to a disaster mitigation and adaptation to climate change (GRD/ACC) fund. For SEDAPAL, this represents, respectively, amounts of PEN 86 million (EUR 23 million) and PEN 315 million (EUR 85 million) over 5 years (2015-19). In September 2019, SEDAPAL raised PEN 60 million (EUR 16 million) for its MERESE fund.

The impact on the household budget is modest. Often, it is less than PEN 1 per month for the MERESE fund, which suggests that the criteria of affordability have been taken into account (Table 3.1). The other side of the coin, however, is that the amounts of reserve funds are often limited (except for Lima given the base of clients served by SEDAPAL). MERESE funds sometimes finance water supply and sanitation infrastructure in addition to the protection of ecosystems, as shown by the example of Cusco (Table 3.2). In Cusco, installing toilets for local communities was a prerequisite for the recovery of a lagoon contaminated by excreta. The PMO logic that underlies the financial functioning of MERESE funds may lead to an imbalance between resources devoted to water supply and sanitation services and those devoted to the ecosystem services for which the fund is normally intended. This is the case for the Cusco EP (Table 3.2).

The activities envisaged vary considerably from one EP to another. Legislative Decree No. 1280 of 2016 establishes three modalities for the use of MERESE funds: within the framework of the programming of public investments (national system of multi-year programming and management of investments); direct payments to PES suppliers; and subcontracting to specialised private entities created by law for the administration of environmental heritage funds. Resolution No. 039-2019-SUNASS-CD of 2019 added the possibility of using MERESE funds for the procurement of goods and services. However, this system of payments for ecosystem services (PES) under the water supply and sanitation policy (aimed at ensuring the protection of upstream water sources) shows its limits in the poor identification of activities providing hydrological services, a step that is essential to calibrate the reserve fund. Among the pricing studies developed by the end of 2018 (Ayacucho, Chachapoyas, Huancayo and Moyobamba, in 2015), only

Moyobamba includes criteria to measure the impact (effectiveness) of payments. The participation of non-governmental organisations (NGOs) and academics in the fund's management committee has certainly contributed to improving the quality of the Moyobamba price study. On the other hand, the Ayacucho and Huancayo price studies do not provide any details on the measures envisaged in their MERESE fund (Table 3.2).

Table 3.1. Creation of MERESE and GRD/ACC reserve funds by the water companies

Water and sanitation service company (EP)		Five-year period	Reserve for Disaster Risk Management (GRD) and Adaptation to Climate Change (ACC)	Reserve for Ecosystem Services Compensation Mechanism (MERESE)		Comments	Official journal
City/Province	Department[1]		Percentage (or amount) of revenues[2]	Average monthly contribution/connection			
				Percentage	In PEN[3]		
Tacna	Tacna	2019-23	0.5	1	0.45		21-Dec-18
Huancavelica	Huancavelica	2019-23	Between 1 and 6.6	Between 2.9 and 5.8	0.93		21-Dec-18
Quillabamba	Cusco	2019-23	0.7, Years 3-4, 0.8, Year 5	0.5 to 1.5	0.33		21-Dec-18
Pucallpa	Ucayali	2019-23	0.72, Year 1	Between 1.27 and 2.1	1.00		14-Dec-18
Chincha	Ica	2019-23	0.8 to 0.6	2.6 to 2.0	1.00		14-Dec-18
Nasca	Ica	2019-23	0.8, Year 3	Between 0.4 and 2.2	0.11 to 0.69		14-Dec-18
Cañete	Lima	2019-23	0.2, Year 2	Between 3.3 and 4.4	0.9 to 1.2		14-Dec-18
Tarma	Junín	2018-22	1, Years 1-2, then 0.8	2.4 to 1.9	0.50		06-Nov-18
Calca	Cusco	2018-22	0.5, Years 2-5	2.0 to 0.5, Years 1-4	0.12		30-Oct-18
Grau	Piura	2018-22	Between 1.09 and 1.97	Between 0.76 and 2.51	0.32 to 1.51		23-Aug-18
Pisco	Ica	2018-22	1	1.5 to 2.0	0.57		30-May-18
Chiclayo	Lambayeque	2018-22	Between 3.2 and 6.2	Between 0.1 and 1.3	0.54 to 0.57	PEN 0.05, Year 1	23-May-18
Moquega	Moquega	2018-22	0.5	1 to 3, Years 2-5	0.85		29-Dec-17
Ica	Ica	2018-22	1	1.0 to 1.5	0.55		29-Dec-17
Bagua Grande	Amazonas	2018-22	Between 0.8 and 2.5	2.2, Years 1-2, then 2.0	0.50		29-Dec-17
Mantaro	Junín	2017-21	1, Years 1-2	3, Years 2-5	0.64		14-Dec-17
Sicuani	Cusco	2017-21	0.5, Year 1, then 0.4	0.6 to 3.2	0.39		14-Dec-17
Cajamarca	Cajamarca	2017-21	1, Years 1-2	4	1.13		14-Dec-17
Puerto Maldonado	Madre de Dios	2017-21	Between 1.4 and 6.7	Between 0.7 and 1.8	1.16	PEN 0.44, Year 1	10-Nov-17
Bagua	Amazonas	2017-21	PEN 12 272-12 832, Years 1-2	PEN 18 223 to PEN 85 377	..		10-Nov-17

Water and sanitation service company (EP)		Five-year period	Reserve for Disaster Risk Management (GRD) and Adaptation to Climate Change (ACC)	Reserve for Ecosystem Services Compensation Mechanism (MERESE)		Comments	Official journal
City/Province	Department[1]		Percentage (or amount) of revenues[2]	Average monthly contribution/connection			
				Percentage	In PEN[3]		
Andahuaylas	Apurímac	2017-21	0.20	2	0.70		22-Sept-17
Rioja	San Martín	2017-21	1.1, Year 3-5	Between 2.2 and 5.4	1.40	PEN 0.80, Year 1	21-Jul-17
Chimbote	Chimbote	2017-21	1.1, Years 2-5		..	Joint GRD/ACC/MERESE	09-Mar-17
Iquitos	Loreto	2016-20	1	0.5, Year 1	..		10-Oct-16
La Oroya	Junín	2016-20	4.7-4.5, Years 1-2	1	..		04-Oct-16
Huánuco	Huánuco	2016-20	1.5	1	..		21-Jul-16
Chanchamayo	Junín	2016-20	1.2	1, Year 1	..		09-Mar-16
Ayacucho	Ayacucho	2015-19	2	2	..		30-Oct-15
Chachapoyas	Amazonas	2015-19	4 to 1	11.8, Year 2	..	PEN 8 317, Year 1	20-Aug-15
Huancayo	Junín	2015-19	2.5	2.5	..		07-Jul-15
Lima	Lima	2015-19	3.8 to 3.5	1	..		15-Jun-15
Moyobamba	San Martín	2015-19	1.1, Years 3-5	..	1.00		18-Dec-14
Abancay	Apurímac	2014-18	..	..	..	Tariff increase[4]	18-Jun-14
Cusco	Cusco	2013-17	..	..	..	Tariff increase[5]	06-Sep-13

Note:
1. 19 out of 26 departments.
2. Revenues refer to the amount billed for drinking water and sewerage services, including the fixed charge, excl. General Sales Tax (*Impuesto General a las Ventas*, IGV) and Municipal Promotion Tax; Percentage (or amount) levied annually over the five-year period unless otherwise indicated.
3. "..''stands for missing value or not available
4. Increased water tariff to finance the protection of Laguna Conococha (7.5% Year 2, 8.3% Year 4).
5. Increased water tariff to finance the pollution prevention of Laguna Piuray by nutrients (4.8% Years 1-2, 4.2% Years 3-5).
Source: SUNASS (n.d.[14]), "SUNASS comprometida con el cuidado de las fuentes de agua".

Table 3.2. Activities covered by MERESE reserve funds of water companies

Water and sanitation service company (EP)	Five-year budget (PEN million)[1]	Financing[1]	Issue[1]	Activities[1]	Effectiveness criteria[1]	Contractual arrangement[1]
Huancayo[2]	..	..	..	..	..	..
Ayacucho[2]	..	..	..	..	..	..
Cusco	136.5 (INV)	EPS (40%), GORE (35%) + loan from JICA (27%)	Shortage of water in the Piuray Lagoon, main source of water for EPS, and pollution by nutrients (nitrogen, phosphorus).	Improved sanitation of rural villages near the lagoon to treat domestic wastewater and, to a much lesser extent, development of organic farming to reduce fertiliser use.	..	Tripartite Co-operation Agreement between EPS, Chinchero District Municipality and the management committee of the basin.
Moyobamba	1.3 (INV) + 0.2 (O&M)	EPS (monthly charge of PEN 1 per connection) and GORE (62% of investment cost)	Bad agricultural practices in micro-basins of Almendra, Mishquiyacu and Rimiyacu cause deforestation and soil erosion. As a result, turbidity of the water collected downstream by EPS Moyobamba is generating service cuts to users.	- Reforestation of protection margins of gorges and areas of greater fragility (90 ha). - Better farming practices: coffee cultivation (300 ha); livestock breeding partly in the open air and agroforestry in existing pastures (120 ha). - Installation of gauges in gorges of the 3 micro-basins; monthly record of flows. - Capacity building: training; studies of flora and fauna; awareness raising.	Daily records of water turbidity at the entrance and exit of the San Mateo Drinking Water Treatment Plant	A management committee with legal status ensures compliance with the agreements. It includes the regional offices of ministries (education, health, production); GORE of San Martin, municipality of Moyobamba, EPS of Moyobamba, ALA of Rioja, local communities, farmers' association, hydroelectric company, non-governmental organisations (NGOs) and academics.

Water and sanitation service company (EP)	Five-year budget (PEN million)[1]	Financing[1]	Issue[1]	Activities[1]	Effectiveness criteria[1]	Contractual arrangement[1]
Chachapoyas	0.5 (INV) + 0.6 (O&M)	Fully funded in the EPS (PEN 8 317 per month the first year, increase of the drinking water supply tariff of 11.8% from the second year)	Livestock raising, pine planting in the grasslands, and slash-and-burn in the Tilancancha Private Preservation Area (ACP) disrupted the upper basin water regulation function and produced sediment in the water collected by the EPS downstream, resulting in a reduction in water supply due to turbidity.	- In the ACP: surveillance (enforcement), information (water regulation service by monitoring rainfall in the recharge area of the EPS; identifying the source of sediments in the Tilacancha Gorge); and reforestation (restoring native forests). - Outside the ACP: improve agricultural productivity (dairy production and irrigation) in the middle and lower basins to reduce pressures (overgrazing and pine plantation) in the ACP.	..	..

Note:
INV = investment; O&M = Operation and Maintenance; GORE = Regional Government; JICA =Japan International Cooperation Agency; ALA = Local Water Authority
1. "..''stands for missing value or not available
2. Although these two EPS implement a MERESE fund, their pricing study does not provide any information on its operation.
Source: SUNASS, various EPS pricing studies (*estudio tarifario*).

Environmental charges

Environmental charges are requited[1] payments made by consumers to providers of environmental management services, including water resource management. In that they differ from environmental taxes, defined as "compulsory, unrequited[2] payments to general government levied on tax bases deemed to be of particular environmental relevance" (OECD, 2001[15]).

A conceptual framework

Effectiveness

Morley and Abdullah (2010[16]) evaluate the effectiveness of environmental taxes and charges, and find a significant relationship between their levels and a reduction in pollution. However, the effectiveness of an individual instrument depends heavily on the specific design of the instrument, the circumstances within which it operates (e.g. the availability of capital) and its primary objective (e.g. reducing water abstraction/pollution or simply revenue-raising) (Dias Soares, 2011[17]; Wakabayashi and Sugiyama, 2009[18]). These aspects also make *ex ante* estimations of the effectiveness of taxation and charging instruments in achieving its objective difficult.

The point of obligation for an environmental charge may be upstream of the point of water abstraction/wastewater discharge (e.g. on irrigated land or fertiliser inputs) at the point of abstraction/discharge itself (e.g. on abstraction volume or pollutant load) or on the "impact" of emissions (e.g. on ambient conditions, such as the minimum flow or pollutant concentration of the affected water bodies, with the tax paid by users/pollutant sources). Each point of obligation has different feasibility constraints and consequences for efficiency.

In a perfect market with perfect competition, the point of obligation does not matter, as the price signal and therefore the incentive for abatement across the system, in the long run, is equivalent. If the instrument is applied upstream, producers (farmers, industry) should pass through 100% of the cost of production (including the tax or charge) to consumers (as the long-run supply curve is flat),[3] reducing demand for a given product or service in line with the elasticity of demand. If the instrument is applied at the point of abstraction/discharge, demand is directly influenced and upstream suppliers would be expected to react to this. However, regardless of the point of obligation, non-perfect markets, along with issues of specific design and feasibility constraints, also impact effectiveness and may act to prevent pricing instruments from achieving their full theoretical potential.

Cost efficiency

Pricing instruments are statically cost-efficient if the explicit or implicit price is applicable to and equalised across all water users/sources of pollution within the scope of the instrument. However, an equalised rate on a given user/pollutant does not consider marginal damages that may vary depending on the timing, location, medium, concentration and other characteristics of its abstraction/release, regardless of the point of application. This renders charges rather blunt instruments, unable to effectively address scarcity/pollutant "hotspots" (OECD, 2008[1]), with consequences for overall efficacy.

This is particularly the case for upstream charges. In addition, an upstream pricing instrument may also prevent the use of "end-of-pipe" abatement measures, which may produce abatement at a lower marginal cost than other options. In upstream pricing, downstream actors may only reduce costs through increasing input efficiency and product substitution, potentially reducing static cost efficiency at the outset. Applying pricing instruments at the point of abstraction/discharge may tackle these difficulties to some extent by allowing rate differentiation between different types of users/pollutant release in different locations (e.g. water abstraction/effluent released in areas of different ecological risk) and allowing the potential for abatement to be achieved where the cost is least. However, there are limits to the feasibility of each approach (see below).

The presence of environmentally harmful subsidies for scarcity/pollution generation (such as irrigation or fertiliser subsidies) may significantly inhibit the effectiveness of pricing instruments. For example, groundwater pumping that is subject to a reduced electricity tariff, producing an implicit water subsidy, counteracts the incentive for water use efficiency (e.g. to adopt modern irrigation technology) produced by abstraction charges.

Pricing instruments, by providing a liability that market actors constantly seek to minimise, theoretically stimulate innovation and adoption of new products, processes and practices, producing high dynamic cost efficiency. Whilst employing effective indicators to measure innovation and its attribution to a single factor is difficult, the empirical evidence suggests that environmental taxes and charges are effective in producing organisational and technical innovation (OECD, 2010[9]), although instrument design and operational context are considerable determinants (Kemp and Pontoglio, 2011[19]). In addition, policy certainty is an important driver for innovation, regardless of the type of instrument in question. A lack of certainty surrounding, for example, the level and scope of application of future charges, and therefore cost liabilities, may dissuade organisations from investing in research and development as the return on such investments becomes inherently riskier.

Feasibility

Generally, environmental charging instruments are highly administratively feasible: most countries have the required institutions and administrative systems already in place. Even so, there are various exceptions and nuances. An upstream charge, for example, is likely to be more administratively feasible than a charge at the point of abstraction/discharge, as the former targets far fewer actors than the latter, reducing transaction costs and increasing the potential for effective monitoring and enforcement, particularly in low-income countries lacking the administrative capacity required for implementing and enforcing instruments applied at the point of abstraction/discharge. Furthermore, by its nature, an upstream charge also reduces the potential for avoidance and evasion.

However, technical challenges remain both for the instruments targeted upstream and those applied at the point of abstraction/discharge. Whilst pollutants such as nitrates or pesticides depend largely on the nitrogen or chemicals content of the fertiliser/plant protection product, the amount of water diverted for irrigation depends largely on the location and technology employed, rendering an efficient upstream pricing instrument infeasible. Conversely, monitoring nitrogen pollution at the point of emission from small stationary sources (e.g. households) or from the multiple and diffuse pathways of non-point source pollution in the agriculture sector may be both technically and administratively infeasible. For such sources of pollution, a tax or charge on ambient conditions (e.g. pollutant concentration in a water body), for example, may be a practical solution. Similarly, although monitoring the use of water at the point of abstraction is theoretically simple, it requires a measuring device, rarely used in small irrigation schemes. For such water users, a charge on ambient conditions (for example, the minimum flow of a river) may also be a practical solution. However, such an approach may only be effective if individual actors believe that their water use/discharges substantially impact the aggregate, producing an incentive to reduce abstractions/discharges. This may be the case concerning water scarcity/pollution in a small watershed with few agricultural producers but not, for example, in an urban area with large numbers of inhabitants individually contributing very marginally to aggregate use/pollution levels (Karp, 2005[20]).

Opposition from industry and the public, which in turn influences political acceptability, often proves to be the most significant impediment to the introduction of environmental taxes and charges. Opposition to charges appears to stem from eight broad roots. The first is a misunderstanding, or a mistrust, of the rationale behind the introduction of such instruments. Both individuals and organisations tend to hold a view of charges as simple revenue-raising instruments, rather than in terms of incentives or welfare-maximisation. Second, even if the principles behind the charge are understood, it is often believed by the general public that they are ineffective in influencing behaviour, and third, the public may doubt that it is even required at all. This belief is influenced by the environmental attitudes of individuals, which are themselves associated with socio-economic circumstances and worldviews. This is linked to the fourth aspect of policy "labelling". A policy labelled a charge is likely to be less popular than the same instrument with a less emotive label. The fifth aspect is the perception of coerciveness and impingement on individual and organisational freedoms resulting from environmental taxes and charges. Linked to this is the sixth aspect of fairness – environmental charges, particularly when associated with goods consumed across the socio-economic spectrum (such as water), may be regressive. Seventh, environmental charges may have or may be perceived to have negative impacts on industrial competitiveness. The eighth and final aspect concerns the use of revenue raised – pricing instruments are less popular when the revenue "disappears" into government budgets, rather than being hypothecated for a given purpose. This is often connected with a mistrust of government.

To reduce the possibility of excessive administrative burden, and distributional and competitiveness impacts, certain entities such as small organisations, households or industries that may otherwise be significantly impacted may be exempt from the provisions of pricing instruments, subject to reduced rates or receive compensation. Whilst this raises political feasibility, it acts to reduce environmental effectiveness and efficiency. Similarly, preferential treatment may be afforded to other users/sources of pollution for which costs would be prohibitive, such as ageing industrial installations. However, in order to prevent perverse incentives to maintain the operation of these installations, such provisions should be time-limited. An alternative option to exemptions and differentiated rates is the use of environmental taxation reform (ETR) principles, where taxes and charges on environmentally harmful activities are offset by reducing taxes on, and therefore stimulating, positive activities (such as labour). This may be combined with some element of revenue hypothecation; increasing transparency, for which empirical evidence suggests strong support, and to the extent to which it helps polluting industries reduce the net cost of pollution abatement, may help to prevent the migration of polluting activities to other jurisdictions (pollution haven effect), maintaining the overall effectiveness of the instrument. However, the ability of ETR principles to achieve revenue and cost neutrality may vary between high- and low-income countries. The latter tend to have a lower proportion of the population employed in the formal economy, for example, making compensation via a reduction in labour taxes less effective. In such instances, the provision of reduced (or no) cost services such as water use efficiency measures, healthcare or education may be a suitable mechanism for revenue recycling.

Environmental taxes and charges are relatively flexible instruments, as rates may be altered relatively easily. However, the hypothecation of revenue for a given purpose may lead to revenue dependency, which may impact the ability to adjust rates (particularly downwards) or alter the instrument in a more structural manner. This may be seen as a positive or negative attribute, depending on the attitude taken towards the instrument.

The state of play in Peru

Since 2009, the National Water Authority (*Autoridades Administrativas del Agua*, ANA) has collected charges on water abstractions and sewage discharges from a range of stakeholders. By law (Article 95 of the 2009 Water Resources Act), charges must cover the costs of governance of integrated water management approved by ANA and rehabilitation of water resources subject to abstraction and discharge of wastewater. However, revenue raised by ANA is insufficient to cover its ordinary operating costs (USD 55 million in 2018 – see below).

Charges for risk management of water shortage

Peru applies water abstraction charges (*Retribuciónes Económicas por el Uso del Agua,* REUA) according to the availability of water (and therefore the risk of shortage), thus applying the polluter pays principle. The Ministry of Agricultural Development and Irrigation (*Ministerio de Desarrollo Agrario y Riego*, MIDAGRI) is the competent body for setting the REUA rates, at the proposal of ANA (which belongs to MIDAGRI) and these rates are set annually through Supreme Decree. The revenues collected from REUAs are assigned to the ANA budget. In this way, the principle of "water pays for water" is applied, as Peru considers that ANA provides services (water management, monitoring, etc.) that users must pay.

In particular, ANA uses REUA revenues for the following actions (ANA, 2015[21]):

- Formulation of water resource management plans per basin; management and administration of water resources in natural sources of water; integrated water management in less-favoured watersheds; and preservation of water resources in basin headwaters.
- Control and monitoring measures to ensure the protection of water quality, an increase of water availability, conservation of sources of production and efficiency of water use.

Though the REUA revenues are allocated to the ANA budget, REUAs are collected by different actors, depending on the rights granted for the use of water (Head Resolution No. 083-2019-ANA):

- Users of surface water for agricultural purposes that receive the water supply service pay their charges to the hydraulic infrastructure operators:
  - After water use, for the volume of water used.
  - Prior to the use of water, for the volume of water requested.
- Users of surface water other than farmers, users of groundwater, users of seawater and users with their own supply system pay to ANA annually, according to the volume of water used during the previous year. In case of failure of reporting, the volume used to calculate the charge is equal to the volume granted in the right of use.
- Users with authorisation to discharge treated wastewater pay to ANA annually and in advance depending on the volume of the authorised discharge.
- Users with water use authorisations pay to ANA annually based on the volume of water used. In case of failure to submit the reports, the volume used will be equal to the volume granted in the right of use.

According to available OECD data,[4] more than half of OECD countries have introduced similar abstraction charges but very few OECD countries take into account the risk of scarcity in the design of the instrument. In this sense, Peru is more advanced. What needs to be corrected is the differential rate of REUAs between sectors (Table 3.3), which must be eliminated because the impact of water withdrawal on the environment is the same regardless of the user.

In Peru, the REUA rate takes into account three factors: i) the volume used (in m^3); ii) a coefficient of value (in PEN/m^3) according to the use (for example, industrial, mining, population, agricultural); and iii) modulation of the value coefficient according to the demand/availability of water (in part, following ANA, (ANA, 2012[22])). The value coefficient takes into account economic criteria – which apply to the productive sectors (industry, mining) – and social criteria – for water use by the population and the agricultural sector. Thus, the value coefficients are higher for the productive sectors, leading to a cross-subsidisation of the productive sector to the population and agricultural sectors. The modulation of the value coefficient is based on environmental criteria, namely the availability of water per capita (m^3/inhabitant/year) for each body of surface water. The modulation is between water bodies in equilibrium (high availability), water bodies in danger (the demand being close to the supply, priorities in use must be assigned and efficiency of use improved) and water bodies already overexploited (compromising all economic and social development). Similarly, Peru's aquifers are classified into three categories: underexploited, in equilibrium and overexploited, depending on the demand/availability ratio of each aquifer. The modulation coefficient for groundwater is based on these three risk categories of scarcity. Such a setting is like trying to kill several birds with a stone. The formula mixes social, economic and environmental criteria. This is the best way to achieve no objective when there is a risk of water scarcity (the problem does not arise in case of high availability of water).

An REUA rate linked to the availability of water creates an incentive to turn to water bodies where the abstraction pressure (the risk of scarcity) is lower, which allows economic development and protection of the environment. But giving a preferential rate to the "social sectors" reduces incentives and can lead these sectors to turn to bodies of water where water is less abundant, increasing the risk of scarcity, compromising the environmental objective and, ultimately, the social goal (when scarcity is proven).

Moreover, In the case of the risk of scarcity, Peru already has an allocation regime that favours social sectors and an ecological flow. The preferential REUA rate is twofold with these direct regulatory instruments, which are sufficient on their own.

Different REUA rates apply to different sectors. More specifically, the REUA rate for the agricultural sector differs according to altitude, with a rate of almost half lower for farmers located in the upper basin (*cuenca alta*) compared to other farmers. This is a social measure that has no justification from the point of view of the protection of the environment (see further discussion below). The protection of the water resource (and natural ecosystems) in the headwaters area is indeed decisive for regulating the hydrology of the entire basin, which justifies the payments for ecosystem services through the MERESE fund. Halving the REUA rate in the upper part of the basin runs counter to the MERESE policy of water management at the watershed scale.

A number of boards of users of the hydraulic sector (JUSH) pay a fixed REUA rate, regardless of the availability of water resources. This is not justified from the point of view of the protection of the water resource, even if some of these JUSHs have to pay a higher rate than those subject to a variable REUA rate and located in an area where water resources are insufficient. A fixed REUA rate does not allow for taking into account the seasonality of water scarcity.

Similarly, the REUA rate in "special projects" is based on the water tariff (i.e. the tariff recovering the operations and maintenance (O&M) cost of the irrigation infrastructure serving an association of water users). Again, there is no reason not to keep the link with water availability, especially since "special projects" often refer to large-scale irrigation projects (e.g. the *Special Project Olmos Tinajores – Proyecto Especial Olmos Tinajones*, PEOT – in the department of Lambayeque) and are therefore major consumers of water.

The same differentiated REUA rates apply equally to surface water and groundwater. However, it is generally more difficult (expensive) to recharge an overexploited aquifer than to restore the flow or volume of a body of surface water. REUA rates should be higher for groundwater than for surface water, as is the case in most OECD countries for which (unpublished) information is available while maintaining the risk-based differentiation as is currently the case.

In order to ensure a regular minimum income for ANA, a first block of water withdrawal must be paid by water users, at the same implicit REUA rate as for volumes beyond the block (Table 3.4). For the population sector, the block for groundwater (and therefore the minimum fixed REUA) is half that for surface water, which encourages the use of groundwater rather than surface water. Communal water companies in rural areas enjoy preferential implicit REUA rates for 3 water withdrawal blocks, with a higher subsidy as the block grows (70% of implicit REUA rate for the first block, 93% for the second and 96% for the third). This decreasing block pricing structure discourages water savings.

Table 3.3. Water abstraction charge (REUA) rates

Water availability		Sector (PEN/m³)[1]						
Surface water	Groundwater	Agriculture[2]		Population	Energy[3]	Mining	Other uses[4]	Tourism[5]
High	Underexploited	0.0011	0.0006	0.0050	0.0792	0.1017	0.0330	0.0408
Medium	In equilibrium	0.0022	0.0012	0.0203	0.1583	0.2035	0.0659	0.0817
Low	Overexploited	0.0033	0.0018	0.0356	0.2375	0.3053	0.0988	0.1225

Note:

1. A rate of PEN 0.0020/m³ applies for the use of seawater in productive activities.
2. The left column applies to groundwater use and to users of surface water with their own water supply system. The right column applies to the use of surface water by user organisations in the upper basin (*cuenca alta*) at an altitude greater than 2 000 m (Sierra). Rates between PEN 0.006 and PEN 0.0054/m³ are applied to the use of surface water by other user associations (JUSH), with a rate set for each JUSH regardless of water availability. A charge of 2.61% of the tariff for use of minor hydraulic infrastructure applies to the use of surface water in "special projects" delivered under concession. The use of water for aquaculture is not subject to the payment of REUA.
3. For the use of water in thermoelectric plants. As for the use of surface water for hydropower, the REUA may not exceed 1% of the average price of energy at generation level in accordance with the provisions of article 107 of Decree Law No. 25844 of 1993, Law of Electrical Concessions.
4. For the use of water in: i) studies and works of productive sectors except for energy and mines; and ii) the cleaning of public roads, fountains, public buildings, shops, service stations and others.
5. For the use of water for medicinal, recreational and touristic purposes.

Source: Government of Peru (2019[23]), "Supreme Decree No. 011-2019-MINAGRI of 24 December 2019 approving the charges to be applied in 2020 for the use of surface and groundwater and for the discharge of treated wastewater", https://cdn.www.gob.pe/uploads/document/file/473663/DECRETO_SUPREMO_N__0011-2019-MINAGRI.pdf.

Table 3.4. Fixed water abstraction charge (REUA)

Block (m³)		Sector						
Surface water	Groundwater	Agriculture[1]	Population[2]		Energy	Mining	Tourism[3]	Other uses
High	Underexploited	10 000	22 200	11 000	1 427	1 111	2 721	3 364
Medium	In equilibrium	5 000	5 468	2 710	714	555	1 359	1 684
Low	Overexploited	3 333	3 118	1 545	476	370	906	1 123
Fixed REUA (PEN/block)		11	111	55	113	113	111	111

Note:

1. Applies to groundwater use and to users of surface water with their own water supply system.
2. The left column applies to the use of surface water. The right column applies to groundwater use. Communal organisations in charge of sanitation in rural areas, however, pay only a fixed annual lump sum for their surface water withdrawal: PEN 68 for less than 45 000 m³; PEN 136 between 45 000 and 90 000 m³ and PEN 204 between 90 000 and 135 000 m³; for withdrawals of more than 135 000 m³, the volumetric rate applies (see Table 3.4).
3. For the use of water for medicinal, recreational and touristic purposes.

Source: Government of Peru (2019[23]), "Supreme Decree No. 011-2019-MINAGRI of 24 December 2019 approving the charges to be applied in 2020 for the use of surface and groundwater and for the discharge of treated wastewater", https://cdn.www.gob.pe/uploads/document/file/473663/DECRETO_SUPREMO_N__0011-2019-MINAGRI.pdf.

Charges for risk management of water pollution

Peru also applies charges on the discharge of treated wastewater (*retribuciónes económicas por el vertimiento de aguas residuales tratadas*, REVART) according to the type of use of the receiving water (and therefore the risk of pollution), thus applying the polluter pays principle. Peru is ahead of many OECD countries in this area. According to available OECD data, about a third of OECD countries have introduced similar pollution charges but very few OECD countries take into account the sensitivity of receiving waters in the design of the instrument. In this sense, Peru is more advanced.

Unlike the REUA, the method of calculating the REVART does not take into account economic and social factors but only environmental criteria. The REVART takes into account three factors: i) the volume of wastewater discharged (m^3) – annual volumes discharged according to permit; ii) a coefficient of value (PEN/m^3) that considers the persistence and toxicity of the substances contained in the effluent; and iii) modulation of the value coefficient based on the sensitivity of the receiving water body to contamination.

The value coefficient considers the dangerousness of the substances contained in the effluent to the environment, in particular the time necessary to return to a natural reference situation. Under these conditions, differentiated coefficients are obtained depending on the type of activity generating wastewater, whether it is domestic effluents (municipal) or industrial sectors (industry, fishing, mining, energy and agroindustry) (Table 3.5).

Table 3.5. Rates of charges on the discharge of treated wastewater (REVART)

Environmental quality standard (*Estándar de calidad medioambiental*, ECA) of receiving waters[1]	Pollution load by sector (PEN/m^3)[2]						
	Municipal	Industrial					
		Sanitation and others[3]	Energy	Mining	Agroindustry	Industry	Fishery
Public water supply[4]	0.0069	0.0035	0.0554	0.0623	0.0139	0.0276	0.0208
Fish farming[5]	0.0065	0.0033	0.0517	0.0583	0.0129	0.0259	0.0194
Irrigation[6]	0.0059	0.0030	0.0461	0.0520	0.0115	0.0230	0.0174
Environment[7]	0.0061	0.0031	0.0480	0.0540	0.0121	0.0240	0.0180

Note:
1. Established by MINAM, ECAs set the levels of physical, chemical and biological parameters in water that do not represent a significant risk for health and the environment (in accordance with Article 31 of the General Law on the Environment No. 28611 of 2005).
2. A minimum REVART per year is applied by multiplying the values given in the table by 100 000 m^3, even for discharges of less than 100 000 m^3 per year. Communal organisations in charge of sanitation in rural areas, however, pay only a lump sum of PEN 69.00 per year.
3. Others refer to wastewater generated during the process of water purification and desalination of water.
4. ECA1: Surface water intended for the production of drinking water or intended for recreation.
5. ECA2: Surface water intended for fishing and aquaculture in lakes, lagoons and seawater.
6. ECA3: Surface water intended for irrigation and livestock.
7. ECA4: Surface water intended for the conservation of the aquatic environment: lagoons and lakes, rivers, coastal marine ecosystems.
Source: Government of Peru (2019[23]), "Supreme Decree No. 011-2019-MINAGRI of 24 December 2019 approving the charges to be applied in 2020 for the use of surface and groundwater and for the discharge of treated wastewater", https://cdn.www.gob.pe/uploads/document/file/473663/DECRETO_SUPREMO_N__0011-2019-MINAGRI.pdf.

The modulation of the value coefficient reflects the classification of receiving water bodies in accordance with national environmental quality standards for water. Thus, the modulation differs according to whether it is a body of water used by the population, for coastal marine activities, for irrigation or for the conservation of the aquatic environment. The aim is to incentivise the reduction of the pollutant load of authorised wastewater discharges according to the sensitivity of the receiving water bodies to pollution.

As is the case with REUA, a first block must be paid for wastewater discharges, at the same implicit rate of REVART as for volumes beyond the block (Table 3.5). The block size (100 000 m^3) is the same for all sectors. However, a preferential implicit REVART rate of 90% applies within the block to communal water companies in rural areas, although wastewater is generally less treated than in urban areas and therefore carries a higher pollutant load. Although the objective is not to hinder the necessary development of sanitation infrastructure in these areas, this preferential REVART rate discourages the search for advanced wastewater treatment. As a rule of thumb, any public financial support for sanitation infrastructure must be considered temporary, the tariffs having to, in the long term, recover all the investment, operation and maintenance costs of the infrastructure to ensure its proper management (see Cox and Borkey (2015[24]) for more discussion). In addition, the REVART rate should reflect the toxicity of pollutants in wastewater to health and the environment.

Revenue from water abstraction charges (REUA) and water pollution charges (REVART)

Revenues from the collection of water abstraction and sewage discharge charges have increased in constant terms (not adjusted for inflation) since their introduction some 10 years ago (Table 3.6 and Figure 3.2). Most of the revenue continues to come from abstraction charges outside agriculture (over 50% in recent years). Total charge income amounted to PEN 205 million (EUR 55 million) in 2018 (Table 3.6). According to ANA, the revenues are intended to cover ANA's "integrated water management costs", including: i) the development of water resources management plans by basin; iii) the daily administration of water resources (for example, issuing water licenses); and iii) monitoring and enforcement of water regulations (ANA, 2019[25]).

Table 3.6. Charges collection

In PEN million

Year	Surface water abstraction (REUA)		Groundwater abstraction (REUA)	Discharge of treated wastewater (REVART)	Total
	Agriculture	Outside agriculture			
2009	13	33	0	0	45
2010	10	38	0	3	51
2011	10	34	1	6	51
2012	11	37	2	7	56
2013	13	56	11	25	104
2014	13	48	21	42	124
2015	15	53	18	41	126
2016	16	94	24	39	172
2017	15	89	32	41	177
2018	20	112	32	41	205

Source: ANA (2019[25]), Country submission.

Figure 3.2. Revenues from charges on water abstraction and discharge of treated wastewater

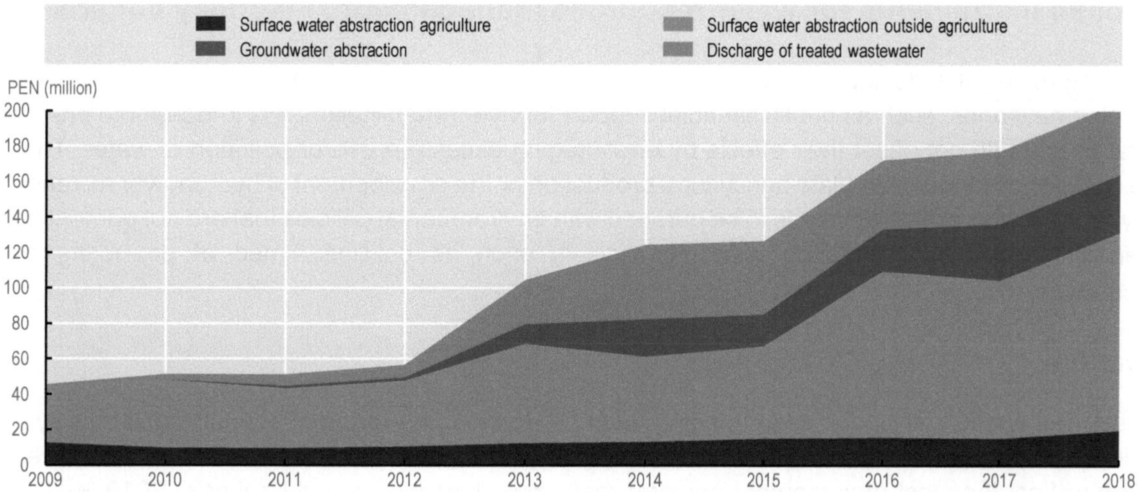

Source: ANA (2019[25]), Country submission.

Public financial support for river rehabilitation

This section discusses how public financial support could be envisaged for the rehabilitation of watercourses, a policy that does not yet exist in Peru but which would greatly contribute to better management of water risks. River development (straightening and channelisation, disconnection of flood plains, land reclamation, dams, weirs, bank reinforcements) to facilitate agriculture, produce energy and protect against floods damages the morphology and hydrology of the water systems. Restoration of good hydromorphological conditions (river rehabilitation) and providing rivers with sufficient space enable them to fulfil their natural functions (connect ecosystems and provide the water needed for life, self-purification of waters and groundwater recharge) and guarantee natural protection against floods.

For all these reasons, public financial support may be granted for river rehabilitation (via environmental policy) and provision of space for waters (via agricultural policy), while electricity consumers (via a tax on electricity bills) may support the ecological improvement of installations related to hydropower use (see Energy Section below). These instruments must be combined with direct regulations on minimum flows and come in addition to any public financial support for flood control (i.e. using grey infrastructure).

The rehabilitation of rivers can benefit from public financial support as it contributes to the protection of aquatic and riverine biodiversity. For the same reason (preservation of biodiversity), the protection of alluvial forests can also benefit from public financial support within the framework of forest policy. Space for water can be cultivated but only as biodiversity protection areas, in which case agricultural land may benefit from public financial support. This is justified to the extent that farmers are paid to go beyond what agricultural policy requires them to do anyway. As long as it contributes to the improvement of agricultural production conditions by land consolidation, the rehabilitation of small rivers in agricultural areas may benefit from public financial support as part of the structural adjustment policy of agriculture. Direct regulation (delineation of risk zones in land use plans) and economic incentives (higher insurance premium in these risk zones) should be favoured to deal with the risk of flooding in populated areas.

Different forms of public financial support can enable landowners to rehabilitate their river in terms of nature protection, provide space for water, protect against floods and improve farmland. It is necessary to ensure synergies and coherence between these different objectives, especially when they are assigned to the same stretch of river. This means assessing the additionality (bundling) of ecosystem services (e.g. flood protection, nature protection, land improvement). In the case of overlapping objectives, no double funding should be allowed for the same service provided.

Economic instruments for water resources management and policy coherence

Beyond improving the design of economic instruments, such as PES and environmental charges, or introducing new ones, such as public financial support for river rehabilitation, it is important to ensure that sectoral policies do not offset their effects by encouraging excessive use or pollution of water. This may be the case for policies to stimulate agricultural production or the development of hydropower as renewable energy. Policy coherence also needs to be pursued with environmental policies that are not primarily aimed at managing water resources but can influence it, such as policies aimed at promoting carbon sequestration.

Agriculture

Because they encourage an increase in agricultural production, the forms of support most closely linked to agricultural production (market price support and payments based on output or input use) are often those that affect the most management of water resources (Henderson and Lankoski, 2019[26]).It can be expected that the effect on water resource management of payments by the number of animals (headage payments) or the area under cultivation (acreage payments) will be smaller and even less so for headage or acreage payments set on a historical basis, unrelated to the actual number of animals or area currently cultivated (decoupled payments).

Thus, the granting of public financial support to modern irrigation techniques would come under "input subsidies" (payment based on the use of inputs) having a distorting effect on agricultural production (and trade) and water use. In addition, this would counteract the incentive of abstraction charges (REUA) to use water more efficiently, in particular by adopting such modern irrigation techniques. In the case of board of users of the hydraulic sector (JUSH), the REUA is passed on to irrigation water tariffs. According to a 2010 survey, only 4.3% of Peruvian farmers had access to modern irrigation techniques (MINAGRI, 2019[27]).

The impact of agricultural support on water resources also varies depending on whether or not it results in a change in land use. For example, agri-environmental payments and agricultural PES can have unintended negative effects on water if they favour cropland over forest land or permanent grassland.

The size of the farm should not be an agricultural policy criterion in terms of water risk management. A small mountain farmer must be as conscientious in managing the water resource as a large irrigator on the coast. If this is not the case, in both cases, it would jeopardise good water management at the basin scale. However, it can be difficult for a low-income farmer to implement a water policy for lack of financial or technological means. The decision to put in place an explicit policy to support farmers' incomes (decoupled from agricultural production) is a political decision. In Colombia, for example, rural development policies are seen as complementary to agricultural policies. Funded by the redistribution of revenues from the exploitation of non-renewable natural resources, they include social measures such as housing subsidies in rural areas.

Aquaculture

Aquaculture in Peru requires a permit to use the aquatic space (sea, rivers or lakes) issued by the Directorate-General of Captaincy and Coast Guard in Peru (DICAPI), a water use permit issued by the ANA and a sanitary authorisation for the use of feedstuff and antibiotics issued by the National Fisheries Health Agency (SANIPES) of the Ministry of Production (PRODUCE). Fish farms must carry out periodic monitoring of their water quality (surface, average and bottom) and submit the results to the Environmental Inspection and Enforcement Agency (OEFA) of MINAM, which monitors compliance of water bodies with environmental quality standards (EQS).

Aquaculture in Peru is not subject to REUA because of non-consumptive use of the water resource. In general, aquaculture effluents do not require a discharge authorisation (Legislative Decree No. 1195, General Aquaculture Law of 2015). However, discharges of aquaculture effluents into a sensitive natural environment are subject to prior authorisation from ANA and payment of the REVART (Table 3.5). However, the use of antibiotics and fungicides, the excess feed used in fish farms as well as faeces pollute the water. The REVART rate is differentiated between sectors according to the persistence and toxicity of the substances contained in their effluents, on average, but with a single rate per sector and type of water use (see Table 3.5). Further differentiation of the REVART, within each sector, would create a better incentive to move towards substances that are less harmful to health and the environment.

Energy

An abstraction charge (REUA) applies in Peru to the (non-consumptive) use of surface water for hydroelectricity. It is justified by the environmental risks associated with hydropower generation: risk of hydropeaking, modification of sediment transport and eutrophication, obstacle to the migration of fish. On the other hand, the REUA is based on the price of electricity at the level of production, which creates a disincentive to produce such renewable and carbon-free energy. Many OECD countries have done the opposite by introducing feed-in-tariffs to promote electricity generated from hydropower. Neither of these two measures is to be recommended given the distortions they cause in the electricity market. Instead, the REUA for the hydropower sector should reflect the environmental risks associated with hydropower generation. In particular, the REUA rate should take into account the negative effects on water flow, sediment transport, pollutant dilution and fish migration, but also the positive role of dams in managing water scarcity and flooding risks. The decision must also take into account energy policy, in particular energy mix objectives. Unlike photovoltaic and wind (and nuclear) plants which generate electricity continuously, hydropower plants with storage dams can adapt the supply of electricity to demand, reducing dependence on fossil-fuelled thermal power plants during peak demand periods.

In accordance with the "polluter pays" principle, hydropower plant operators must cover the cost of upgrading old plants to new hydropeaking standards. This is because frequent fluctuations in flows and water levels downstream and upstream of plants (hydropeaking) hinder the proper management of water resources at the basin level. A tax on electricity bills could finance the costs of upgrading in case of acquired rights of operators guaranteeing them compensation for any limitation of the use of hydroelectric power.

Climate change mitigation

Policy coherence must also be sought with environmental policies that are not primarily aimed at managing water resources. For example, a policy to foster carbon sequestration may help reduce the risks to water. In greenhouse gas emission (GHG) trading systems where GHG emitters may offset their emissions with carbon credits, as provided by the Clean Development Mechanism of the Kyoto Protocol to the United Nations (UN) Framework Convention on Climate Change, farmers who agree to sequester carbon can receive financial compensation if they commit to converting agricultural or pastoral land into forests, often reducing pressure on water resources.

Ways forward to strengthen the use of economic instruments for greater water security

Increase the use of payments for ecosystem services (PES) to protect headwaters

MERESE funds set up in 2013 as part of Peru's water supply and sanitation policy should continue to expand as the optimised master plans of water companies are updated. The turnover of EPs devoted to MERESE could be revised depending on the cost-effectiveness of the PES compared to investment spending in traditional grey infrastructure. Cost-effective use of MERESE funds requires identifying the appropriate projects to finance following a cost-benefit analysis. Local communities living in highlands in Peru have high expectations from the PES instrument, which also has social benefits (avoid migration of these populations to cities) and tourism benefits (preservation of cultural landscapes). There is an urgent need to estimate the needs and costs of protecting headwaters by assessing the risks of water scarcity and pollution in the watershed in the absence of such protection. The beneficiaries of PES payments (populations living in the headwaters) must fully adhere and commit to the proposed PES projects; the feasibility of PES projects depends on it. Equally important is the willingness to pay on the part of beneficiaries of ecosystem services, which implies that they are explicitly informed of the purpose of payments. MERESE fund-raising could extend to other beneficiaries of the protection of mountain ecosystems, namely farmers and industry. Finally, consistency must be sought in the use of MERESE funds and funds for disaster mitigation and adaptation to climate change (GRD/ACC) to avoid duplication and promote synergies in achieving objectives. Below, some options for an efficient effective and feasible design and use of the PES instrument are proposed.

Carry out a water risk analysis for effective use of MERESE funds (Ecosystem Services Compensation Mechanism)

Defining the MERESE fund envelope primarily based on affordability does not allow the identification of needs and the technical cost of protecting upstream water sources. Key sources of hydrological services among terrestrial ecosystems (including wetlands) must first be identified and their contribution to mitigating the risks of water scarcity and pollution of the watershed assessed. A cost-benefit analysis of the proposed MERESE projects can then be carried out. The "rapid diagnosis of water" proposed by SUNASS as part of the implementation of MERESE is a positive step in this direction.[5] The diagnostic aims to facilitate the understanding of the hydrological processes in the basins in order to characterise the hydraulic ecosystem services and their benefits. Governing Council Resolution Resolución N° 039-2019-SUNASS-CD provides for the EPs to set priorities in the implementation of MERESE funds. However, it does not provide clear information on how to do it.

Pending a a better understanding of the hydrological services of ecosystems, prioritisation of the use of MERESE funds could seek synergies with biodiversity policy. Thus, the use of MERESE funds for terrestrial ecosystems could consider protected natural areas that lack public financial support. In the absence of analysis of terrestrial ecosystem services, the use of the MERESE fund will tend to focus on easily identifiable impacts. So far, priority has been given to the protection of lagoons. This is the case, for example, with the protection of the Piuray lagoon, which supplies the city of Cuzco with drinking water. There is greater difficulty in estimating water flow regulation services provided by terrestrial ecosystems (e.g. forests) than the risk of pollution or drying of a lagoon in the headwaters (Cuenca alta). Thus, the priority of use of MERESE funds for terrestrial ecosystems could be given to protected natural areas (*Áreas Naturales Protegidas*, ANPs, national and regional) in order to mobilise private finance for the protection of biodiversity. It is recommended to intervene as a priority in the ANPs also because they have a management plan and are placed under the supervision of MINAM via the National Service of Natural Areas Protected by the State (SERNANP). For example, the MERESE fund of the Chiclayo EP could prioritise the financing of measures to preserve 71 000 ha of ANPs in the district of Carmen de la Frontera located in its headwaters zone (Lambayeque Department). Payments could include helping communities living near the regional ANP to prevent illegal activities in the ANP (by creating a kind of buffer zone around the ANP).

Prioritisation of the use of MERESE funds could also seek synergies with river basin management policy. The MERESE fund could usefully contribute to the implementation of the Basin Water Resources Management Plan (*Plan de Gestión de Recursos Hídricos*, PGRHC) approved by the National Water Authority (ANA), and vice versa. On the one hand, the design of the MERESE fund (the percentage taken from EPs revenues) could aim for consistency with the PGRHC in addressing water risks. On the other hand, the PGRHCs could pay greater attention to ecosystem services and not only to inter-basin water transfers (*trasvase,* Box 3.1) and grey infrastructure (dams, reservoirs).

Box 3.1. Inter-basin water transfers in Peru

Peru implements inter-basin transfers, often through Special Projects. The objective is to bring water to the water-scarce area, in order to support socio-economic development. In particular, water is diverted from river basins that flow into the Atlantic Ocean (via the Amazon) to river basins that flow into the Pacific Ocean (via the coast). There are also transfers within basins that flow to the Pacific Ocean. The table below shows the transfers between different hydrographic units that are currently operational and which aim to mitigate the effects of water scarcity.

Table 3.7. Inter-basin water transfers in Peru

River basin	Origin			Destination			Volume transferred (hm3/year)
	Basins (number of hydrographic units)	AAA	RRHH (hm^3/year)	Basins (number of hydrographic units)	AAA	RRHH (hm3/year)	
Transfers between basins of the Pacific hydrographic region							
Chira-Piura	Chira (56)	V. Jequetepeque-Zarumilla	2 535	Piura (55)	V. Jequetepeque-Zarumilla	1 157	981
Sistema San Lorenzo	Chira (56)	V. Jequetepeque-Zarumilla	2 535	Piura (55)	V. Jequetepeque-Zarumilla	1 157	593
Chavimochic	Santa (43)	IV. Huarmey-Chicama	4 464	Chao (44)-Virú (45)-Moche (46)	IV. Huarmey-Chicama	536	671
Chinecas	Santa (43)	IV. Huarmey-Chicama	4 464	Casma (40)-Nepeña (41)-Lacramarca (42)	IV. Huarmey-Chicama	274	785
Majes-Siguas	Camaná (11)	I. Caplina-Ocoña	2 366	Quilca (10)	I. Caplina-Ocoña	439	396
Sistema Chili	Camaná (11)	I. Caplina-Ocoña	2 366	Quilca (10)	I. Caplina-Ocoña	439	146
Pasto Grande	Tambo (9)	I. Caplina-Ocoña	1 054	Ilo-Moquegua (7)	I. Caplina-Ocoña	67	72
Mauri-Tacna	Uchusuma (149)	I. Caplina-Ocoña	14	Caplina (4)	I. Caplina-Ocoña	25	37
Mauri-Tacna	Mauri (147)	I. Caplina-Ocoña	108	Locumba (6)	I. Caplina-Ocoña	118	13
Total volume mobilised							**3 694**
Transfers between the Pacific hydrographic region and the Amazonas							
Huancabamba-Olmos	Chamaya (118)	VI. Marañón	3 227	Olmos (53)	V. Jequetepeque-Zarumilla	19	406
Huancabamba-Chancay-Lambayeque	Chamaya (118)	VI. Marañón	3 227	Chancay-Lambayeque (51)	V. Jequetepeque-Zarumilla	1 365	238

Mantaro-Rímac	Mantaro (143)	X. Mantaro	14 013	Rímac (31)	III. Cañete-Fortaleza	822	188
Mantaro-Chancay-Huaral	Mantaro (143)	X. Mantaro	14 013	Huaral (33)	III. Cañete-Fortaleza	523	7
Tambo-Ccaracocha	Pampas (145)	XI. Pampas-Apurímac	8 174	Ica (22)	II. Cháparra-Chincha	267	111
Total volume mobilised							**950**

Note: AAA: *Autoridades Administrativas del Agua*, Administrative Water Authorities.
Source: ANA (2019[25]), Country submission.

In sum, the following actions could be considered by MINAM, EPs, regional governments (GORE) and local communities to make cost-effective use of MERESE funds:

- Develop a set of criteria (technical, social and economic) for the cost-effectiveness analysis (CEA) of hydrological services provided by ecosystems in upper parts of the basin and systematise the CEA of PES initiatives, current (*ex post*) and future (*ex ante*).
- While waiting for a better understanding of the hydrological services provided by ecosystems in upper parts of the basin, continue to use MERESE funds primarily to protect the ecosystems surrounding the high mountain lagoons, given the essential role of these lagoons in the regulation of hydrology in Peru.
- Consider protected natural areas (national and regional) as another priority in the use of MERESE funds, in particular those which lack public financial support.
- Also prioritise the allocation of MERESE funds to the promotion of the traditional practice of storing and collecting runoff water (*siembra y cosecha*), for example through payments to build or strengthen terrace systems, as this practice has proven its effectiveness in improving the water supply to downstream water bodies.
- Design the MERESE scheme in a more global approach to water risk management by basin;
- Seek consistency of the use of MERESE funds with the river basin management plans, where they exist.
- Match the use of MERESE funds to the water risks of the basin and undertake a cost-benefit analysis of the proposed MERESE projects.
- New York City, United States, is an interesting example of a city that relies on watershed protection to protect its drinking water supply (Box 3.2).

Box 3.2. New York City Watershed Protection Program

New York City (NYC) is supplied with water by two forested watersheds north of the city, the Croton Basin and the larger Catskill/Delaware Basin. About 10% of NYC's water demand is supplied by water from the Croton Basin, which is now filtered, with the Catskill/Delaware Basin providing the remaining 90%. The Watershed Protection Program (WPP), launched in 1997 and covering both watersheds, has enabled the NYC Department of Environmental Protection, which manages water supply, to obtain a series of exemptions from the filtration requirements of the US Environmental Protection Agency's Surface Water Treatment Rule, thereby generating substantial savings for NYC. Since 1997, USD 2.5 billion has been spent on the WPP, an average of USD 100 million per year. The WPP has two primary objectives: to protect the water quality and to improve the vitality of the communities in the two watersheds. The WPP controls water pollution in the basins by promoting better farming practices, the protection of terrestrial and aquatic ecosystems (forests, wetlands), the restoration of rivers, the treatment of wastewater (sewage treatment plants, septic tanks) and disinfection to combat waterborne pathogens, such as faecal bacteria and viruses. In agriculture, the WPP focuses on nutrients and pesticides. Farms voluntarily enrolled in the WPP must have a Whole Farm Plan that specifies the best management practices to prevent pollutants from entering nearby water bodies. River restoration aims to reduce streambank erosion and sediment transport (with co-benefits in flood risk mitigation and aquatic habitat enhancement). The WPP further provides for the acquisition of land to prevent certain activities or development that may adversely affect water quality.

Source: National Academies of Sciences, Engineering, and Medicine (2020[28]), *Review of the New York City Watershed Protection Program*, https://doi.org/10.17226/25851.

Ensuring the full adherence to MERESE initiatives

Populations living in the upper parts of the basin need to fully adhere to proposed MERESE initiatives. In order to do this, the minimum payment should be at least as attractive to the landowner as the conversion to another legally permitted land use. In other words, the "consent to be paid" for PES activities of populations living in the upper parts of the basin (often farming communities) should be assessed to ensure their full adherence to the MERESE initiatives. It is only with this information that the percentage collected on EPs revenues can be defined. As such, cost estimates should be re-evaluated according to the economic principles of the PES, which entails a detailed socio-economic study of the populations concerned. The MERESE Act of 2014 could introduce the concept of minimum payment and maximum payment. The minimum payment must make ecosystem conservation at least as attractive to the landowner as conversion to another land use permitted by law. The maximum PES payment should represent the cost for downstream populations of reduced water services.

Enhancing the willingness to pay for beneficiaries of ecosystem services

For reasons of cost effectiveness and transparency, the PES must be linked to individual water consumption. Making the individual contribution of PES beneficiaries explicit (for example, by linking urban households' payments to their water consumption instead of taking a percentage of EPs revenues) increases the transparency and consistency of the PES mechanism and thus its sustainability. Progress has been made in this regard in Peru. SUNASS requires that the individual water bills mention the amount allocated to the MERESE fund. Ideally, this should be accompanied by an assessment of "willingness to pay" by city dwellers and other PES beneficiaries. Linking the PES payment to the individual water bill will lead to cost effectiveness (result-based payment) and transparency (the beneficiary knows why he/she is paying).

The MERESE scheme should be further developed in the irrigation sector and extended to the industry and hydropower sectors. The costs of PES payments (whether they are minimum or maximum payment levels as defined above) need to be passed on to the downstream beneficiaries of ecosystem services, including cities, but also farmers, industry and hydropower plants. The scheme is currently implemented by cities and, on a voluntary basis, some associations of irrigators. By participating in the scheme, industry would benefit from increased security of water supply and an increased brand reputation. The extension of the MERESE scheme to hydropower companies should also be considered, as hydropower generation also benefits from upstream source protection (e.g. reduced sedimentation in reservoirs); however, care should be taken not to discourage the production of such renewable energy (compared to fossil fuel-fired plants). If a design similar to the EPs were to be introduced (i.e. allocate part of the revenues of utilities), it could be passed on to the electricity bill of end users. *Ex ante* cost-effectiveness analysis can help select

MERESE projects which do not penalise hydropower in the energy mix. As for board of users of the hydraulic sector (JUSH), they can finance MERESE projects as part of the maintenance of the hydraulic infrastructure for which they are responsible (major or minor), through POMDIH, on a voluntary basis. The resulting MERESE expenses should be passed on to the tariff collected from irrigators, as is the case for city dwellers connected to an EP. This mutualist approach considerably increases the feasibility and effectiveness of the MERESE programme, by increasing the sums available and the capacity to assess the ecosystem services provided (compared to the implementation of a PES by an isolated farmer or a city dweller). In the case of JUSH, it would not prejudge the voluntary nature of MERESE, each JUSH remaining free to participate in a MERESE initiative. Expanding the MERESE system beyond city water companies would strengthen actions to conserve, restore and monitor ecosystems in protected natural areas that regulate the water used by the various beneficiaries. This is the case, for example, with the Nor Yauyos Cochas Landscape Reserve, which supplies water to the El Platanal hydropower plant and the Cañete JUSH. Other examples are Huascarán National Park, which feeds the Chavimochic irrigation project, and Cerros de Amotape National Park, which feeds irrigation projects in Piura and Tumbes.

Ensuring coherence between the various PES systems

Consistency must be sought between the MERESE funds and the funds for disaster risk management (GRD) and adaptation to climate change (ACC) to avoid duplication, promote synergies and thus improve cost effectiveness in their use. The percentage from EPs revenue to fund the GRD/ACC funds is not set by the PMO; this gives EPs greater flexibility in deciding what measures to put in place and how much to allocate to the GRD/ACC funds than it does for the MERESE fund. The decision is often linked to the visible effects of climate change. For example, the drying up of a lagoon in Arequipa caused its eutrophication; the GRD/ACC funds were used to control eutrophication by activated carbon. More generally, the GRD fund is used more often than the ACC fund; disasters are easily visible while there is uncertainty about what to cover in terms of adaptation. Fostering coherence between the MERESE fund and the GRD/ACC funds would avoid duplication, promote synergies and thus improve cost effectiveness in their use.

Win-win approaches must be sought between payments for hydrological ecosystem services and payments for carbon sequestration, so that projects are mutually reinforcing (for example, sustainable forest management). PES for water regulation services in natural water sources can improve the carbon sequestration services of the ecosystems concerned (e.g. forests) and vice versa. Win-win approaches must be pursued by ensuring, however, that projects prioritise the purpose for which they were designed (water regulation services or carbon services). JUSH are also involved in MERESE interventions that use reforestation and the protection of natural ecosystems. The Quiroz-Chira Water Fund project (Piura Department) is a good example. This project has been very well designed and has the financial and technical support of an NGO (Table 3.8). Another example worth mentioning is the Regional Water Fund (FORASAN) which aims to improve the management of water resources in the Chira-Piura Basin by promoting the protection of ecosystems (e.g. *páramos*, cloud forests) and reforestation of degraded areas in the upper parts of the basin. FORASAN receives technical support from ANA and financial support from two JUSH (Chira and Middle and Lower Piura) and agribusiness (Central America Bottling Corporation, CBC). Sustainable forest management and reforestation do not need to be implemented by the state; the private sector can do that too. For example, the Public Works in Lieu of Taxes Act No. 29230 (*Ley de Obras por Impuestos*) facilitates the financing and execution by private companies of priority projects of public entities (for example, central, regional or local governments) by allowing the recovery of investments via concessions on the corporate tax. However, the National Forest and Wildlife Plan to implement the Forest and Wildlife Act should be published without delay in order to provide a global framework for forest management.

The traditional practice of storing and collecting runoff water (*siembra y cosecha*) is also to be considered, for example by payments to build or reinforce terrace systems, as it has proved its effectiveness in supplying water bodies downstream. The provision on the creation of MERESE funds of the Law No. 30045 of 2013 on the modernisation of sanitation services (repealed by Legislative Decree No. 1280 of 2016) has no equivalent in the field of agricultural and industry legislation. In other words, although addressed by the MERESE Regulation (Supreme Decree No. 009-2016-MINAM), there is no legal obligation to implement the MERESE mechanism in the agricultural sector as is the case for the sanitation sector. Nevertheless, payments for hydrological ecosystem services (PHES) have been put in place in the agricultural sector in accordance with the Operation, Maintenance and Development Plan of the Hydraulic Infrastructure (POMDIH), which water user associations (JUHS) are legally required to prepare for effective O&M of irrigation systems. One of the seven objectives of the POMDHI is indeed to preserve the upstream waters (*cuenca alta*). As a result, PHES developed voluntarily (without government intervention) between farmers and local communities. For example, an association of irrigators in the Cañete Basin devoted PEN 10/ha/year (EUR 2.7/ha/year) to protect water sources through reforestation in Yauyos District (a similar practice has developed in the Lurín Basin). The payment was recently suspended pending an evaluation of its effectiveness. Farmers in Valle Viejo (Olmos Basin, Lambayeque) donate part of their harvest to communities in the district of Carmen de la Frontera located in the area of their water sources. The principle is as follows. The water user associations (JUHS) located in the middle of a river basin (*cuenca media*) pay farmers located upstream (*cuenca alta*) to store rainwater through soil and water conservation practices. The water stored upstream (for example by terraces systems) infiltrates the soil (instead of running off) to supply surface water bodies and aquifers in the central part of the basin downstream. This age-old practice of storing and collecting rainwater (*siembra y cosecha*) can very well be considered as a type of green infrastructure and be given increasing attention in PHES policy. Peru's agricultural policy encourages the re-evaluation of traditional practices in agriculture and, in July 2019, Law No. 30989 declared the implementation of the *siembra y cosecha* practice of national interest. In France, the mineral water company Vittel pays farmers to adopt more traditional farming practices to avoid contamination of aquifers by nitrates (see Perrot-Maitre (2006[29])).

Consistency with ANA groundwater monitoring is required to co-ordinate efforts and methodologies. A portion of the EPs revenues feeds into the groundwater monitoring fund. This fund is designed to help EPs monitor groundwater levels, which is essential to prevent the risk of groundwater shortage and to evaluate the effectiveness of measures taken under the other two funds, where applicable.

The MERESE system must be part of a more global approach to risk management by basin. Indeed, it would be pointless to protect the headwaters without also managing the risks associated with economic activities along the watershed, between the headwaters and the coastal waters (agriculture, industry, hydroelectric production, in particular). This involves dealing with policy coherence to manage risks of water shortage, water pollution, flooding and the risk of undermining the resilience of freshwater systems along watersheds (see below).

In sum, the following actions could be taken into account by MINAM, EPs, GORE, local communities, ANA and sectoral ministries (MIDAGRI, PRODUCE, Ministry of Energy and Mining [MINEM]) to ensure: i) that beneficiaries of PES payments fully adhere to proposed PES initiatives; ii) the willingness to pay on the part of beneficiaries of ecosystem services; and iii) consistency in the design of MERESE projects, projects for disaster risk management and adaptation to climate change (GRD/ACC funds) and other PES schemes:

- Estimate the costs of PES projects in accordance with the economics of PES; in particular, the minimum payment must be at least as attractive to the landowner as converting his/her land to another legally permitted use.
- Link the PES payment to the individual water bill for reasons of cost effectiveness (result-based payment) and transparency (the beneficiary knows why he is paying).

Table 3.8. The Quiroz-Chira Water Fund project

Location	Five-year budget (PEN million)	Financing	Issue	Activities	Effectiveness criteria	Contractual arrangement
Quiroz Basin (Piura Department)	2.1 (INV + O&M)	2 JUSH (51%), 2 municipalities (13%) and 1 NGO (36%). JUSH San Lorenzo (5% of water tariff) and JUSH Chira (PEN 28 000/year)	Fog forests and moors (*bosques de neblina y paramos*) in the upper Quiroz River Basin are the sources of water for the Quiroz Basin. In the ecosystems, slash-and-burn practices to expand the agricultural frontier and leaving the farmland uncovered (e.g. burning of crop residues) causes soil erosion. Extensive livestock farming has a direct impact on water storage and retention capacity.	Reforestation with native species such as alder. Irrigation of pastures increases forage production, thus preventing the entry of livestock into natural ecosystems. The ultimate goal is to intervene on the whole upper basin of the Quiroz River (156 000 ha), which includes degraded lands, agricultural lands and natural ecosystems (fog forests and moors). Priority has been given to protecting existing natural ecosystems (18 000 ha), which host the most important water sources and for their functions of water retention and regulation of the water regime.	Natural ecosystems allow to maintain a base flow during the dry season. On an annual average, the base flow is estimated to contribute 4 m^3/second to the hydrological regime of the Quiroz River Basin. A baseline of water quality in the basin has been developed which will be used to assess the impact of the measures.	The Quiroz-Chira Water Fund, a non-profit association with legal status, selects investment projects. The fund comprises an NGO, a provincial municipality, a district municipality and the water users' councils of Chira and San Lorenzo. The Transparency and Oversight Committee, an organ of the fund, brings together leaders of peasant communities in "accountability assemblies" to monitor compliance with the agreements.

Note: JUSH = water user association.

Source: Contreras, L.E.A. (2017[30]), "El Fondo del Agua Quiroz-Chira, Un mecanismo de gestión para los ecosistemas de montaña de Piura, Perú", http://www.bosquesandinos.org/wp-content/uploads/2017/02/FAQCH-FINAL-WEB.pdf.

- Extend the MERESE scheme to industry, which also benefits from increased security of water supply – MERESE is currently only funded by cities (EPs) and, on a voluntary basis, farmers' associations (JUSH); this would increase funding for PES projects and the industry would benefit from a better brand reputation.
- Consider extending the MERESE scheme to hydropower companies, since hydropower production also benefits from the protection of upstream water sources (for example, reduced sedimentation in reservoirs); however, it is important not to discourage hydroelectric production which is a renewable energy.
- Clarify the scope of MERESE and GRD/ACC funds in the areas of flood risk management and climate change adaptation.
- Seek win-win approaches between payments for hydrological services and payments for carbon sequestration so that the respective projects are mutually reinforcing (e.g. sustainable forest management)
- MINAM could usefully keep a register of the various MERESE/PES projects and publish it (to contribute to synergy/avoid any duplication between these projects).

Strengthen economic incentives of abstraction and pollution charges based on water risks (scarcity, pollution) to develop a "water culture"

There is an urgent need to strengthen economic incentives based on water risks (scarcity, pollution) in order to sensitise stakeholders to the knowledge of the risks (to develop a "water culture"). Abstraction/pollution charge rates must be aligned between sectors (cities, farmers, industry) because the impact of water abstraction or wastewater discharges on the environment depends on the availability of the resource and the quality of the receiving water, regardless of the user/polluter. Estimating which charge rates, or which new charges, are necessary to fulfil the legal obligations to manage scarcity and pollution risks of water bodies is a prerequisite for creating incentives to reduce abstraction and discharges. It would also raise revenues, which could be redistributed in the form of financial aid to local communities, industry and farmers in accordance with the master plan for each basin. These options are discussed below.

According to the OECD Principles on Water Governance (2015[31]), water charges will only be viable: if responsible authorities are clearly in charge and endowed with the needed capacity; if they are designed, collected and disbursed at the right scale; if they are documented with robust information-based systems to guide decisions; if they are driven by solid, realistic and policy coherent planning; if they are properly regulated, with effective enforcement and compliance; if stakeholders are engaged well upstream to raise their awareness and secure their buy-in; if their design implementation is transparent; and if they are properly monitored and evaluated. Box 3.3 provides tailored guidance for water abstraction and pollution charges in Brazil (OECD, 2017[32]).

Agreeing on *acceptable* levels of risk for the community and each would give ANA an extremely powerful "entry point" to bring together stakeholders and inform on-the-ground discussion on water resource management. The freezing of major investments for the Peruvian economy (in the mining sector, for example) in the absence of a prior agreement on the risks to water could have been avoided if a risk-based approach had been followed. This approach would also reduce the need for legal proceedings (e.g. Water Conflict Resolution Court for the day-to-day management of water resources).

Setting a maximum level of water withdrawal or wastewater discharge that is acceptable to all stakeholders is at the heart of water risk management. The aim is to ensure a sustainable and cost-effective allocation of the resource among the different sectors while preserving the needs of ecosystems, cultural heritage and the resilience of water systems. Such a risk-based approach (see OECD (2013[33]) for further discussion) should take account of the water allocation regime that prevails in Peru and complement it by specifying how much each user will be able to benefit.

Box 3.3. OECD Principles on Water Governance applied to water charges in Brazil

OECD Principles	Tailored guidance for water abstraction and pollution charges in Brazil
1. Clear roles and responsibilities	• Clearly allocate and distinguish roles and responsibilities amongst federal, state and basin authorities for setting, implementing and regulating water charges, and adjust where need be based on results. • Identify and address duplications, overlaps, gaps or grey areas across levels of government, given the multiplicity of state and federal agencies involved. • Overcome the legal gap concerning water agencies, in charge of allocating revenues from water charges. • Ensure the consultative and deliberative functions of state/interstate river basin committees and state/national water councils are outcome-driven.
2. Appropriate scales within basin systems	• Design, collect and disburse water charges at the appropriate scale to reflect distinctive local capacity, hydrographic situations and water-related risks. • Foster co-ordination between hydrographic and administrative scales, which often do not correspond, with due attention to the higher complexity and multiplicity of stakeholders involved in federal rivers and the double dominion. • Foster co-ordination between local, state and federal levels of government.
3. Policy coherence	• Ensure that decisions taken in agriculture, energy, spatial planning, land use and environmental licensing do not undermine the water use efficiency rationale of charges. • Foster planning tools that drive water charges decisions and policy complementarity between water-related domains.
4. Capacity	• Identify and address capacity gaps to design and implement water charges in state/interstate river basin committees, agencies and councils.
5. Data and information	• Produce, update and share consistent and comparable data and information to guide, assess and improve the design and implementation of water charges. • Ground the level of charges on sound technical criteria, building on economic analysis to support decision-making, and impacts on affordability and competitiveness.
6. Financing	• Ensuring that governance arrangements help raise and spend revenues from water charges in an efficient, transparent and timely manner. • Ensure that the "polluter pays" and "user pays" principles are properly taken into account when designing charges. • Consider pros and cons of earmarking to show the benefits of water charges to end users (e.g. allowing them to access some funds for water conservation measures).
7. Regulatory framework	• Ensure that regulatory frameworks support the efficiency, effectiveness and inclusiveness of water charges and are effectively implemented and enforced. • Ensure sound inspection and control mechanisms as well as sanctions and penalties in case of non-enforcement and compliance.
8. Innovative governance	• Promote innovative practices for the design and implementation of water charges, for example integrating behavioural dimensions into water charge design. • Enhance pilots and experimentation, building on the proposed OECD typology of states, to test some ways forward before upscaling.
9. Integrity and transparency	• Mainstream integrity and transparency practices in the water charge cycle, in particular: who pays for what across water users; and how revenues collected are spent and according to which criteria.
10. Stakeholder engagement	• Raise the awareness of stakeholders on water risks to secure the political/social buy-in for water charges. • Build capacity and share information for outcome-oriented debates and actions to charges in committees, councils and agencies. • Manage the risks of consultation capture, vested interests and low representativeness in deliberative and consultative fora.
11. Trade-offs across users, rural and urban areas and generations	• Use water charges as a contribution to managing trade-offs across users, rural and urban areas, current and future generations. • Evaluate the possibility of cross-subsidies and solidarity mechanisms across users in periods of drought.
12. Monitoring and evaluation	• Promote regular monitoring and evaluation of the adequacy, implementation and results of water charges to assess to what extent they fulfil the intended outcomes and adapt where necessary.

Source: OECD (2017[32]), *Water Charges in Brazil: The Ways Forward*, https://doi.org/10.1787/9789264285712-en.

Developing incentives based on water risks (scarcity, pollution) would sensitise stakeholders to the knowledge of risks (to develop the "water culture"). This is why the differential REUA and REVART rates between sectors (cities, farmers, industry) should be eliminated. The impact of water withdrawals or wastewater discharges on the environment depends on the availability of the resource and the quality of the receiving water, regardless of the user/polluter. As such, the REVART rate should reflect the health and environmental toxicity of pollutants in wastewater. For example, a preferential rate applies for the REVART to communal water companies in rural areas. Although this encourages the necessary development of sanitation infrastructure in these areas, it reduces the incentive to build modern infrastructure (e.g. advanced wastewater treatment). The single REUA rate that applies to some boards of users of the hydraulic sector (JUSH) does not take into account the risk of water scarcity; it must be replaced by a differentiated rate according to the availability of water, as is the case for other users. For the same reason, the REUA rate applied to "special projects", a percentage of the tariff to cover the cost of operation and maintenance of the irrigation infrastructure (*tarifa por el servicio de agua*), must be replaced by a differentiated REUA rate according to the availability of water.

Moreover, some options to be considered are:

- *Farmers*: Eliminate the preferential electricity tariff for pumping groundwater in areas where it applies (e.g. Tacna), as it counteracts the incentive, through REUA, to use water more efficiently (for example, by adopting modern irrigation technology).
- *Hydropower plants*: Set the REUA according to the environmental risks and benefits associated with hydropower generation – hydropeaking, modification of sediment transport and eutrophication, obstacles to fish migration, the positive role of dams in managing water scarcity and flooding risks – and not on the basis of the price of electricity ex-factory, as is currently the case.
- *ANA and EPs*: Ensure that groundwater monitoring by ANA and the water companies (the latter financed by the water bill) complement each other and are consistent.

Extending ANA's inspection fee coverage for water resource use would improve regulatory compliance and knowledge of water scarcity risks; the same recommendation applies to the Ministry of Health with respect to inspection fees for the discharge of wastewater. ANA and the Ministry of Health apply inspection fees. An extension of their coverage, both for the use of resources and for effluent discharges, would increase the number of inspections and, consequently, increase compliance with regulations and knowledge of the risks associated with water. There is an urgent need to improve knowledge of the water risks (scarcity, pollution) in Peru and to sensitise stakeholders (to develop a "water culture").

The imposition of an REUA on seawater abstraction in Peru is surprising because there is no risk of depletion of the seawater resource. On the contrary, desalination increases the availability of freshwater. However, it can have negative effects on the marine environment in the form of brine discharges to the sea that can lead to a substantial increase in salinity and temperature, as well as the accumulation of metals, hydrocarbons and other toxic compounds in receiving waters (Roberts, Johnston and Knott, 2010[34]). The imposition of a REVART on the discharge of concentrated brine by marine outfalls of desalination plants, as is already the case in Peru, makes more sense from the point of view of the protection of the environment.

In sum, the following actions could be taken into account by ANA, MIDAGRI, MINAM, MINEM and EPs to strengthen economic incentives to develop a "water culture" based on the risks of water scarcity:

- Farmers located in the upper basin (*cuenca alta*): Remove the preferential rate of abstraction charges (REUA) in areas at risk of water scarcity because this goes against any PES to protect headwaters.
- Boards of users of the hydraulic sector (JUSH): Replace the single rate of REUA that applies to some JUSH by a differentiated rate according to the availability of water (i.e. the risk of water shortage), as is the case for other users.

- "Special projects" under concession: Pass on the REUA paid by the water collector (*concedente*) to the irrigation water supply tariff (*tarifa por el servicio*), instead of applying a fixed rate of 2.61% of the tariff.
- Farmers: Eliminate the preferential electricity tariff for pumping groundwater, as it thwarts the incentive of REUA to use water more efficiently (for example, by adopting modern irrigation technology).
- Hydropower plants: Set the REUA according to the environmental risks and benefits associated with hydropower generation – hydropeaking, modification of sediment transport and eutrophication, obstacles to fish migration, the positive role of dams in managing water scarcity and flooding risks – and not on the basis of the price of electricity ex-factory, as is currently the case.
- ANA: Broaden the base of ANA's water resource use inspection fees to improve compliance with water legislation and awareness of water scarcity risks.
- ANA and EPs: Ensure that groundwater monitoring by ANA and the water companies (the latter financed by the water bill) complement each other and are consistent.

The following actions could be taken into account by ANA, MIDAGRI, MINAM and the Ministry of Health (MINSA) to strengthen economic incentives to develop a "water culture" based on the risks of water pollution:

- Communal sanitation organisations (rural areas): Replace the preferential rate of the charge on the discharge of treated wastewater (REVART) by a differentiated rate according to the quality of the receiving water, as is the case for other sectors.
- All: Set the REVART rate according to the toxicity of the effluents for health and the environment.
- MINSA: Broaden the base of MINSA wastewater discharge inspection fees to improve compliance with water legislation and raise awareness of water pollution risks.

Bring together different sources of financial support to launch a policy of "river rehabilitation"

In Peru, an explicit river rehabilitation policy is lacking. As such, it could usefully bring together different sources of financial support to restore the natural course of rivers (*inter alia* to avoid significant damage from floods). Restoring good hydromorphological conditions in rivers (river rehabilitation) can help improve water supply (self-purification of water and recharge of groundwater), ensure natural protection against floods and protect nature (providing sufficient space to rivers allows them to connect ecosystems). It is necessary to ensure synergies and coherence between these different objectives and policies to encourage them. To introduce such a river rehabilitation policy, Peru should estimate the river sections to be restored and the financial support to be mobilised. In particular:

- Assess the ecosystem services provided by river rehabilitation (improvement of water resources, protection against floods, nature protection, land consolidation).
- Consider river rehabilitation as part of MERESE payments for hydrological services.
- Provide public financial support for river rehabilitation as it contributes to the protection of natural ecosystems and their services (such as floodplains).
- Provide public financial support for the protection of alluvial forests.
- Provide public financial support for the rehabilitation of small rivers located in agricultural areas to the extent that it contributes to the improvement of agricultural production conditions through land consolidation.
- In case of overlapping policies for the same stretch of river, no double funding should be allowed for the same service provided.

In sum, the following actions could be taken into account by MIDAGRI and MINAM to bring together different sources of financial support to launch a policy of "river rehabilitation":

- Target agricultural policy support for flood risk management.
  - Provide agricultural policy support for the rehabilitation of flood plains and their natural habitats in agricultural areas as part of agri-environmental measures.
  - Provide agricultural policy support for the rehabilitation of small rivers in agricultural areas as part of land consolidation policies.
- Target PES and public financial support to alluvial forests and natural riparian ecosystems.
  - Consider river rehabilitation as part of MERESE payments for hydrological services.
  - Provide environmental policy support for the protection of alluvial forests and natural riparian ecosystems.

An interesting example is provided by the Swiss river rehabilitation policy. In 2011, Switzerland embarked on a long-term effort to restore its rivers. The Swiss river rehabilitation policy was triggered by a popular initiative of fishermen to strengthen the biological functions of rivers through habitat creation and riparian zone management (Box 3.4).

Box 3.4. River rehabilitation policy in Switzerland

Around 40% of Swiss rivers are in poor morphological status and about a quarter have a high degree of fragmentation due to artificial structures that affect the passage of migratory fish, change the natural habitat distribution within rivers and modify their ecological capacity. The Swiss policy of river rehabilitation, initiated in 2011, aims to strengthen the biological functions of watercourses by creating habitats and managing riparian zones. It led to the amendment of several federal laws: the Waters Protection Act, the Watercourse Management Act, Energy Act and Rural Land Act.

A national target was set to rehabilitate about 25% of waters with poor morphological status in the next 80 years, i.e. some 4 000 km of river length by about 2090. The Swiss cantons must delimit sufficient space to allow the rivers to fulfil their natural functions and to guarantee protection against floods and the use of water. This "space for waters" must be included in their master plan and land use plan.

Public financial support is granted for rehabilitation works (via environmental policy) and provision of space for waters (via agricultural policy), while electricity consumers (via a tax on electricity bills) support the ecological improvement of old hydropower plants. This is combined with direct regulations on minimum flows and come in addition to the public financial support for flood control.

Source: OECD (2017[35]), *OECD Environmental Performance Reviews: Switzerland 2017*, https://doi.org/10.1787/9789264279674-en.

Strengthen policy coherence between the economic instruments deployed to manage water risks and instruments related to sectoral and environmental policies

Sectoral policies should not offset the effects of policies to pay for hydrological services and river rehabilitation, as well as charges on water abstraction and wastewater discharges, by encouraging overuse or water pollution. This may be the case for policies to encourage agricultural, aquaculture or hydroelectric production (Table 3.9). Coherence must also be sought with carbon sequestration policies.

For the purpose of strengthening policy coherence, the following actions could be considered:

- Evaluate the impact of agricultural support, in its different forms, on water resources.

- Evaluate the impact of hydropower development on fluctuations in flows and water levels downstream and upstream of plants (hydropeaking), sediment transport and eutrophication, and fish migration.
- Manage the risk of water pollution by antibiotics, fungicides and feed used on fish farms.
- Promote forest carbon credits for farmers who commit to converting their land to forests, thereby reducing pressure on water resources.
- Within the framework of strengthening links for the management of water resources and water and sanitation services. It is suggested to articulate them with the Quality Control Plans of the sanitation services and the Health Adaptation Plan promoted by the Ministry of Health/ Directorate-General for Environmental Health and Food Safety (DIGESA).

Climate mitigation and water policies can help each other. In New Zealand, for example, in places where it has induced farmland conversion into forests, carbon emission trading has reduced nitrogen releases into water (Box 3.5).

Table 3.9. Summary of actions to strengthen policy coherence between the economic instruments

Practical steps	Potential indicators	Objectives	Relevant OECD experience	Champion
- Evaluate the impact of agricultural policy support (market price support, direct payments, input subsidies, irrigation subsidies) on water resources.	- Water resource withdrawals, irrigated area and irrigation water application rates. - Water quality: nitrates, phosphorus and pesticides.[1]	- Agriculture	The information contained in the OECD Producer Support Estimate (PSE) can be used as a starting point to assess the impact of agricultural policies on the environment, either at the sector level or the farm level.[2]	- MIDAGRI - MINAM
- Manage the risk of water pollution by antibiotics, fungicides and feed used on fish farms.	- Reporting of the use of antibiotics and fungicides to assess trends. - Nitrogen balance for each fish farm.	- Fish farming	Several OECD countries have taken steps to manage the externalities generated by aquaculture.[3]	- PRODUCE - MINAM
- Evaluate the impact of the development of hydropower on fluctuations in water flows and levels downstream and upstream of dams (hydropeaking), sediment transport, eutrophication and fish migration.	- Number of hydropeaking events. - Siltation of dam reservoirs. - Number of eutrophication episodes in dam reservoirs. - Share of dams with fish ladder.	- Hydropower	Guiding principles on sustainable hydropower development have been developed in the Danube Basin.[4]	- MEM - MINAM
- Promote a forest carbon credits policy for landowners who commit to preserving their forest lands or converting their lands to forests, thereby reducing pressure on water resources.	- Forest carbon credits (in tonnes of CO_2 equivalent).	- Forest carbon sequestration	In New Zealand, GHG emitters can pay (via a trust) farmers who agree to sequester carbon by converting farmland into forests, thus helping to reduce agricultural pollution of water.[5]	- MINAM - MIDAGRI's SERFOR (National Forest and Wildlife Service)

Source: 1. OECD (2013[33]), *Water Security for Better Lives*, https://doi.org/10.1787/9789264202405-en; 2. Henderson, B. and J. Lankoski (2019[26]), "Evaluating the Environmental Impact of Agricultural Policies", https://doi.org/10.1787/add0f27c-en; 3. OECD (2010[9]), *Paying for Biodiversity: Enhancing the Cost-Effectiveness of Payments for Ecosystem Services*, https://doi.org/10.1787/9789264090279-en; 4. ICPDR (2013[36]), *Sustainable Hydropower Development in the Danube Basin - Guiding Principles, International Commission for the Protection of the Danube River*, https://www.icpdr.org/main/activities-projects/hydropower; 5. Leining, C. and S. Kerr (2018[37]), *A Guide to the New Zealand Emissions Trading Scheme*, https://www.mfe.govt.nz/publications/climate-change/guide-new-zealand-emissions-trading-scheme.

Box 3.5. Synergies between water and climate policies in New Zealand

In New Zealand, a combination of tradeable permit systems (TPS) helps reduce carbon dioxide emissions and at the same time reduce the risk of water pollution by nitrates.

On the one hand, a GHG emissions trading scheme (ETS) allows GHG emitters (for example industry) that do not wish to reduce their emissions to enter into an agreement (via a trust) with farmers. To receive financial compensation, farmers must commit to converting their pastoral lands to forests, thereby helping to sequester carbon. GHG emitters receive ETS credits in exchange for pastoral land converted to forestry. The trust is financed by the GHG emitters through the purchase of ETS credits.

On the other hand, to reduce nitrogen pollution in Lake Taupo, New Zealand's largest lake, a nitrogen cap-and-trade system has been put in place for farmers in the lake basin. Instead of selling their nitrogen pollution rights, farmers can opt for permanent nitrogen reductions, for which they are compensated financially by the GHG trust. This opens up the possibility for farmers to be paid to reduce nitrogen emissions, at the same time as receiving income from forest credits.

Source: OECD (2018[38]), *Human Acceleration of the Nitrogen Cycle: Managing Risks and Uncertainty*, https://doi.org/10.1787/9789264307438-en.

References

ANA (2019), "Country submission". [25]

ANA (2015), "Determinando el valor del agua, Agua y Más", *Revista de la Autoridad Nacional del Agua*, N°01 Abril 2015, Autoridad Nacional del Agua. [21]

ANA (2012), *Retribución Económica por el Uso del Agua y por Vertimiento de Aguas Residuales Tratadas: Metodología para Determinar su Valor*, Autoridad Nacional del Agua, Lima, Perú. [22]

Asquith, N., M. Vargas and S. Wunder (2008), "Selling two environmental services: In-kind payments for bird habitat and watershed protection in Los Negros, Bolivia", *Ecological Economics*, Vol. 65/4. [3]

Contreras, L.E.A. (2017), "El Fondo del Agua Quiroz-Chira, Un mecanismo de gestión para los ecosistemas de montaña de Piura, Perú", Programa Bosques Andinos de la Agencia Suiza para el Desarrollo y la Cooperación (COSUDE) and Naturaleza y Cultura Internacional, http://www.bosquesandinos.org/wp-content/uploads/2017/02/FAQCH-FINAL-WEB.pdf. [30]

Cox, A. and P. Borkey (2015), "Challenges and policy options for financing urban water and sanitation", in Barajas, I. et al. (eds.), *Water and Cities in Latin America, Challenges for Sustainable Development,*, Earthscan, London. [24]

Dias Soares, C. (2011), "The design features of environmental taxes", MPhil thesis, The London School of Economics and Political Science. [17]

Engel, S., S. Pagiola and S. Wunder (2008), "Designing payments for environmental services in theory and practice: An overview of the issues", *Ecological Economics*, Vol. 65, https://doi.org/10.1016/j.ecolecon.2008.03.011. [4]

FAO (2007), *The State of Food and Agriculture: Paying Farmers for Environmental Services*, Food and Agricultural Organization of the United Nations, Rome. [12]

Görlach, B. (2013), *What Constitutes an Optimal Policy Mix? Defining the Concept of Optimality, Including Political and Legal Framework Conditions*, Ecologic Institute, Berlin. [39]

Government of Peru (2019), "Supreme Decree No. 011-2019-MINAGRI of 24 December 2019 approving the charges to be applied in 2020 for the use of surface and groundwater and for the discharge of treated wastewater", https://cdn.www.gob.pe/uploads/document/file/473663/DECRETO_SUPREMO_N__0011-2019-MINAGRI.pdf. [23]

Greiber, T. (2009), *Payments for Ecosystem Services: Legal and Institutional Frameworks*, International Union for Conservation of Nature and Natural Resources, Bonn. [11]

Henderson, B. and J. Lankoski (2019), "Evaluating the Environmental Impact of Agricultural Policies", *OECD Food, Agriculture and Fisheries Papers*, No. 130, OECD Publishing, Paris, https://doi.org/10.1787/add0f27c-en. [26]

ICPDR (2013), *Sustainable Hydropower Development in the Danube Basin - Guiding Principles, International Commission for the Protection of the Danube River*, International Commission for the Protection of the Danube River, https://www.icpdr.org/main/activities-projects/hydropower. [36]

Karp, L. (2005), "Nonpoint source pollution taxes and excessive tax burden", *Environmental and Resource Economics*, Vol. 31. [20]

Kemp, R. and S. Pontoglio (2011), "The innovation effects of environmental policy instruments - A typical case of the blind men and the elephant?", *Ecological Economics*, Vol. 72/C. [19]

Leining, C. and S. Kerr (2018), *A Guide to the New Zealand Emissions Trading Scheme*, Motu Economic and Public Policy Research, https://www.mfe.govt.nz/publications/climate-change/guide-new-zealand-emissions-trading-scheme. [37]

MINAGRI (2019), *Aprovechamiento de los Recursos Hídricos Para Uso Agrario; Contenidos Mínimos del Programa Presupuestal, Anexo 2*, Ministerio de Agricultura y Riego, Lima, Perú. [27]

Morley, B. and S. Abdullah (2010), "Environmental taxes and economic growth: Evidence from panel causality tests", *Bath Economics Research Working Papers*, No. 04/10, University of Bath, UK. [16]

National Academies of Sciences, Engineering, and Medicine (2020), *Review of the New York City Watershed Protection Program*, The National Academies Press, Washington, DC, https://doi.org/10.17226/25851. [28]

OECD (2018), *Human Acceleration of the Nitrogen Cycle: Managing Risks and Uncertainty*, OECD Publishing, Paris, https://doi.org/10.1787/9789264307438-en. [38]

OECD (2017), *OECD Environmental Performance Reviews: Switzerland 2017*, OECD Environmental Performance Reviews, OECD Publishing, Paris, https://doi.org/10.1787/9789264279674-en. [35]

OECD (2017), *Water Charges in Brazil: The Ways Forward*, OECD Studies on Water, OECD Publishing, Paris, https://doi.org/10.1787/9789264285712-en. [32]

OECD (2015), *OECD Principles on Water Governance*, OECD, Paris, https://www.oecd.org/cfe/regionaldevelopment/OECD-Principles-on-Water-Governance-en.pdf. [31]

OECD (2013), *Water Security for Better Lives*, OECD Studies on Water, OECD Publishing, Paris, https://doi.org/10.1787/9789264202405-en. [33]

OECD (2010), *Paying for Biodiversity: Enhancing the Cost-Effectiveness of Payments for Ecosystem Services*, OECD Publishing, Paris, https://doi.org/10.1787/9789264090279-en. [9]

OECD (2008), "An OECD Framework for Effective and Efficient Environmental Policies", Meeting of the Environment Policy Committee (EPOC) at Ministerial Level, 28-29 April 2008, OECD, Paris. [1]

OECD (2001), *Environmentally Related Taxes in OECD Countries: Issues and Strategies*, OECD Publishing, Paris, http://dx.doi.org/10.1787/9789264193659-en. [15]

Pagiola, S. and G. Platais (2007), *Payments for Environmental Services: From Theory to Practice*, World Bank, Washington, DC. [6]

Pattanayak, S., S. Wunder and P. Ferraro (2010), "Show me the money: do payments supply environmental services in developing countries?", *Review of Environmental Economics and Policy*, Vol. 4/2. [7]

Perrot-Maitre, D. (2006), "The Vittel payments for ecosystem services: A 'perfect' PES case?", International Institute for Environment and Development, London, https://pubs.iied.org/pdfs/G00388.pdf. [29]

Roberts, D., E. Johnston and N. Knott (2010), "Impacts of desalination plant discharges on the Mmarine environment: A critical review of published studies", *Water Research*, Vol. 44. [34]

Schomers, S. and B. Matzdorf (2016), "Payments for ecosystem services: A review and comparison of developing and industrialized countries", *Ecosystem Services*, Vol. 6. [2]

Schwarz, G. et al. (2008), *An Analysis of the Potential Effectiveness of a Payments-by-results Approach to the Delivery of Environmental Public Goods and Services Supplied by Agri-environment Schemes*, Report to the Land Use Policy Group, UK, Macaulay Institute, Pareto Consulting, and Scottish Agricultural College. [10]

SUNASS (2020), "Pasco: Sunass fortalece implementación de mecanismos de conservación de fuentes de agua para consumo humano | Gobierno del Perú", https://www.gob.pe/institucion/sunass/noticias/318025-pasco-sunass-fortalece-implementacion-de-mecanismos-de-conservacion-de-fuentes-de-agua-para-consumo-humano (accessed on 11 February 2021). [13]

SUNASS (n.d.), "SUNASS comprometida con el cuidado de las fuentes de agua", https://www.sunass.gob.pe/websunass/index.php/eps/sunass-comprometida-con-el-cuidado-de-las-fuentes-de-agua. [14]

Tomich, T., D. Thomas and M. Noordwijk (2004), "Environmental services and land use change in Southeast Asia: from recognition to regulation or reward?", *Agriculture Ecosystems and Environment*, Vol. 104. [5]

Wakabayashi, M. and T. Sugiyama (2009), “Case studies and its effectiveness of environmental taxation”, *SERC Discussion Paper*, SERC09005, Central Research Institute of Electric Power Industry. [18]

Wunder, S., S. Engel and S. Pagiola (2008), “Taking stock: A comparative analysis of payments for environmental services programs in developed and developing countries”, *Ecological Economics*, Vol. 65. [8]

Additional references

Agence de l'eau Seine-Normandie (2019), “Les redevances de l’Agence de l'eau Seine-Normandie 2019-2024”, https://en.calameo.com/agence-de-l-eau-seine-normandie/read/004001913990170881f15.

Albán Contreras, L.E. (2017), “El Fondo del Agua Quiroz-Chira, Un mecanismo de gestión para los ecosistemas de montaña de Piura, Perú”, Programa Bosques Andinos de la Agencia Suiza para el Desarrollo y la Cooperación (COSUDE) and Naturaleza y Cultura Internacional, http://www.bosquesandinos.org/wp-content/uploads/2017/02/FAQCH-FINAL-WEB.pdf.

Notes

[1] Görlach (2013[39]) identified five feasibility factors that may act to limit the ability to introduce instruments in the most theoretically desirable manner: administrative feasibility (e.g. transaction costs), side effects (e.g. distributional and competitiveness impacts), political and public acceptability, legal feasibility, (compatibility with existing legal frameworks) and flexibility (e.g. the ability to respond to new information).

[2] See also discussion on “stacking” and “bundling” ecosystem services in https://www.forest-trends.org/wp-content/uploads/2018/11/Stacking-Bundling-Resource-Paper-01-11-18.pdf.

[3] The WTO provides three “traffic light boxes” for subsidies, from Green (permitted), Amber (to be reduced) and Red (forbidden).

[4] Decree-Law No.1280 of 2016 regulates the inclusion of GRD and ACC funds in the water tariff structure. Resolution No. 039-2019-SUNASS-CD of the Board of Directors of SUNASS of 20 November 2019 provides that GRD and ACC funds can be used to finance MERESE projects provided that the latter include measures of adaptation to climate change or disaster risk management.

[1] Levied approximately in proportion to services provided.

[2] Benefits provided by government to taxpayers are not normally in proportion to their payments.

[3] Over time, the competitive price level will emerge, set at the marginal cost of production (zero profit), producing a flat supply curve.

[4] For countries for which information is available (unpublished data from the OECD Database on Policy Instruments for the Environment).

[5] Draft Resolution of the Board of Directors No. 027-2019-SUNASS-CD of 3 September 2019.

4 Regulatory framework for water supply and sanitation services in Peru

The chapter starts with an overview of the water supply and sanitation (WSS) services in Peru, recent government policies and goals for the sector, and a description of the structure of the water industry. It then turns to the legislative framework and allocation of regulatory functions before looking in more detail at the governance and performance of Peru's independent water regulator, the *Superintendencia Nacional de Servicios de Saneamiento* (SUNASS). The chapter concludes with a series of policy recommendations to support the policy goals of universal coverage of WSS services.

Peru's water supply and sanitation (WSS) services

There are significant gaps in access to WSS services in Peru, with rural areas particularly affected. Peru is below the Latin America and the Caribbean (LAC) regional standards for access to safely managed drinking water services (Figure 4.1): 9.2% of the population (3 million people) lack access to public water supply networks and 25.2% (8.2 million people) lack access to public sewerage services (INEI, 2019[1]). Furthermore, when looking at subjective measures, only 61% of individuals in Peru report that they are satisfied with the quality of the water (Figure 4.2) (OECD, 2015[2]). Access to WSS services in rural areas is significantly lower than in urban areas. Key statistics include (INEI, 2019[1]):

- 24.8% of the rural population and 4.9% of the urban population do not have access to public water supply networks (i.e. water is supplied by water tanker trucks, wells, rivers, springs, canals or other sources).
- Only 37.1% of the population consumes water from public networks with appropriate disinfection concentration; in rural areas, the figure is just 2.4%.
- Only 55.6% of the population (54.9% of the urban population and 58.1% of the rural population) has 24-hour access to a water supply.
- 24.5% of the population lacks access to public sewage networks (10.2% of the urban population and 80.8% of the rural population).
- 8.7% of the population lacks any kind of sewage system (4.4% of the urban population and 24.0% of the rural population).

Figure 4.1. Access to safely managed drinking water services is low in Peru compared to the LAC region

Percentage of the population, 2017

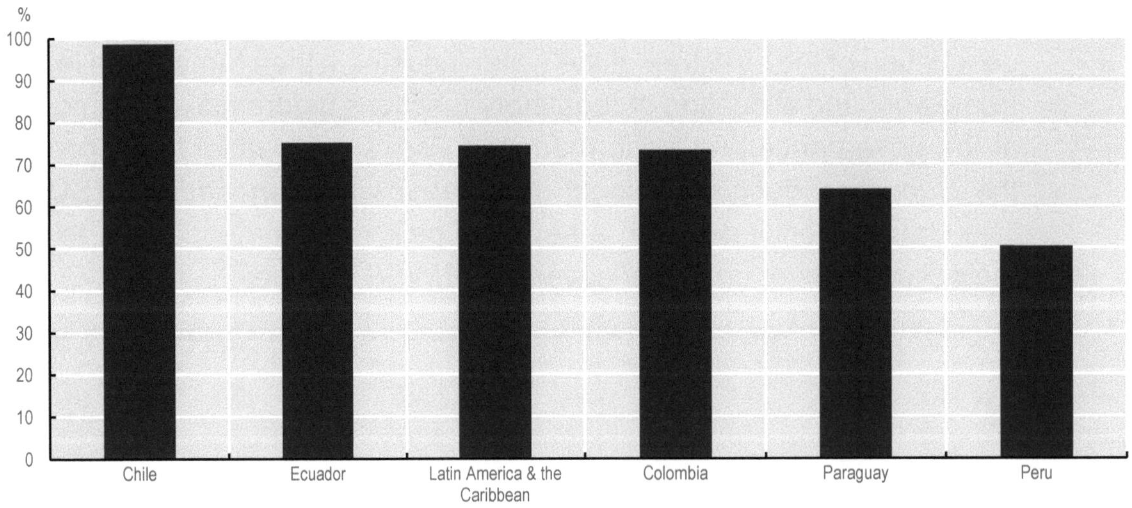

Note: The percentage of the population using drinking water from an improved source that is accessible on premises, available when needed and free from faecal and priority chemical contamination. Improved water sources include piped water, boreholes or tubewells, protected dug wells, protected springs and packaged or delivered water.
Source: World Bank (2019[3]), *World Development Indicators*, World Bank, Washington, DC.

Figure 4.2. Satisfaction rates with the quality of water in Peru

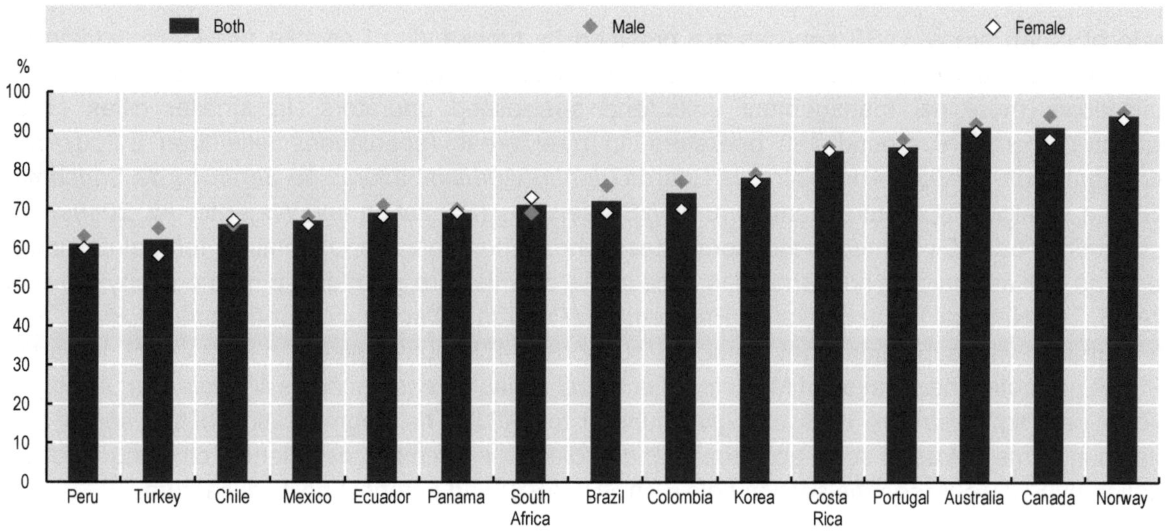

Source: Gallup Organisation (2015[4]), *Gallup World Monitor (database)*, in OECD (2015[2]), *Multi-dimensional Review of Peru: Volume 1. Initial Assessment*, https://dx.doi.org/10.1787/9789264243279-en.

The OECD Principles on Water Governance (2015[5]) recommend that countries "ensure that sound water management regulatory frameworks are effectively implemented and enforced in pursuit of the public interest". In line with common practice in OECD countries and internationally, this chapter uses the term WSS services, which can be considered equivalent to the term sanitation (*saneamiento*) used commonly in Peru and which refers to the full range of water supply, disposal of human excreta and sewage, and wastewater treatment services, as defined in Title I, Article 2 of Legislative Decree No. 1280. In Peru, there are still significant gaps in access to WSS services, especially in rural areas, and the sector remains highly fragmented. While the role of WSS sector policy lead (*ente rector*) of the Ministry of Housing, Construction and Sanitation (*Ministerio de Vivienda Construcción y Saneamiento*, MVCS) and the role of economic regulator for the supervision and monitoring of WSS service provision of SUNASS are clearly defined in legislation,[1] a lack of co-ordination and capacity, as well as potentially overlapping or unclear mandates of a number of public bodies and levels of government, undermine role clarity and the effective achievement of policy goals. In order to overcome these gaps, these policy goals must be approached from a perspective of unity and a high-level pact for ownership and support of all stakeholders for their achievement. Along the same line, responsible institutions should co-ordinate and streamline data collection for measuring progress and impact.

Sector structure

The water supply and sanitation (WSS) sector is highly fragmented in Peru, with different modes of market organisation in urban and rural areas (Figure 4.3). In urban areas (cities above 15 000 inhabitants), 50 water and sanitation service providers (*Empresas Prestadoras del Servicio de Saneamiento*, EPs) provide drinking water to 18.4 million people, who represent 57% of the national population, 72% of the total urban population and 90% of the population within the EPs' scope of responsibility (the geographical area in which the EPs should provide WSS services, defined under contract) (SUNASS, 2020[6]). The 50 EPs, all publicly-owned, are categorised by size: SEDAPAL, the EP that serves Lima is in a category of its own with over 1 million connections; 4 "Large 1" companies with 100 000-1 million connections; 14 "Large 2" companies with 40 000-100 000 connections; 15 medium-sized companies with 15 000-40 000 connections; and 16 small companies with less than 15 000 connections (SUNASS, 2018[7]). This fragmentation of the urban market limits economies of scale, with a consequent loss of efficiency in WSS services delivery.

Outside of urban areas, WSS services are provided by thousands of diverse providers, adding to the fragmentation of the sector and potentially hindering efficient service delivery. Providers include community organisations, municipal management units and specialised operators. In smaller cities (<15 000 inhabitants), there are around 450 operators. In rural areas (populations less than 2 000), around 25 000 Sanitation Services Administrative Boards (*Juntas Administradoras de Servicios de Saneamiento,* JASS) and municipal operators manage rural WSS services (Sanitation and Water for All, 2019[8]). JASS are community-based, volunteer water committees whose members are responsible for maintaining WSS systems as well as charging household fees, the levels of which are guided by a methodology provided by SUNASS. The National Rural Sanitation Programme (*Programa Nacional de Saneamiento Rural*, PNSR), in co-ordination with subnational governments, supports 1 458 municipalities to form JASS. In particular, the PNSR promotes the creation of Municipal Technical Areas (*Areas Tecnicas Municipales*, ATMs) within municipalities, administrative units that give support to JASS. The fragmentation of the sector creates problems in terms of loss of scale economies and additional sources of inefficiency, challenges for sound regulation by SUNASS (see the section below on SUNASS) and potential political capture.

Figure 4.3. Market structure of WSS services providers in Peru

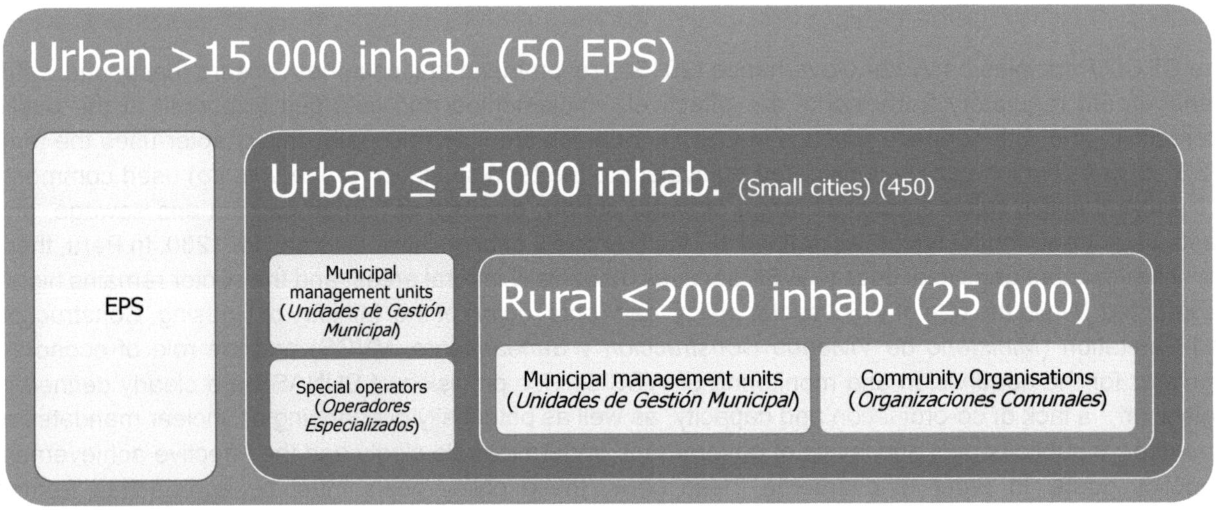

Source: SUNASS (2019[9]), "Presentation summarising the classification of service providers, as per Supreme Decree No. 019-2017-VIVIENDA", at OECD workshop, Santo Domingo, September 2019.

Moving towards a more consolidated water industry faces resistance at the local level. The merging of EPs could enable WSS service provision at a regional (or larger) scale – encompassing rural, urban and peri-urban areas – that would facilitate EPs to reap economies of scale. Local authorities currently have decision-making authority on whether to integrate WSS providers but there is generally resistance to this process which can stand in the way of achieving economies of scale within EPs. Any public policies to address the fragmentation of the WSS sector will need to take into account such political economy considerations.

The financial sustainability of WSS operators is a serious concern in Peru, with many urban EPs operating at a loss and many rural operators failing to meet basic financial sustainability. Water utilities in Peru tend to be small public agencies with low business income, often leading to shortcomings in terms of financial feasibility. Inefficient management (e.g. high leakage rates) can compound these challenges. In urban areas, many EPs are undergoing reforms to improve services. The EPs are supported by the Technical

Agency for the Administration of Sanitation Services (*Organismo Técnico de la Administración de los Servicios de Saneamiento*, OTASS). Currently, 19 EPs are under the Transitional Support Scheme (*Régimen de Apoyo Transitorio*, RAT) due to insolvency or poor business performance and are undergoing bailout procedures overseen by OTASS, responsible for improving their management. In rural areas, poorly determined tariffs also result in income that does not cover costs (Ministerio de Vivienda, Construcción y Saneamiento, 2016[10]). Furthermore, investment in physical infrastructure in rural areas has often not been complemented by sufficient resourcing for the development of local capacity for operation and management, or adequate social awareness by users on the costs of WSS provision (Oblitas de Ruiz, 2010[11]).

Institutional framework

The Ministry of Housing, Construction and Sanitation (MVCS) sets the overall public policy goals that provide the framework for the development of sector regulation. The MVCS is the governing body for sanitation and has exclusive power over the development, planning, co-ordination, implementation and overseeing of national specific and related policies within its legal powers, issuing guidance and technical standards, planning and funding of sanitation services as a public service. The MVCS leads, manages and administers the Water and Sanitation Information System (*Sistema de información en agua y saneamiento*, SIAS).[2] OTASS, attached to the MVCS,[3] promotes and implements the policy of the MVCS regarding the management, administration and provision of sanitation services. In particular, it executes the policy of the governing body regarding administration for the provision of sanitation services and takes control of public EPs under municipal ownership in the event of financial and operational insolvency so as to improve their performance (Chapter 1). The Ministry of Health (MINSA), through the Directorate-General for Environmental Health and Food Safety (*Dirección General de Salud Ambiental e Inocuidad Alimentaria*, DIGESA), regulates and monitors the compliance in terms of quality parameters of water for human consumption. The Ministry of Development and Social Inclusion (*Ministerio de Desarrollo e Inclusión Social*, MIDIS) is also responsible for interventions in terms of investments in sanitation services in rural areas and for the maintenance and rehabilitation of water and sanitation systems, as per Supreme Decree No. 18-2017-VIVIENDA.

The regulatory framework for water supply and sanitation (WSS) services in Peru is organised around the establishment of dedicated agencies with regulatory functions. The National Water Authority (*Autoridad Nacional del Agua*, ANA) is the regulatory body for the use and management of water resources that include surface and groundwater (and extends to the sea and atmospheric water where applicable). SUNASS is the economic regulator for WWS. Other agencies intervene in the sector as part of their overall responsibilities, including the Agency for Environmental Assessment and Enforcement (*Organismo de Evaluación y Fiscalización Ambiental*, OEFA) and a public health authority (MINSA via DIGESA). In addition, regional governments have some health regulatory functions (notably monitoring the application of the nationally-defined quality standards) through the Regional Health Directorate (DIRESA)/DIGESA (Table 4.1). Moreover, a number of ministries – the Ministry of Agricultural Development and Irrigation (*Ministerio de Desarrollo Agrario y Riego*, MIDAGRI), the Ministry of the Environment (*Ministerio del Ambiente*, MINAM) and the MVCS – have WSS in their portfolios, making governance arrangements around the former authorities complex (Figure 4.4).

Within the context of legal powers of the MVCS, an instrument for the Ecosystem Services Compensation Mechanism (MERESE), which allows for an explicit connection of urban and rural water services delivery and water resources management, has been implemented. Article 27.1 of Legislative Decree No. 1280 establishes that water utilities (EPs) must further agreements to set up an Ecosystem Services Compensation Mechanism and that SUNASS must include in the water and sanitation services tariff the amount the Ecosystem Services Compensation Mechanism that corresponds to each user.

Table 4.1. Regulatory functions for water in Peru

Function	Responsible authority
Tariff regulation	SUNASS
Ecosystem Services Compensation Mechanism (MERESE)	MINAM SUNASS
Environmental quality standards for water	MINAM
Quality standards for drinking water Maximum permissible limits	MINSA through DIGESA (national level) in co-ordination with other sectoral ministries Monitored at the regional level by DIRESA/GERESA
Quality standards for wastewater treatment	MINAM
Defining public service obligations	MVCS SUNASS
Defining technical/industry and service standards	MVCS SUNASS
Setting incentives for efficient use of water resources	ANA MVCS SUNASS
Promoting climate change adaptation and mitigation measures and monitoring the implementation progress of those measures	MINAM Sector ministries
Setting incentives for efficient investment	PROINVERSION MVCS SUNASS
Promoting innovative technologies	CONCYTEC MVCS Regional governments
Promoting demand management of water and sanitation services	ANA SUNASS
Defining the geographic area for WSS service provision	SUNASS
Information and data gathering	MVCS: manages, administers and updates information included in SIAS ANA: through the National Water Resources Information System EPS Regional governments Local governments SUNASS: "collect, process and incorporate in the SIAS or other approved by the Governing Body, under responsibility, the information on the infrastructure and management indicators of the sanitation services of the EPS and small cities" MINAM: National Environmental Information System (SINIA)
Monitoring of service delivery performance	SUNASS
Customer engagement	INDECOPI EPS
Consumer protection and dispute resolution	INDECOPI SUNASS
Licensing of water operators	ANA

Function	Responsible authority
Supervision of contracts with utilities/private actors	SUNASS
Uniform systems of accounts, e.g. for financial accounts	SUNASS
Analysing water utilities' investment plans/business plans	SUNASS (through EPS Optimised Master Plans) OTASS approves the Emergency Action Plan and the Bailout Plan of the service providers incorporated in the Transitional Support Regime (RAT) and finances its preparation and implementation
Supervising utilities' financing activities (e.g. issuing bonds, seeking equity investments)	PROINVERSION
Carrying management audits on utilities	SUNASS

Note: ANA = National Water Authority; CONCYTEC = National Council of Science, Technology and Innovation; DIGESA = General Directorate of Environmental Health (within the Ministry of Health); EPS = Water and sanitation service companies; INDECOPI = National Institute for the Defence of Competition and the Protection of Intellectual Property; MVCS = Ministry of Housing, Construction and Sanitation; MERESE = Ecosystem Services Compensation Mechanism; MINAM = Ministry of the Environment; MINSA = Ministry of Health; OTASS = Technical Agency for the Administration of Sanitation Services; PROINVERSION = Private Investment Promotion Agency; SIAS = Water and Sanitation Information System; SUNASS = Economic regulator for WSS; WSS = Water supply and sanitation.
Source: OECD (2019[12]), OECD Survey on Water Governance in Peru.

Figure 4.4. Responsibilities in the WSS sector in Peru

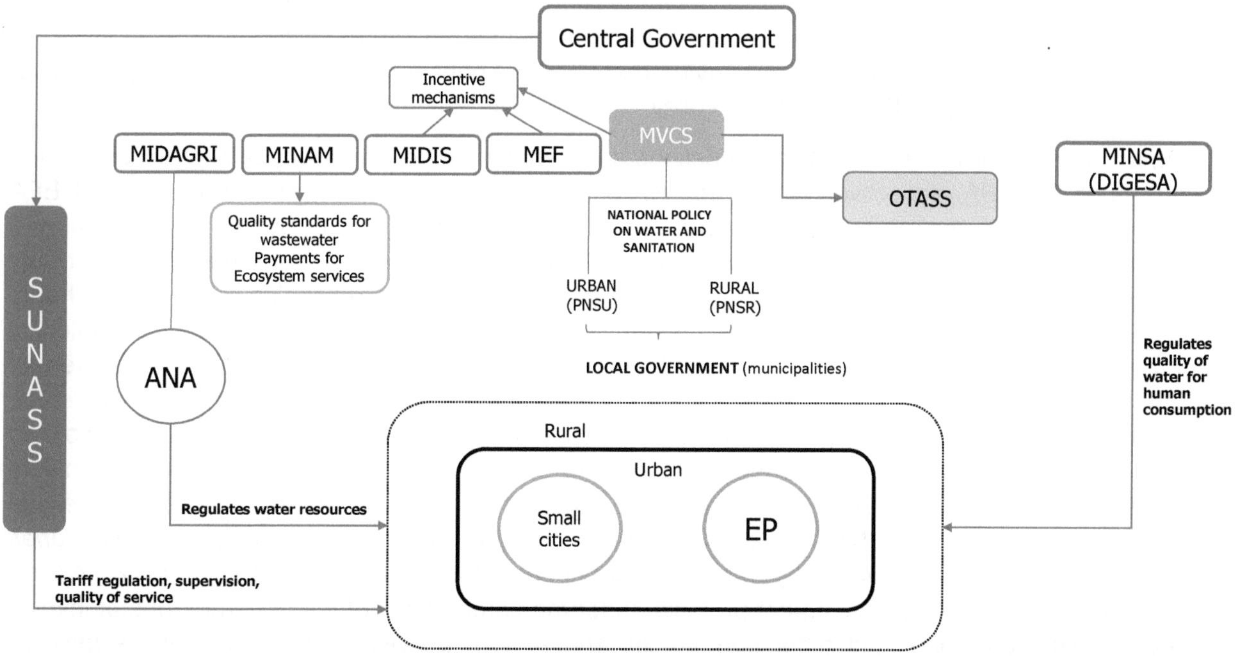

Note: ANA = National Water Authority; DIGESA = General Directorate of Environmental Health (within the Ministry of Health); EPS = Water and sanitation service companies; MVCS = Ministry of Housing, Construction and Sanitation; MEF = Ministry of Economy and Finance; MIDIS = Ministry of Development and Social Inclusion; MIDAGRI = Ministry of Agricultural Development and Irrigation; MINAM = Ministry of the Environment; MINSA = Ministry of Health; OTASS = Technical Agency for the Administration of Sanitation Services; SUNASS = Economic regulator for WSS.
Source: SUNASS (2019[9]), "Presentation summarising the classification of service providers, as per Supreme Decree No. 019-2017-VIVIENDA", at OECD workshop, Santo Domingo, September 2019.

MINAM also regulates payments for ecosystem services via– MERESE. Payments for ecosystem services seek to conserve or restore the ecosystem and the services provided by the ecosystems, which enables water users (in this case, the EPs) access to water in sufficient quantity and quality. According to Law No. 30215 and Decree-Law No. 1280, these payments for ecosystem services are included in tariff schemes set by SUNASS for EPs in order to finance investments in natural infrastructure (ecosystems) as water sources. As a matter of fact, the National Sanitation Plan 2017[4] establishes that SUNASS is responsible for making the necessary provisions aimed at promoting, designing and implementing MERESE. Law No. 30125 on MERESE clearly states that these payments for ecosystem services are voluntarily aimed at the conservation, recovery and sustainable use of aquatic ecosystems, in line with similar systems in other countries. These payments for ecosystem services are included in tariff schemes set by SUNASS for EPs in order to finance investment in natural infrastructure (ecosystems) as water sources. MERESE, albeit a very promising instrument, still faces significant lock-ins at different levels (social, legal, institutional, operational, analytical, etc.). ANA regulates the use of water resources via water abstraction charges (*retribuciones económicas*) and the discharge of wastewater, i.e. water users must pay a pollution charge for the wastewater they produce (Box 4.3; see Chapter 3). It emits regulations that classify different types of water resources and determine which water resources can be used for water supply.

The MINAM is responsible for proposing environmental targets and ensuring the protection of the environment and the conservation of natural resources within the framework of the National Environmental Policy. This is done through its main Directorates-General: DG Policies and Regulation on Building and Sanitation (DGPRCS) and the attached Directorate of Sanitation, DG Programmes and Building and Sanitation Projects (DGPPC) and DG Environmental Issues (DGAA). The Directorate-General for Environmental Issues (*Dirección General de Asuntos Ambientales*, DGAA) is the body responsible for setting environmental objectives, drafting guidance and strategies for the development of the MINAM's legal powers, ensuring the protection of the environment and the conservation of natural resources within the framework of the National Environmental Policy.

Environmental and public health regulatory functions are primarily the responsibility of MINAM/OEFA and MINSA through DIGESA respectively, although ANA also has environmental regulation functions. OEFA monitors wastewater to ensure quality standards are in line with those set out by MINAM and has the power to sanction. OEFA also contributes to the reduction of contamination of water resources that may occur in the energy, mining, industry, etc. sectors within the scope of its competencies. On the other hand, OEFA, through its supervisory power, issues preventive measures in order to control the affectation of environmental components, including water. Finally, OEFA, as the governing body of National System of Environmental Evaluation and Inspections (*Sistema Nacional de Evaluación y Fiscalización Ambiental*, SINEFA), can verify the exercise of environmental control in wastewater exercised by the public authorities in charge of environmental inspections and enforcement on certain regulated subjects and/or objects (*Entidades de Fiscalización Ambiental* -. EFAs). (OECD, 2020[13]) For water resources, a specialised technical body under MINAM – SNACE (*Servicio Nacional de Certificación Ambiental para las Inversiones Sostenibles*) – is in charge of evaluating environmental impact studies (regulated in Law No. 27446) on public, private or mixed capital investment projects under the competency of the government that involve activities, construction works and other commercial and service activities that may cause significant environmental impact, which may include the use of water resources.

While OEFA is the primary entity for the enforcement of environmental regulation, ANA also carries out some regulatory functions for environmental regulation. In particular, ANA's favourable opinion is needed for the approval of any Environmental Management Instruments (*Instrumentos de Gestión Ambiental*, IGAs) related to water resources. Its opinion is binding. ANA also grants a binding opinion in the environmental certification process, in accordance with the provisions of the SEIA Law Regulation, approved by Supreme Decree No. 019-2009-MINAM. The Ministry of Health (MINSA) via DIGESA/DIRESA, in the framework of monitoring the quality of water for human consumption, carries out the characterisation of water (microbiological, physical, chemical analysis) in the water supply system for human consumption (water sources, treatment plant of water, reservoirs, distribution networks, housing, etc.).

SUNASS is independent from the public utility operators, the government and consumers. It was created in 1992 when arms-length economic regulators were created to accompany the liberalisation of Peru's economy (regulators were also created for e-communications, energy [later energy and mining], and transport infrastructure). This model allows separation of powers between the regulator and the executive and limits potential conflicts between policy formulation and enforcement. In both OECD and non-OECD countries in recent years, the development of dedicated regulatory bodies for WWS stands out as a consistent response to some of the challenges to regulating water services, including the fragmentation of roles and responsibilities in the sector and the difficult political economy of tariff setting (OECD, 2015[14]).

SUNASS is responsible for tariff setting, monitoring and enforcing compliance with quality-of-service levels and prices, and consumer protection (see the section below for a more detailed discussion of SUNASS). It is also charged, since 2020, with defining the geographic area (*área de prestación*) for WSS service provision. In addition to its responsibilities over WSS, SUNASS has other responsibilities related to the economic regulation of water resources (primarily ANA's responsibility, as noted above), reflecting its strong technical capacity among Peru's water-related institutions. In particular, it approves the methodology for determining the tariffs of the groundwater monitoring and management service for non-agricultural users with their own wells.

Legislative and planning tools for WWS services

The legislative framework in Peru provides a strong basis for the provision of WWS services, although there is room for streamlining and improvements. Legislative Decree No. 1280 approved the Framework Law for the Management and Provision of Sanitation Services. It aims to strengthen the efficient management of WSS operators and sets out the roles and responsibilities of water and sanitation authorities with the aim to increase coverage, ensure quality and secure the sustainable provision of services. An example of a potential improvement includes a legal amendment to generate the enabling conditions for further reclaimed wastewater reuse (see discussion below on regulating wastewater services).

National policies set out ambitious targets for improving access to WSS services. The National Sanitation Policy 2017-21 (Supreme Decree No. 007-2017-VIVIENDA) sets out Peru's objective to achieve sustainable, universal access to sanitation in urban areas by 2021 and in rural areas by 2030, in line with the United Nations (UN) Sustainable Development Goals (SDGs) (Sanitation and Water for All, 2019[8]). The term sanitation in this context refers to the full range of water supply, disposal of human excreta and sewage, and wastewater treatment services. The country's National Environmental Policy (approved by Supreme Decree No. 012-2009-MINAM) and associated instruments, such as the National Environmental Action Plan (Supreme Decree No. 014-2011-MINAM), are aligned with the 2021 goal to reach 100% wastewater treatment in the urban areas.

The National Sanitation Policy builds on several programmes and initiatives in the sector over the past two decades. Successive administrations have made improving access to WSS services a political priority. In 2007, the Water for All programme (created through Supreme Decree No. 006-2007-VIVIENDA) aimed to provide poorer populations with potable water and sewerage services. In 2012, the National Rural Sanitation Programme (PNSR) was created through Supreme Decree No. 002-2012-VIVIENDA, with the purpose of providing rural populations most in need of comprehensive, quality and sustainable WSS services. In the framework of the PNSR, the MVCS works with regional and local levels and has supported the development of action plans for intervention in rural areas, including diagnosis on WSS. Bilateral co-operation partners have also significantly supported the rural sanitation sector in Peru. For example, the current SABA+ programme is the fourth generation of rural sanitation programmes supported by the Swiss Development Co-operation (SDC/COSUDE). To date, rural providers have focused on improving water supply, with relatively less attention to and progress made on the disposal of human excreta and sewage, which requires significant investment and can also encounter cultural barriers to implementation. Furthermore, much emphasis has been placed on bridging gaps in access rather than sustaining the level of service.

Ways forward to strengthen the regulatory framework

A number of policy recommendations, based on international practices, are proposed below. They aim to strengthen and modernise the regulatory framework.

Assess legislative framework and capacity for implementation

While Peru has the necessary legislation to a large extent, implementation is lagging due to a lack of capacity as well as significant differences in capacity between institutions. The economic regulator for WSS, SUNASS, is among the strongest institutions in the sector but overall institutional capacity in the sector is still developing. Fundamentally, there appears to be a mismatch between the sophisticated legal framework and the capacity of Peru's institutions to implement it. In this context, the absence of policy action to tackle an existing or emerging problem can lead to an institution favouring action and outcomes over the defined distribution of roles and responsibilities. An assessment of the current sectoral capacities combined with a prioritisation exercise of goals for the sector over the short, medium and long terms could help translate the aspirations of the laws into realistic and workable objectives that evolve as institutional capacity develops. The necessary degree of improvements in administrative, technical and financial capacity will need to be supported by strong political will over time at the national, regional and local political levels.

The lack of capacity contributes to and is compounded by a lack of clarity around roles and responsibilities, undermining the road to the achievement of Peru's ambitious WSS goals. Role clarity is the bedrock of a well-functioning regulatory framework with different actors knowing their role and purpose that is complementary and not duplicative or detrimental towards each other (OECD, 2014[15]). The role of all actors should be clearly defined in legislation in terms of their objectives, functions and co-ordination with other entities. These should be clear to all relevant authorities and the regulated bodies, but also for citizens and other stakeholders. In Peru, relationships between national institutions and subnational levels of government are very complex (see chapter on multi-level governance). Furthermore, mandates and perimeters of activity are not always clearly defined. For example, both the MVCS and MIDIS have roles in rural sanitation: while the MVCS leads on policy-setting and investment in the sector, MIDIS works through its International Co-operation Fund for Social Development (*Fondo de Cooperación para el Desarrollo Social*, FONCODES) to channel development assistance funds to programmes targeting poor rural populations, including supporting local governments with basic WSS services (MIDIS, 2019[16]).

There is a need for an assessment led by the centre of government of implementation capacities and the level to which they match requirements set in law. This can support a prioritisation exercise of goals for the sector over the short, medium and long terms and helps translate the aspirations of the law into realistic and workable objectives that evolve as institutional capacity develops. Such a prioritisation exercise can support the important aim of managing expectations across public administration and in relation to citizens. The exercise should also seek to clearly define the role of all actors in terms of their objectives, functions and co-ordination with other entities. While some areas of overlap will always inevitably exist, roles should be as clear as possible to all relevant authorities and regulated bodies, but also citizens and other stakeholders.

In sum, the PCM (*Presidencia del Consejo de Ministros,* Presidency of the Council of Ministers), the MVCS, MINAM, ANA, SUNASS, OTASS could consider the following actions:

- Signal strong, lasting political commitment to delivering affordable and good quality WSS by political leaders at the national, regional and local levels including the promotion of infrastructure investment.
- Identify and advocate for opportunities to update and streamline legislation, for example in order to generate the enabling conditions for further reclaimed wastewater reuse.
- Assess current capacities to implement laws and carry out a prioritisation exercise of goals for the sector over the short, medium and long terms. This could help translate the aspirations of the laws into realistic and workable objectives that evolve as institutional capacity develops.
- Clearly define the role of all actors in terms of their objectives, functions and co-ordination with other entities (e.g. the MVCS, SUNASS, OTASS). These should be clear to all relevant authorities and the regulated bodies, but also for citizens and other stakeholders.

Box 4.1. Portugal's 20-year "Strategic Cycle of Public Water Policy"

In Portugal, the provision of water and sanitation services is a shared responsibility between the 308 municipalities and the national, public holding company Águas de Portugal (AdP) and its subsidiaries.

In 1993, Portugal adopted Law No. 372 which established a Strategic Cycle of Public Water Policy, a clear roadmap for the sector with a 20-year horizon that included significant flexibility to adapt to different realities in the country. This reform introduced the adoption of the corporate management model, opened up the sector to the private sector, aggregated and merged several regional systems, actively promoted multi-municipal companies, created Águas de Portugal as the overarching corporate structure of the water sector and saw the establishment of the economic regulator ERSAR.

Since 1993, Portugal experienced a growth in the private sector participation in the water sector, both as a unique shareholder through public service concessions and as a minority shareholder, through institutional PPPs.

For the past 20 years, the implementation of WSS sector reforms in Portugal has been guided by 3 successive strategic plans: PEAASAR 2000–06 (PEAASAR I) focused on the restructuring of the sector and defining objectives and policies to guide social, environmental and economically sustainable solutions; PEAASAR 2007–13 (PEAASAR II), emphasising the rational use of public expenses; and PENSAAR 2020 – A New Strategy for the Water Supply and Wastewater Sector, still under implementation.

Today, 26 years since the approval of the 1993 sector policy reform, Portugal has witnessed remarkable progress in the provision of drinking WSS public services while substantially increasing social well-being, public health and environmental standards.

Source: Godinho, R. (2013[17]), "A brief approach to water sector in Portugal", APDA, May 2013, https://www.apda.pt/site/upload/A%20Brief%20Approach%20to%20Water%20Sector%20in%20Portugal_EU2_RG.pdf; Francisco da Silva Costa, F. (2018[18]), "Water policy(ies) in Portugal", https://doi.org/10.4000/mediterranee.10078; World Bank (2019[19]), *Outline for a New Strategic Plan: Potential Option*, http://documents1.worldbank.org/curated/en/633581580714106097/pdf/Outline-for-a-New-Strategic-Plan-Potential-Options-Deliverable-C-1.pdf; LIS Water (n.d.[20]), *Lessons Learned from Water Reform in Portugal.*

Implement a high-level pact between all actors involved in the Peruvian WSS sector

On many aspects, efforts to improve co-ordination between actors need to continue, along the line of a high-level pact between all actors involved in the Peruvian WSS sector. For example, WSS sector plans drawn up at different levels (national, subnational) are not always coherent with each other. This risks sending mixed investment signals and hindering an optimal allocation of resources. The MVCS has been carrying out actions to better co-ordinate investments in the sector, in particular the coherence between plans at the subnational level (Regional Sanitation Plans) and the National Sanitation Plan.

In addition, a high-level agreement between all actors involved in WSS policy design and implementation, regulation and its delivery, based on legal attributions and complementarities would complete these efforts and present a unified implementation plan for the country's 2021 and 2030 policy goals. The achievement of this crucial objective must begin with the signalling of strong, lasting political commitment to delivering affordable and good quality WSS by political leaders at the national, regional and local levels, through the creation of a high-level pact supported by all actors, including line ministries and arms-length agencies.

Box 4.2. Examples of co-ordination among regulatory agencies

The challenges faced by regulators often transcend sectoral and geographical boundaries; hence, greater co-ordination and collaboration are needed. There are a number of experiences with co-ordination among regulatory agencies domestically, including:

- **Australia**: The Utility Regulators Forum aims to facilitate the exchange of information, understanding of the issues faced by regulators, consistency in the application of regulatory functions and the review of new ideas about regulatory practices. The newsletter of the forum is published quarterly and contains articles on common challenges, summaries of recent journal articles on regulatory matters, and updates on regulatory decisions.
- **France**: The Club des Régulateurs provides a forum for both established and new economic regulators to share common problems with a few thematic meetings every year, most recently on issues of data privacy and data handling. A third party, currently an academic institution, hosts it.
- **United Kingdom (Scotland)**: As part of the Strategic Review of Charges for 2021-27, stakeholders in Scotland meet on a monthly basis to ensure collective buy-in and collaborative working around the key issues faced by the water and wastewater sectors. The meetings involve high-level representatives from the water operator (Scottish Water), economic regulator (Water Industry Commission for Scotland, WICS), the quality regulator (Drinking Water Quality Regulator for Scotland, DWQR) and the environment regulator (Scottish Environment Protection Agency, SEPA), as well as the Customer Forum and the consumer association. More granular analysis from the working groups feeds into those high-level discussions.
- **Ireland**: A new Economic Regulators' Network is convened around four times a year and hosts discussions on common challenges such as the legal interpretation of new regulations. Participants recognise that further work is needed to address technical regulatory issues across sectors.

Source: Information compiled by the OECD Network of Economic Regulators (NER) (2021[21]) .

Improve clarity in the allocation of regulatory functions

Some gaps exist in the allocation of regulatory functions, including:

1. Regulatory requirements regarding the efficiency of water use apply only to the supply of drinking water for human consumption, regulated by SUNASS but do not apply to water use (or treated wastewater use) for other sectors that consume the largest volumes of water, in particular agriculture. Legislative Decree No. 1280 and its regulation Supreme Decree No. 019-2017-Vivienda establishes that EPs can sell treated (and untreated) wastewater (for example, for use in irrigation), and prices are not regulated. Before tariffs can be introduced, it must be declared that there is no competition, hence justifying the intervention of the regulator; however, it is not clear which is the competent authority to make this decision. This gap in the regulatory framework could result in technical and economic inefficiency in the reuse of treated wastewater in Peru. Regulating the use of treated wastewater, in particular linking it to regulations for the use of water for irrigation purposes, is an option that Peruvian authorities could consider.
2. EPs under RAT: When under this special regime overseen by OTASS, certain regulatory obligations designed to improve the financial sustainability of the EPS may result in reduced access to drinking water service for consumers. Regulations and the framework need to ensure the financial sustainability of EPs after their graduation from RAT status, through good corporate governance as well as appropriate tariff levels.

For all institutions, a large informal sector limits regulatory reach. Informality, at close to 60% of workers, is one of the highest in Latin America (OECD, 2015[2]). Small businesses often opt for informality in order to save significant opportunity costs in the face of complicated administrative procedures. The consequences for the water sector are high levels of non-compliance with water-related and other environmental regulations by the informal sector. As such, regulatory norms and frameworks should be reviewed so as to support the following objectives:

- Consolidating the water industry, as fragmentation of the market limits economies of scale, leading to a consequent loss of efficiency in WSS service delivery.
- Consider regulating the use of treated wastewater, in particular linking to regulations for the use of water for irrigation.
- Regulatory norms and framework need to ensure the financial sustainability of EPs, with a focus on ensuring good corporate governance.

Box 4.3. Paying for water in Peru: Charges, tariffs and family fees

Charges

Charges (*retribuciones*) are levied for water abstraction (both consumptive and non-consumptive uses, both surface water and groundwater abstraction) and for treated wastewater discharge. For both water abstraction and sewage discharge, all permit holders must pay the state an amount per cubic meter of water withdrawn/sewage discharged (Water Resources Law No. 29338 of 2009), as water is considered a natural resource that is national property. The charges are set by the National Water Authority (ANA) and vary by type of use (municipal, industrial, agricultural): charges applied to the productive sector respond to economic criteria; charges applied to the water used for the general population and the agriculture sector respond to social criteria. The revenue raised is used to finance ANA.

For water abstraction, the rate-setting process (volumetric and flat rates) takes account of water availability in river basins and aquifers. JASS are only subject to flat rates and only for surface water; the rates are progressive (i.e. they increase with the demand for water).

For authorised discharge of wastewater treated in a recipient body, ANA assesses the charge rates (volumetric rates only) according to the quality of the receiving water and the cost of recovery at the affected source. The rates charged for discharges of municipal wastewater are much lower than those applied to the productive sector. The agricultural sector is exempt, given the diffuse nature of agricultural pollution. JASS are an exception because they are subject to a flat rate (very low).

Legislative Decree No. 1285 of 29 December 2016 amends the Water Resources Law No. 29338 to remove the requirement of the favourable prior technical opinion of the Environmental and Health Authorities for the granting of wastewater discharge permits, which remain under ANA's responsibility. The stated aim is to speed up and simplify licensing procedures and "avoid duplication". However, this may overwhelm ANA's existing capacity to assess the quality of the receiving waters and therefore the risk of pollution.

Tariffs

The regulator SUNASS sets tariffs for EPs (operating in urban areas with populations over 15 000) using a methodology that aims to ensure economic and financial viability, taking into account projected demand and cost developments, approved investment plans and payments for ecosystem services (Ter-Minassian, 2018[22]). Tariffs are set for five-year periods, with increases in the last two years contingent upon the EPs meeting performance targets. There are different tariffs according to user type: residential, commercial, industrial, public. Tariffs include a fixed charge and some variable charges based upon consumption levels. Residential tariffs for the poorest households are subsidised, through cross-subsidisation. The Ministry of Development and Social Inclusion (MIDIS) determines the process for identifying the beneficiaries of targeted subsidies. As per Legislative Decree No. 1280, SUNASS also sets tariffs for service providers established based on public-private partnerships, municipal management units, special operators and communal organisations

Household fees

In rural areas and small cities, where WSS provision is carried out by JASS, users are required to pay a "household fee". On 7 February 2018, SUNASS published a methodology to allow JASS to set a household fee that allows them to cover at least the operation and maintenance (O&M) costs of drinking water supply services and sanitary disposal of excreta in rural population centres (less than 2 000 inhabitants), as well as the replacement of minor equipment and rehabilitation. As provided by Legislative Decree No. 1280, Framework Law for the Management and Provision of Sanitation Services, the role of SUNASS includes guaranteeing the financial sustainability of drinking water and sewerage services in the rural sector. JASS ultimately decide the level of the family fees.

Source: Ter-Minassian, T. (2018[22]), "State-owned enterprises and fiscal risks in Peru", *Discussion Paper No. IDB-DP-575*, Inter-American Development Bank (IDB).

Improve data collection and management for the WSS sector

Data on WSS is produced by a number of actors and covers many sector dimensions but is not always shared which may hinder its quality and relevant use. Several actors have responsibility for collecting data but the lack of interoperability between data systems hinders information sharing and creates data silos. Duplication of efforts may also divert resources from producing unified and high-quality data and create unnecessary burdens on service providers. For example, in the field of water quality, MINSA collects data on water quality from testing in the pipe network and homes, MIDIS collects data on the coverage of chlorinated water in rural areas and SUNASS collects information from water utilities on the water quality in drinking water and, in some cases, from wastewater plants although this is not systematic. On the other hand, ANA has an information portal on the quality of water from sources (National Water Resources

Management System, *Sistema Nacional de Gestión de los Recursos Hídricos*, SNIRH) that can be accessed by companies depending on the type of permit they have obtained. Current plans include the standardisation of concepts and units of measurement with respect to potable water supply systems (to code water supply systems) by the Ministry of Housing, Construction and Sanitation (MVCS) and MINSA.

Efforts are ongoing to integrate WSS data into a unified data platform but careful attention should be given to ensuring that data collection and management efforts are not duplicated by different actors. The MVCS leads the management and administration of the Water and Sanitation Information System – SIAS – and its related Rural Water, Sanitation and Hygiene (WASH) Information System (DATASS) platform covering rural areas, that is intended to integrate sanitation information and provide the basis for water risk management. Separately, SUNASS has developed a data capture system called SICAP that collects information on management variables of the 50 EPs. This information is used among others for benchmarking and management indicators. SUNASS also operates the GEOSUNASS platform that displays water and sanitation information and reports to the minister as an input into policymaking, in line with the new Management and Provision of Sanitation Services Law. The platform integrates different kinds of information to support decision-making about the regulation and supervision of water and sanitation services. The regulator is also putting in place structures to give access to this information to other ministries, of Health, Development and Social Inclusion, the Environment, Defence and Education, among others. The interoperability of the systems and databases described above is not yet effective across the board.

SUNASS has put in place two methods for its data collection on WSS service providers depending on location but all data is integrated into a single digital system that SUNASS systemises. The EPs (covering urban areas) submit their data directly to SUNASS and in January 2019, the framework law was modified to give municipalities (ATM) the responsibility of reporting information to SUNASS for supervision and oversight of community organisations. To date, around 80% of municipalities report performance data to the ATM web system (SUNASS, 2021[23]) . Additionally, as part of its supervision activities, SUNASS collects primary information from community organizations in the field and places it in a database, as well as verifying the information from the ATM web system, if applicable. This information serves as the basis for the benchmarking of community organization and too for supervising the quality of the service. .

There are concerns about the quality of data submitted by water utilities to SUNASS due to inconsistency in data management practices and capacity constraints, undermining the capacity to monitor the achievement of sector goals. In particular, there is a lack of reliable, standardised and timely data. SUNASS requires EPs to submit data in a specific format to its data system that has been in place since 2004. The regulator uses this data to calculate the management indicators for utilities. Information requested by SUNASS includes data on infrastructure, such as reservoirs and the number of drinking water connections. However, not all EPs gather this information and those that do have different practices for managing, processing and saving data, making comparability a challenge. Furthermore, water utilities often miss deadlines for submitting information and data can be unreliable, despite being submitted as an affidavit. SUNASS trains the water utility personnel responsible for processing and submitting the information; however, the high turnover of staff in water utilities means that this capacity is frequently lost and the regulator must regularly invest in training new personnel.

As part of high-level pact and definition of roles and responsibilities, it would be key to include the collection and management of data and its use for monitoring the implementation of policy and regulation as a priority area of attention. It would also be important to: define specific targets with regard to burden reduction on WSS actors for data submission; better co-ordinate public sector data collection and sharing; the MVCS to work with other ministries and advocate for a clear definition of roles and responsibilities in relation to data collection on sanitation; and continue work to build up a holistic view of the performance of the sector throughout the country, and report this information to all relevant stakeholders.

Governance of SUNASS

Mandate and functions

Peru's dedicated water regulator, the *Superintendencia Nacional de Servicios de Saneamiento* (SUNASS) is in charge of regulating, supervising and monitoring the provision of drinking water and sewerage services. Established in 1992 by Decree-Law No. 25965 and subject to the general framework for all Peruvian regulators (Law No. 27332, issued in 2000), SUNASS has built up a solid reputation as a technically sound and credible independent WSS regulator, one of the strongest in the region. The establishment of water regulators is both a recent and consistent trend across OECD and non-OECD countries in the past 25 years (OECD, 2015[14]), although the majority (23 out of 34 surveyed) of regulators covered in the OECD survey are multi-sector, often combined with energy regulation.

SUNASS has the following powers:

1. Regulatory: it can dictate regulations, guidance and standards.
2. Tariff setting: it sets tariffs for the services and activities under its economic regulation.
3. Surveillance: it can verify the compliance of legal, contractual or technical obligations by entities, companies or supervised activities, as well as the power to verify compliance with any provision, mandate or resolution issued by the regulatory body or any other obligation that is in charge of the supervised entity or activities.
4. Sanctioning: it can impose sanctions and corrective measures on EPs for the breach of obligations derived from legal or technical regulations, as well as the obligations of the concessionaires in their respective concession contracts.
5. User claims (*solución de reclamos*): it can resolve conflicts that arise between water service operators and users through administrative channels.
6. Conflict adjudication (*solución de controversias*): it can resolve conflicts that arise between companies through administrative channels.
7. Definition of the geographic area for WSS service provision.
8. Additionally, with regard to water resources management, SUNASS has the function of approving the methodology for determining the rate of the groundwater monitoring and management service tariff for non-agricultural users with their own well, as well as its corresponding approval for water utilities qualified according to the relevant regulation.

SUNASS regulates the provision of WSS services based on a long term (30-year) strategic approach and its implementation in the short and medium terms. To support this, each EPs prepares a strategic plan for the provision of WSS services that has a 30-year horizon. SUNASS then establishes the management goals related to performance and quality of the service that the EPs must achieve in each regulatory year and that are established in the tariff review process that is carried out every five years. In addition, SUNASS pursues a long-term water security strategy, notably in Greater Lima but also in other areas of the Pacific Coast.

SUNASS also regulates the WSS services market structure via several powers. It approves the efficient scale for WSS services delivery (updated every five years), sets the service delivery area that EPs should serve, determines whether small cities are of a viable size to incorporate water utilities and must give a favourable opinion before a water utility can be created. Through these powers, SUNASS is attempting to promote market integration in order to reap economies of scale and improve performance.

Situated under the PCM, the contribution of SUNASS to public policy is highly appreciated by the executive although its opinions are not binding. SUNASS, as with all regulators in Peru, is placed under the PCM. It depends on the PCM for approval of several procedures, from changes in organisational structure to international travel of staff. The MVCS is responsible for the design of the regulatory framework for the

WSS sector; while the opinions of SUNASS are not binding, it reports that they are taken into account and evaluated.

SUNASS counts with technical and administrative independence as defined in law and has demonstrated a strong culture of independence in its actions. This culture of independence is essential given the context within which the regulator operates, in particular, the attempts at political interference in rate-setting at the local level. SUNASS has demonstrated independence in its regulatory functions in the face of this political pressure. For example, in 2019, the regulator stood firm in its decision on the revised tariffs for the area of Tacna, in the Atacama Desert in the south of Peru, insisting that tariffs would not be suspended, and also ensured that the rates applied in Moquegua were in line with its assessment. This resistance to political pressure followed a case in April 2018 in Moquegua in which the local government announced that the planned rate increases would not go ahead, in defiance of the decision of SUNASS (Gestion, 2019[24]).

The expansion of SUNASS' functions to smaller towns and rural areas is a major undertaking

The scope of SUNASS' functions changed dramatically in 2016 as the regulation of WSS services in rural areas was added to its portfolio (El Peruano, 2016[25]) . Previously, the regulator was responsible for supervising WSS services only in cities with a population of over 15 000 inhabitants, which in practice entailed supervising 50 urban EPS. In 2016, its functions were expanded to include the supervision of 26 885 community-organised water and sanitation services boards (JASS) in rural areas[5] and 450 operators in smaller urban areas (<15 000 population) to ensure quality of service and financial sustainability. Prior to this, regional offices of the MVCS regulated water services in areas outside of the larger urban areas but the lack of supervision of sanitation services in these areas was recognised as a weakness in the sector.

The expansion of its mandate presents a challenge for SUNASS, as it is now charged with the supervision of a huge number of operators that have different capacities, coverage, types of network connections, and that operate in very different contexts. Few water regulators have responsibility for supervising such a large number of water operators (Figure 4.5). The expansion of functions represents a challenge for the regulator as it demands a different regulatory approach to the one used so far, requires interaction and co-ordination with bodies it did not previously work with (ATM, regional governments…), has implications for the regulator's financing model and raises important questions about the governance of SUNASS in terms of capacity, competencies and powers, which are evolving in step with this change. Italy's national water regulator (ARERA) interacts with intermediate regional institutions, which in turn oversee water operators within their respective regions. This approach is to enable the oversight of a large number of operators (more than 2 000).

SUNASS has adapted its governance and approach to take on this new mandate and has made progress in several areas. For example, importantly, SUNASS has created a local presence nationwide through 24 regional offices. Other progress includes, among others: a methodology to determine the areas of service delivery that will be implemented through the 24 local offices of SUNASS; multidisciplinary teams with detailed knowledge in each of the regions; a roadmap for co-ordinated work among the institutions in a given territory; a strategy for the regulation of sanitation services in rural areas, which seeks to strengthen and complement prevailing institutions; and approval of the Small Cities Service Quality Regulations . Moreover, during 2018, 2019 and part of 2020, SUNASS has begun monitoring service providers in rural areas and small cities in order to assess the provision and quality levels of the services they provide, in the interest of making recommendations for their improvement. This information has been systematised through a web-based monitoring system that displays six indicators to measure the performance of service provision. In addition, the Regulations on the Quality of Sanitation Services Provided by Community Organisations in Rural Areas (RCOC) and the Regulations on the Monitoring of Sanitation Services have been approved (SUNASS, 2020[26]). In 2020, SUNASS approved the Quality Regulation for the Provision of Sanitation Services in Small Cities with the objective of establishing the measures that regulate the quality conditions for the provision of such services (SUNASS, 2020[27]).

Given the fragmentation of the sector, different regulatory approaches will be used for each of the 3 categories (urban area with a population over 15 000; smaller urban areas between 2 000 and 15 000 population, and rural areas with populations of less than 2 000). SUNASS is in the process of designing and implementing the new regulatory approaches for smaller urban areas cities and rural areas. A modification to the Framework Law made in 2019 endows municipalities with responsibility for building capacity of JASS and reporting on their performance to SUNASS. Newly-created technical support teams (ATMs) within each municipality liaise directly with local operators, creating an intermediary between the operators and SUNASS. In some cases, where capacity at the municipal level is weak, SUNASS will inspect JASS directly and collect benchmarking information through field visits. Regulatory approaches of water regulators in other countries may provide ideas for ways to effectively and efficiently supervise large numbers of WSS operators in rural areas.

Figure 4.5. Number of active water operators in the water and sewerage sector supervised by water regulators

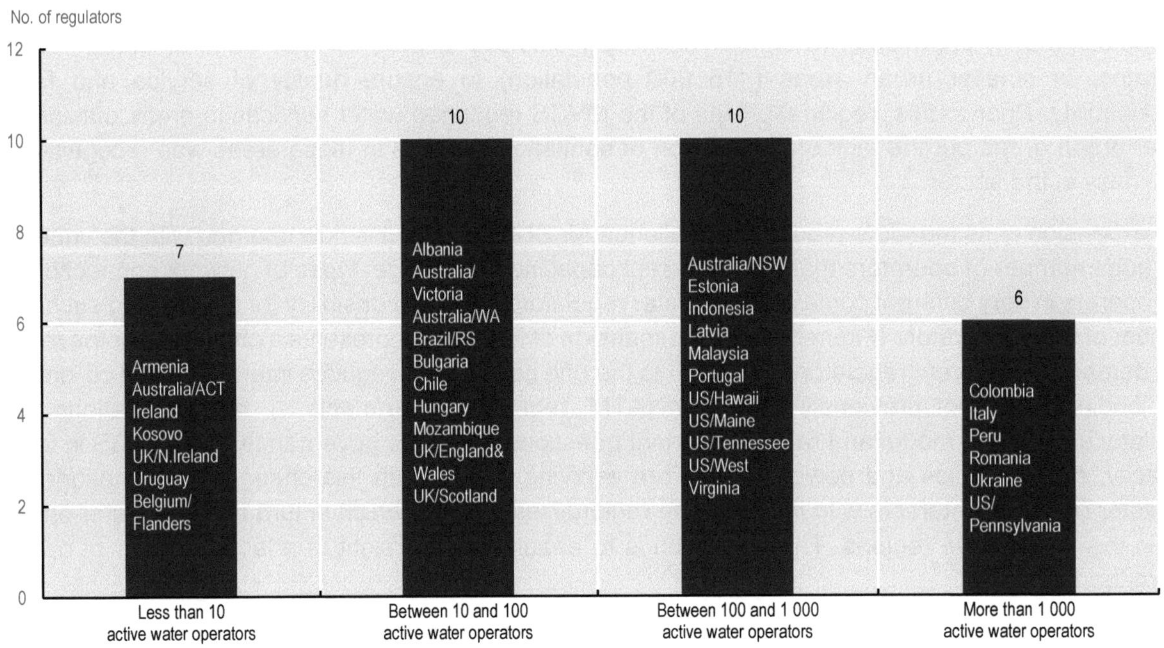

Note: This figure, originally presented in OECD (2015[14]) has been updated to reflect the change in category for Peru. Previously Peru was included in the category 'Between 10 and 100 active water operators'.
Source: OECD (2015[14]), *The Governance of Water Regulators*, https://dx.doi.org/10.1787/9789264231092-en.

As well as expanding the scope of SUNASS actions, Legislative Decree No. 1280 establishes new functions for the regulator designed to address weaknesses in the WSS sector. These include: determining the geographical area for which providers would be responsible for delivering WSS services and sanctioning companies in case of non-compliance; evaluating the performance of EPS to determine whether they need to enter the RAT under OTASS; determining and approving the efficient scale of WSS service delivery to determine whether WSS service providers should be merged.

SUNASS also supervises companies' compliance with legal or technical obligations in relation to corporate governance and that they approve and execute the instruments established by the Framework Law and its Regulations, such as the Code of Good Corporate Governance. This also includes verifying that the powers and responsibilities are correctly assigned between the board of directors, the general management, its shareholders (municipalities), those who temporarily exercise the right of property (mayors or their representatives) and other interested parties; as well as that these relationships are clear, transparent, explicit and objective.

The regulator's strategic framework

SUNASS operates within the framework of an Organisational Strategic Plan (*Plan Estratégico Institucional*, PEI) 2017-22 that sets out five strategic objectives and associated goals. The strategic objectives are established by a special working group selected by the board, in line with the Guide for Institutional Planning issued by the National Centre for Strategic Planning (*Centro Nacional de Planeamiento Estratégico,* CEPLAN). The PEI was approved in December 2017 by a Resolution of the Board of Directors and the extension of the term to the year 2022 was approved by Resolution of the Board of Directors in April 2019. SUNASS revised and modified the PEI for the period 2020-24 in 2019. The strategic objectives are translated into an annual operational plan which lists all operational activities, providing coherence between day-to-day activities and the overarching strategic plan.

The current objectives form a fairly balanced strategic framework with a focus on external impact and outcomes (objectives 1-3 on quality of service, equity and the rational and sustainable use of water) (Table 4.2). Objective 5 (to strengthen disaster risk management) is a requirement set by CEPLAN[6] rules and is required in strategic frameworks of all public bodies in Peru. The plan establishes indicators, baselines and measurable targets, and progress is monitored and reported to CEPLAN annually.

Table 4.2. SUNASS strategic objectives, according to the OECD input-process-output-outcome framework

	Strategic objective	Type of indicator
1	Optimise the quality of sanitation services provided to users	Outcome
2	Contribute to the equitable provision of sanitation services to users	Outcome
3	Contribute to the rational and sustainable use of water by users and sanitation service providers	Outcome
4	Improve institutional management	Process
5	Strengthen disaster risk management	Process

Note: The OECD Framework for Regulatory Policy Evaluation uses an input-process-output-outcome logic, which breaks down the regulatory process into a sequence of discrete EPs. The logic is flexible and can be applied both to evaluate practices to improve regulatory policy in general and to evaluate regulatory policy in specific sectors, based on the identification of relevant strategic objectives.
Source: OECD analysis based on SUNASS' strategic objectives.

Funding of the regulator

The reform of SUNASS' mandate dramatically changed the regulator's financing model, making government budget its majority source of financing. Prior to the expansion of its functions to rural areas, SUNASS was funded solely from the EPs that it regulated, collecting a maximum of 1% of income after sales taxes. While this funding scheme represented a strength that contributed to the independence of the regulator (OECD, 2016[28]), it was already inadequate to carry out its functions fully, as water utilities in Peru tend to be small public agencies with low business income. The regulator is now funded by a mix of fees and government funds, with government funds providing the majority of the budget. In order to cover the expansion of supervision to rural WSS services, in 2019, a Supreme Decree allocated PEN 70 million to SUNASS from the MVCS, after approval by the Ministry of Economy and Finance. The income from regulated entities therefore represents just 30% of its PEN 100 million annual budget. These financing arrangements set SUNASS apart from practice for water regulators internationally (Figure 4.6): data from the OECD Database on the Governance of Sector Regulators show that only 15% of water regulators receive funding from a combination of fees and budget appropriations (Casullo, Durand and Cavassini, 2019[29]).

Figure 4.6. Regulators funded through budget appropriations, fees or both

By sector, percentage of all answers, all countries

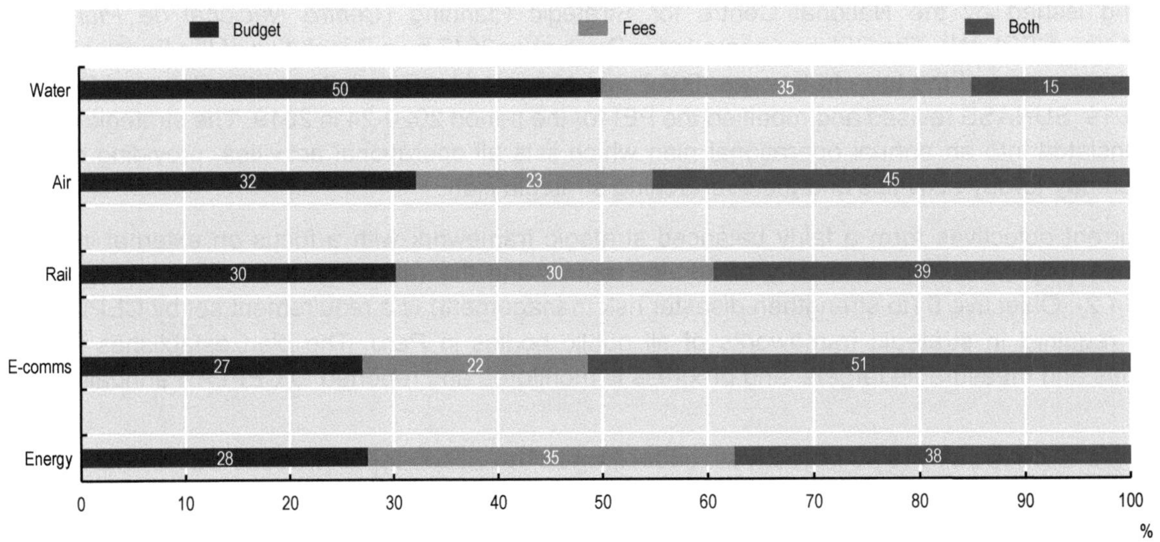

Note: The figure reflects the answers of regulators included in the 2018 survey on the governance of sector regulators; Peruvian regulators/SUNASS are not included in the sample.

Source: OECD (2018[30]), Database on the Governance of Sector Regulators, OECD, Paris, in Casullo, L., A. Durand and F. Cavassini (2019[29]). "The 2018 Indicators on the Governance of Sector Regulators - Part of the Product Market Regulation (PMR) Survey", https://dx.doi.org/10.1787/a0a28908-en.

Co-ordination of SUNASS with other actors

The picture is mixed with regards to co-ordination with public sector actors: some relationships are institutionalised but co-ordination with other regulators in the sector appears weak. SUNASS has signed inter-institutional co-operation agreements with the Ministry of the Environment (MINAM) and the National Water Authority (ANA), through which it carries out activities and meetings on topics of common interest. In 2020, SUNASS entered an agreement with the Ministry of Development and Social Inclusion (MIDIS), DIGESA, the MVCS and MEF to implement multi-sectoral collaboration through its regional offices with regard to levels of residual chlorine content in reservoirs in small towns. Aside from these formal arrangements, co-ordination with sector agencies, in particular the Vice Ministry of Construction and Sanitation (VMCS) and its national urban and rural programmes, and the Technical Agency for the Administration of Sanitation Services (OTASS), is carried out through meetings to discuss and co-ordinate on specific issues, such as the corporate governance of the EPs. SUNASS generally participates in and contributes to consultations on proposed legislation, legislative amendments or related regulations, but there have been occasions where its opinions have not been sought. For example, a recent modification to Legislative Decree No. 1280 (DU 011-2020) was published without prior consultation with SUNASS.

SUNASS shares relevant information with other regulators and state bodies – sometimes systemically, sometimes ad hoc – but co-ordination does not appear to extend beyond this. For example:

1. SUNASS monitoring information, indicators and evaluations of EPs are sent to OTASS as well as to the General Directorate of the General Office of Statistics and Information.
2. SUNASS monitoring and recommendations reports on water suppliers in small and rural cities are systematically sent to municipalities and copied to the MVCS Citizen Service Centres (CACs), in order to improve the provision of services in the interventions carried out by the CACs.
3. SUNASS sends the results of water samples analysis from its monitoring activities to the National and Regional Health Authority.
4. ANA has requested from SUNASS information on the analysis of water samples taken upstream of drinking water treatment plants and at the exit of wells.
5. MINAM periodically requests information related to wastewater treatment in water companies, which SUNASS provides.

A lack of institutionalised co-ordination is a common shortcoming among water regulators but improvement in this area would increase the clarity and legitimacy of the regulatory framework. Among the 34 water regulators surveyed for *The Governance of Water Regulators* report (OECD, 2015[14]), co-ordination with entities with related responsibilities was mainly pursued on an ad hoc basis rather than through systematic and institutionalised mechanisms. Co-ordination will be particularly important as SUNASS expands its functions into rural areas: building relationships and co-ordinating with other public agencies and ministries that are active in the rural sector with whom it has not needed to interact before. For example, the Ministry of Development and Social Inclusion has responsibilities for improving sanitation services in rural areas, alongside the MVCS. The Modernisation of Public Management rule, overseen by the PCM, includes inter-institutional co-ordination as one of its pillars; however, SUNASS reports that this has not had benefitted its role as a regulator.

Good regulatory practices

SUNASS, along with other economic regulators in Peru, has made steady progress on good regulatory practices such as the use of regulatory impact assessments (RIAs) and administrative simplification, and could strengthen its performance in this area through a renewed focus on co-ordinating with other public bodies involved in the regulatory space (e.g. on inspections) and its stakeholder engagement processes. SUNASS is currently designing the process for the systematic use of RIAs. This will improve the evaluation of draft regulation that at present relies primarily on a limited approach to cost-benefit analysis. The practices of Peruvian economic regulators on transparency and accountability are also more advanced compared to obligations in the central government (OECD, 2016[28])), although there are opportunities for further improvement

Regulatory activities, whether for tariff regulation or quality standards enforcement, are confronted with behavioural and cultural barriers in Peru. There is a widespread unwillingness to pay for water in Peru (as in many countries) and the regulator encounters significant resistance within the tariff-setting process. As a result, in general, tariffs are set at levels that are far from full cost recovery. Furthermore, the high level of informality in Peru contributes to a situation whereby people are less likely to pay for water. What constitutes "good quality" water also differs between official standards and the views of local populations. For example, whereas SUNASS tracks the proportion of chlorinated water as an indicator of quality, local populations sometimes oppose treated water on grounds of taste.

In response, SUNASS alongside the international donor community has undertaken activities to educate communities on the necessity of tariffs and the importance of treated drinking water for health. Following good regulatory practices for stakeholder engagement and applying behavioural insights could supplement and reinforce these efforts.

Inspections and enforcement

Operational co-ordination with other public agencies on inspections could be improved. Inspections are an important function of SUNASS that requires effective co-ordination with other public bodies that inspect for different policy objectives, such as environmental inspections by OEFA and the DGAA (the environmental inspection body for WSS) of the MVCS and public health inspections by MINSA through DIGESA. In line with the principles identified in the *OECD Regulatory Enforcement and Inspections Toolkit*, co-ordination and, where needed, consolidation of inspections can ensure better use of public resources, minimise the burden on regulated entities and improve compliance, but there needs to be a clear authority for co-ordination to remove uncertainty about the legality of any arrangements. Currently, there are no structured mechanisms in place to co-ordinate these functions with other public bodies.

The expansion of SUNASS' responsibilities to cover rural areas could pose a challenge for its inspections and enforcement function, given the relatively resource-intensive nature of the work in terms of personnel. This further strengthens the need for close co-ordination and co-operation with other public bodies with inspection functions in order to promote efficiency and effectiveness. Furthermore, in a context of financial constraints, strengthening good practices such as prioritisation, using risk-based approaches and outcome-focused inspections would also help to carry out inspection functions efficiently and effectively (see OECD (2018[31])). The regulator is aware of the challenge and has started taking a number of actions including, for example, carrying out over 700 visits to ATMs to provide technical assistance.

Stakeholder engagement

Engagement with regulated entities and other stakeholders is provided for under legislation but the process is not leading to the expected results in terms of quality of relationships. Tariff setting and any reforms of the regulatory framework are subject to stakeholder consultation, with different processes followed for each. SUNASS advertises its public hearings as well as the elections for its user councils through several channels, including traditional media (radio, television, written press, flyers), its website, social media, newsletters, emails and EPs websites. As with other economic regulators in Peru, SUNASS prepares a matrix that assembles stakeholders' comments. For example, for proposals for changes to regulations, this matrix includes: the regulation under consultation; the proposed modifications; the name of the stakeholders providing comments; the specific comments, opinions or point of view of the stakeholders; and the evaluation of the regulator regarding these comments which includes whether and how the comment will be considered.

- Consultation on regulations: SUNASS carries out public consultations when developing regulations. In the first instance, SUNASS uses public consultation to collect evidence to correctly identify the problem to be solved through the intervention of the regulator. SUNASS then invites comments from stakeholders on any proposed regulations. All comments are published and responded to through the matrix that is available on the SUNASS website.
- Consultation on tariffs (tariff approval procedure): Public hearings for tariffs have been carried out in co-ordination with the 50 urban-based EPs since 2005. SUNASS presents the EPs with a proposal of tariffs, management goals and an investment plan for each five-year regulatory period. As part of this tariff approval procedure, the regulator organises public hearings to enable the participation of the EPs, local authorities, professional associations, user councils, the media and civil society representatives, among others. Public hearings aim to provide information on the issues regarding WSS services, the foreseen solutions and their impact on tariffs. The results of consultation with regulated entities and the views of the participants in the consultation process are all made public. Through these hearings, SUNASS collects comments and proposals which inform the tariff levels, the management goals and the investment plan. These are then included in the Final Tariff Study which is intended to explain how the comments and proposals made by civil society were taken into account, or why they were not.

- SUNASS does not yet carry out public consultations in smaller urban areas (the regulatory scheme is currently being designed).
- SUNASS does not carry out public consultations in rural areas, where household fees are set by the communities.

The SUNASS reports that the organisation of public hearings as part of the tariff approval procedure have resulted in several benefits, including:

- Better-informed populations on the situation of their EPs and the proposals for improvements in sanitation services for the subsequent five-year period.
- Strengthened EPs-SUNASS-user interaction as a result of communications campaigns around the tariff study projects.
- Reduction of negative reactions to or social conflicts in relation to proposals for tariff increases.

However, reports of poor communication around tariff announcements and frequent resistance to tariffs suggest that engagement processes could benefit from some redesign, perhaps informed by behavioural insights SUNASS could try to reach out to those who are usually least represented in the rule-making process, proactively searching to include those who are either "able but unwilling" or "willing but unable" to participate and make every effort to remove any obstacles to their participation (in line with *OECD Best Practice Principles on Stakeholder Engagement*). Behavioural insights could also be used to support better-informed stakeholder engagement. Surveys and focus groups can provide a broad overview of user trends and some ideas on preferences. However, they can be fraught with biases depending on the framing of the questions, their sequencing and the words chosen. Experiments that control for these biases can provide a better sense of the preferences of users when taking regulatory decisions (OECD, 2018[32]).

Performance monitoring and reporting

Monitoring and reporting on the performance of the sector

SUNASS is making steady progress in building up a holistic view of the performance of the sector; work remains to close the outstanding gaps. SUNASS reports on the performance of utilities and selected community organisations (EPs, community organisations) using benchmarking tools but it does not report on municipal providers and specialised operators *(prestadores municipals, operadores especializados*). For the EPs, SUNASS collates indicators in four categories (access to services, quality of service, financial and environmental sustainability, governance and governance and disaster risk management) in order to benchmark operators with the aim of improving the performance of EPs and sharing good practices among them. SUNASS also benchmarks providers of water and sanitation services in rural areas. Different benchmarking indicators are used for community organisations. SUNASS uses the information submitted by ATMs through the online system as a way to identify which community organisations will be monitored. SUNASS may also choose to monitor certain community organisations in cases where it wants to verify that previous recommendations have been implemented or following complaints about service delivery. It publishes the data and reports on the performance of EPs and the performance of selected community organisations on its website.

Table 4.3. Benchmarking indicators to measure utility performance

Type of indicator	Area	Indicator	Unit
Access	Drinking water	Population coverage	%
	Sewerage	Population coverage	%
Quality	Drinking water	Continuity of service	Hours/day
		Water pressure	m.c.a.

Type of indicator	Area	Indicator	Unit
		Frequency of claims	No. of claims/1 000 connections
		Prevalence of leakage	Leakage/km
	Sewerage	*Densidad de atoros*	atoros/km
Sustainability	Financial	Staff costs in total operating costs (*Relación de trabajo*)	%
	Prevention and mitigation	Disaster risk management	%
	Environmental	Non-domestic users within maximum permissible limits (*Usuarios No Domésticos en la aplicación de los Valores Máximos Admisibles*, VMA)	%
		Wastewater treated	%
		Metered active connections (*Conexiones Activas con Micromedición*)	%
		Metered water (*Micromedición*)	%
		Non-revenue water	%
Governance (*Gobernabilidad y Gobernanza*, GYG)	Good corporate governance	Indicator of good corporate governance	

Source: SUNASS (2018[7]), *Benchmarking Regulatorio de las empresas prestadoras*, https://cdn.www.gob.pe/uploads/document/file/1098028/Benchmarking_regulatorio_de_las_EPS_2018.pdf; OECD (2019[12]), OECD Survey on Water Governance in Peru. .

The recently introduced system of data collection for WSS operators in rural areas is starting to build up a holistic view of WSS services in the country for the first time. This new, systematic data on the WSS sector should be a valuable input for policymaking and the overall governance of the sector. It can also provide essential information for decisions regarding investments and monitoring their impact on the quality of services. The utility of this information rests on its accuracy and will be defined by the regulator's approach and effectiveness in collating and verifying the data.

While SUNASS carries out market surveillance (e.g. monitoring inflation rates adjustment, monitoring the use of investment funds and financial reserves), it does not appear to carry out horizon scanning exercises to identify major issues that may affect the sector in the medium to long terms.

Monitoring and reporting on the performance of SUNASS

While SUNASS is not required to so do so by law, it prepares an annual report and reports on its performance to a number of central government entities; these efforts could be continued in favour of accessible and transparent reporting overall. While there is no legislative requirement for the regulator to produce a report on its activities on a regular basis, SUNASS publishes an annual report. The annual report is the public document through which the actions and interventions of the regulator and how they affect the provision of WSS services are reported. SUNASS reports relevant information to different institutions of the central government, according to the regulatory framework (OECD, 2016[28]). For instance, it reports the implementation of recommendations to the General Audit Office of the Republic (*Contraloría General de la República*), budget execution to the Ministry of Economy and Finance, strategic and operational plans and performance indicators to the PCM, among others. It also responds to information requests and enquiries from Congress on a regular basis. However, there is no obligation to provide performance reports to Congress on a systematic basis. It is important to be accountable to external public powers that could evaluate the regulator's performance as a whole. Better reporting on SUNASS performance could also go some way to improving understanding of the value of its role (Box 4.4).

Its annual reports contain rich information on outcomes for the sector (e.g. indicators of water quality and quality of service), SUNASS activities (e.g. numbers of people reached through educational campaigns to promote the responsible use of water) and some indicators on the performance of the regulator itself (e.g. on the number of days taken for an appeal to be processed by SUNASS' dispute resolution mechanism [*Tribunal Administrativo de Solución de Reclamos de Usuarios de Servicios de Saneamiento*, TRASS] or outcomes of cases where SUNASS' decisions have been challenged. Other useful indicators of the regulator's performance could include:

- Efficiency and effectiveness of inputs (e.g. organisational and financial performance).
- Output from regulatory activity (e.g. effectiveness of regulatory decisions and reaching out to citizens/users).
- Direct outcome of regulatory decisions (e.g. compliance with the regulator's decisions).

Annual reports could be further strengthened by reporting on progress against the objectives set out in the strategic plan (PEI).

Box 4.4. Scotland's Outputs Monitoring Group

The Outputs Monitoring Group (OMG) is chaired by the Scottish Government and comprises senior (executive level) representatives from the Drinking Water Quality Regulator, the Scottish Environmental Protection Agency, the Water Industry Commission (the economic regulator), Consumer Futures Unit (the customer representative body) and Scottish Water.

The primary function of the group, which meets quarterly, is to oversee the delivery of the investment objectives set by Scottish ministers for the regulatory period. These objectives set out high-level outcomes for the industry: such as meeting defined drinking water quality standards, environmental performance targets and customer service standards.

As part of the regulatory process, these high-level objectives have been translated, prior to the start of the regulatory period, into an agreed set of programme outputs, for example, the "number of water treatment works to be improved" or "environmental performance assessments to be carried out". In turn, these output programmes are linked to an agreed list of projects – termed the Technical Expression – which details the investment works and studies that will deliver the output programmes. This provides the OMG with clarity on the projects that will deliver the output programmes and the ministerial objectives.

Going into the regulatory period, Scottish Water provides a baseline delivery plan for the regulatory period which details the expected profile of completion of these output programmes. This then allows the OMG to monitor output delivery performance against Scottish Waters' planned delivery profile.

The OMG owns and maintains this agreed baseline of outputs: ensuring that any changes arising from study outputs or new information during the period are incorporated into the baseline in a controlled and transparent way. This is achieved through a well-defined change mechanism that requires regulatory sign-off of changes.

The preparation of reports and information for the OMG is carried out by the OMG working group (OMGWG) which comprises senior representatives from the same set of stakeholders as OMG. The OMGWG also meets quarterly, a month ahead of the OMG meeting, and focuses on the preparation of accurate reports for the OMG, as well as overseeing the change mechanism.

At the OMG meetings, based on the information provided by the OMGWG, output delivery progress across the investment programme is discussed and any shortfalls against the targets are highlighted. The OMG reviews progress at five key delivery milestones – such as "financial approval" and "regulatory sign-off of output delivery". Scottish Water is required to provide explanations in respect of any shortfall against a milestone target: highlighting what corrective action is underway. This provides a high degree of transparency in respect of the delivery of the outputs for which customers have paid.

The OMG produces a quarterly report on progress which is published on the Scottish Government website. At the end of the regulatory control period, the group also provides a final report that details progress with the delivery of the agreed set of outputs and the ministerial objectives.

Source: Information provided by the Water Industry Commission of Scotland (October 2016).

Ways forward to enhance the governance and performance of the economic regulator

Monitor the evolving role and objectives of SUNASS

The significant expansion of functions raises important questions about the governance of SUNASS, in terms of capacity, competencies and powers, which will need to evolve in step with this change. For example, it is likely that the regulator will have to take on a stronger capacity-building role, given the fragmented water industry structure in Peru that it now oversees (OECD, 2015[14]). While SUNASS has made important steps in implementing its new role and functions, these efforts will require consistent follow-up, investment and monitoring going forward.

While SUNASS is an independent regulator, its vision and strategic goals should be aligned with the national policy set by the government. SUNASS strategic objectives are designed to be in line with the objectives of the PCM, the MVCS and MINSA. It assesses that there are no overlaps or conflicting objectives with these other actors in the current strategic plan but it remains a perennial challenge to seek coherence with all actors. Some goals in the current framework do not appear to be aligned with national policy goals: for example, the plan includes the goal that 57% of the urban population would have access to chlorinated water (*agua segura*) by 2019, up from a baseline of 54% in 2015. These targets do not seem to be in line with the ambition of the national policy to achieve universal access to WSS in urban areas by 2021.

The reform of SUNASS objectives and scope of action (to include small cities and rural areas) must be approached through an explicit and proactive strategy of institutional transformation. Such an agenda will include a review of the capacity, competencies and powers of SUNASS and how each of these will need to evolve in step with the expansion of its functions and new objectives. The identification of necessary changes to the resources, structure and ways of working of the agency will need to be accompanied by a new identity, vision and mission for SUNASS, wich provides a common sense of purpose for staff internally and communicates a clear message to external stakeholders. As such, coherence must continue to be sought between SUNASS' vision and strategic goals and those of other public bodies in the sector through careful co-ordination and consultation (e.g. SUNASS in co-operation with other relevant actors, including CEPLAN) and ensure transparent monitoring and reporting around the strategic plan (PEI), for example through the annual report.

The in-depth review and modernisation of the institution could be reflected in an updated strategic framework (PEI), priority action and performance indicators, which can be used to communicate to government and stakeholders progress in implementing the reform. SUNASS' new role will also require the institutionalisation of co-ordination with other actors in the sector to increase the clarity and legitimacy of the regulatory framework. Formal co-ordination mechanisms could include memoranda of understanding (MoUs) or similar agreements.

In order to closely monitor the process of expanding SUNASS' functions to small cities and rural areas and communicate the results to the government, the following would be needed:

- Review capacity, competencies and powers, which will need to evolve in step with the expansion of functions. For example, if capacity building becomes a greater focus on work, ensure that SUNASS has the necessary competencies and powers to carry out these tasks.
- Adopt a risk-based approach to regulation that recognises that the hands-on supervision of all operators may be impracticable, specifically those operating at a very small scale.
- Monitor its performance in carrying out its new functions, in order to provide feedback on the system and whether the new regulatory approach is meeting objectives for the sector: identify what is working well as well as areas that may need adjustment.

Ensure adequate and predictable resourcing of SUNASS

Uncertainty over the sustainability of government funding is an additional challenge that SUNASS must manage. Water regulators' reliance on funding from government funding can potentially undermine their independence, although there are a number of mechanisms that can be put in place to mitigate this risk. For example, one mechanism to bolster independence can be multi-annual budgeting and Peru follows this good practice of establishing multi-annual budget estimates. However, recent fiscal consolidation efforts have resulted in SUNASS receiving less funding than expected (as is the case for other Peruvian public sector bodies that rely on transfers from the Treasury). This uncertainty in financing risks undermining the regulator's ability to fully carry out its functions.

Advocating for budget-setting according to an estimation of the costs related to the regulation and supervision of the sector, rather than on available resources, could ensure sufficient resources. This could strengthen the regulator's case for more resources and flexibility. The Peruvian national administration implements a performance-based budgeting system whereby budgets are to be aligned with the goals and objectives of the institution and budget execution is monitored in parallel with progress in performance indicators. In 2018, the Commission for Consumer Defence and Regulators of Public Utilities (*Comisión Defensa del Consumidor y Organismos Reguladores de los Servicios Públicos*) discussed and approved raising the cap on fees from regulated entities from 1% to 2% of income after sales taxes but the decision has not passed through Congress.

The review of the impact of the new functions on the capacity and competencies of SUNASS should at least take into account the following aspects: i) internal structure and organisation of technical teams; ii) competencies and professional profiles among technical staff; iii) staffing plan including recruitment and training to existing staff; iv) use of external experts and providers, such as for inspections and supervision activities; v) new financial needs. The review of SUNASS' funding scheme will ensure that the regulator can carry out its functions and reach its policy objectives effectively, while preserving its independence, in order to:

- Advocate for budget-setting according to an estimation of the costs related to the regulation and supervision of the sector, rather than available resources.
- Continue the good practice of multi-annual budgeting.
- Ensure new financing arrangements with the executive (MEF, PCM) are transparent.

Continue to strengthen good regulatory practices at SUNASS

Peru's regulators are advanced in the use of good regulatory practices and SUNASS has undertaken significant steps to develop and fully implement the systematic use of regulatory impact assessment (RIA). The regulator can build on this work to continue improving transparency and engagement with all stakeholders. Immediate steps can include the publication of the actual costs of service provision as an initial step to addressing resistance to tariff increases and enhancing the engagement of user councils, building on the experience of other Peruvian economic regulators. Moreover, SUNASS can seek to improve the accessibility and readability of its stakeholder engagement and outreach by using innovative approaches such as behavioural insights in tariff setting and other consultation processes and by using plain language and appropriate communications materials adapted to a range of audiences, especially non-technical ones. Some options to strengthen good regulatory practices are described below:

- Continue to develop and fully implement the process for the systematic use of RIA.
- Explore ways to better manage stakeholder expectations around tariffs.
  - Publish the actual costs of service provision as an initial step to addressing resistance to tariff increases.
  - Review stakeholder engagement processes: explore using innovative approaches such as behavioural insights in tariff setting and other consultation processes.
  - Enhance engagement with user councils to improve understanding of the issues and foster a willingness to pay the necessary price for water services.
- Build on existing strong transparency practices to include the use of plain language and appropriate communications materials adapted to a range of audiences, especially non-technical ones. SUNASS must ensure that the information it publishes can be easily understood by its wide range of stakeholders. This is particularly important for its engagement with new regulated entities and stakeholder groups in rural areas, i.e. JASS, which were not previously under its supervision.
- Improve operational co-ordination with other public agencies on inspections: review whether there are opportunities to consolidate inspections to ensure better use of public resources, minimise the burden on regulated entities and improve compliance; ensure that there is clear authority for co-ordination to remove uncertainty about the legality of any arrangements.

Improve performance monitoring of WSS services provision by SUNASS

The collection and analysis of data are key to improve the performance of the WSS sector. SUNASS could design a staged strategy for data collection and analysis, given the need for building capacity for data collection and reporting by EPs, municipalities and JASS, and for the creation and uptake of digitised data collection systems that are co-ordinated across the public sector. The staged strategy will need to be designed with representatives of decentralised actors and central government bodies, with both short- and medium-term objectives. A staged approach differentiated between regions may be included so as to focus attention on specific geographic zones and learn from this experience before upscaling to cover the entire country. The strategy will aim to keep burden on actors required to submit data as low as possible, by streamlining forms, reducing information requests and digitising submission for a live quality check when submitting data. The draft forms and systems could be designed by working groups that include representatives of EPs, municipalities and JASS, to test feasibility.

Data collected from the sector will be a key ingredient for SUNASS reporting on the performance of the sector and the implementation of the reform. This data and indicators will also need to be complemented with indicators on the performance of the regulator, to be included in the updated PEI, for a comprehensive vision of its performance. Reporting on the regulator's performance can be further systematised, including through greater engagement with Congress around the annual report.

Options to improve performance monitoring of WSS services provision by SUNASS are described below:

- Build capacity for data collection and reporting by EPs, municipalities and JASS.
- Carry out horizon scanning exercises to identify major issues that may affect the sector in the medium to long terms.

- Systematise reporting on the regulator's own performance to improve accountability and clarify roles in the sector (e.g. greater engagement with Congress around the annual report). It is important to be accountable to external public powers, which could evaluate the regulator's performance as a whole. Better reporting on SUNASS' performance could also go some way to improving understanding of the value of its role.
- Use data and indicators to assess and report on SUNASS' own performance in terms of:
  - Efficiency and effectiveness of inputs (e.g. organisational and financial performance).
  - Quality of processes for regulatory activity (e.g. accuracy, timeliness, accessibility of regulatory decisions, use of evidence and data in taking decisions).
  - Output from regulatory activity (e.g. effectiveness of regulatory decisions and reaching out to citizens/users).
  - Direct outcome of regulatory decisions (e.g. compliance with the regulator's decisions).
- Build links with other economic regulators in Peru and internationally to exchange on institutional and organisational challenges and share best practice.

References

Casullo, L., A. Durand and F. Cavassini (2019), "The 2018 Indicators on the Governance of Sector Regulators - Part of the Product Market Regulation (PMR) Survey", *OECD Economics Department Working Papers*, No. 1564, OECD Publishing, Paris, https://dx.doi.org/10.1787/a0a28908-en. [29]

da Silva Costa, F. (2018), "Water policy(ies) in Portugal", *Méditerranée*, Vol. 130, http://journals.openedition.org/mediterranee/10078. [18]

El Peruano (2016), *Decreto Legislativo que aprueba la Ley Marco de la Gestión y Prestación de los Servicios de Saneamiento*, https://busquedas.elperuano.pe/normaslegales/decreto-legislativo-que-aprueba-la-ley-marco-de-la-gestion-y-decreto-legislativo-n-1280-1468461-1/ (accessed on 17 March 2021). [25]

Gallup Organisation (2015), *Gallup World Monitor (database).* [4]

Gestion (2019), *Sunass: No se suspenderá la aplicación de nuevas tarifas de agua en Tacna*, https://gestion.pe/economia/sunass-suspendera-aplicacion-nuevas-tarifas-agua-tacna-267473-noticia/?ref=gesr. [24]

Godinho, R. (2013), "A brief approach to water sector in Portugal", Presentation, APDA, May 2013, https://www.apda.pt/site/upload/A%20Brief%20Approach%20to%20Water%20Sector%20in%20Portugal_EU2_RG.pdf. [17]

INEI (2019), *Perú Formas de Acceso al Agua y Sanaemiento Basico*, El Instituto Nacional de Estadística e Informática, https://www.inei.gob.pe/media/MenuRecursivo/boletines/boletin-el-agua-3.pdf. [1]

LIS Water (n.d.), *Lessons Learned from Water Reform in Portugal.* [20]

MIDIS (2019), *Quiénes Somos?*, http://www.foncodes.gob.pe/portal/index.php/nosotros/quienessomos3. [16]

Ministerio de Vivienda, Construcción y Saneamiento (2016), *Propuesta de bases para una política nacional de saneamiento: Logros, experiencias compartidas y dialogo de política*, http://www3.vivienda.gob.pe/popup/Latinosan/PROPUESTA%20DE%20BASES%20PARA%20UNA%20POL%C3%8DTICA%20NACIONAL%20DE%20SANEAMIENTO.pdf. [10]

Oblitas de Ruiz, L. (2010), *Servicios de agua potable y saneamiento en el Perú: Beneficios potenciales y determinantes del éxito*, https://repositorio.cepal.org/bitstream/handle/11362/3819/lcw355.pdf;jsessionid=5742CF2. [11]

OECD (2021), *The OECD Network of Economic Regulators*, https://www.oecd.org/gov/regulatory-policy/ner.htm (accessed on 17 March 2021). [21]

OECD (2020), *Regulatory Enforcement and Inspections in the Environmental Sector of Peru,*, https://doi.org/10.1787/54253639-en. [13]

OECD (2019), *OECD Survey on Water Governance in Peru.* [12]

OECD (2018), *Database on the Governance of Sector Regulators*, OECD, Paris. [30]

OECD (2018), *OECD Regulatory Enforcement and Inspections Toolkit*, OECD Publishing, Paris, https://dx.doi.org/10.1787/9789264303959-en. [31]

OECD (2018), *OECD Regulatory Policy Outlook 2018*, OECD Publishing, Paris, https://dx.doi.org/10.1787/9789264303072-en. [32]

OECD (2016), *Regulatory Policy in Peru: Assembling the Framework for Regulatory Quality*, OECD Reviews of Regulatory Reform, OECD Publishing, Paris, https://dx.doi.org/10.1787/9789264260054-en. [28]

OECD (2015), *Multi-dimensional Review of Peru: Volume 1. Initial Assessment*, OECD Development Pathways, OECD Publishing, Paris, https://dx.doi.org/10.1787/9789264243279-en. [2]

OECD (2015), *OECD Principles on Water Governance*, OECD, Paris, https://www.oecd.org/gov/regional-policy/OECD-Principles-on-Water-Governancebrochure.pdf. [5]

OECD (2015), *The Governance of Water Regulators*, OECD Studies on Water, OECD Publishing, Paris, https://dx.doi.org/10.1787/9789264231092-en. [14]

OECD (2014), *The Governance of Regulators*, OECD Best Practice Principles for Regulatory Policy, OECD Publishing, Paris, https://dx.doi.org/10.1787/9789264209015-en. [15]

Sanitation and Water for All (2019), "Peru: Closing sanitation gaps with evidence-based investments in the sector", http://sanitationandwaterforall.org/news/peru-closing-sanitation-gaps-with-evidence-based-investments-in-the-sector/?category=11. [8]

SUNASS (2021), *Reporte/Indicador: Porcentaje de municipalidades que cuentan con área técnico municipal formalizada*, http://aplicaciones.sunass.gob.pe:8080/RegistroATM/indicadoresATM.html (accessed on 17 March 2021). [23]

SUNASS (2020), *Benchmarking Regulatorio 2020 de las Empresas Prestadoras (EP)*, https://www.sunass.gob.pe/wp-content/uploads/2020/11/BENCHMARKING-REGULATORIO-DE-LAS-EPS-2020-DATOS-2019.pdf. [6]

SUNASS (2020), *Informe sobre la prestación de los servicios de saneamiento en el ámbito rural y de pequenas ciudades (N. 434-2020-SUNASS-DAP-ESP)*, https://www.sunass.gob.pe/wp-content/uploads/2020/09/RCD-014-2020cd-INFORME.pdf. [26]

SUNASS (2020), *Sunass aprobó el Reglamento de Calidad para la Prestación de Servicios de Saneamiento en Pequeñas Ciudades*, https://www.sunass.gob.pe/lima/sunass-aprobo-el-reglamento-de-calidad-para-la-prestacion-de-servicios-de-saneamiento-en-pequenas-ciudades/ (accessed on 17 March 2021). [27]

SUNASS (2019), "Presentation summarising the classification of service providers, as per Supreme Decree No. 019-2017-VIVIENDA", OECD workshop, Santo Domingo, September 2019. [9]

SUNASS (2018), *Benchmarking Regulatorio de las empresas prestadoras*, https://cdn.www.gob.pe/uploads/document/file/1098028/Benchmarking_regulatorio_de_las_EPS_2018.pdf. [7]

Ter-Minassian, T. (2018), "State-owned enterprises and fiscal risks in Peru", *Discussion Paper No. IDB-DP-575*, Inter-American Development Bank (IDB). [22]

World Bank (2019), *Outline for a New Strategic Plan: Potential Option*, World Bank, Washington, DC, http://documents1.worldbank.org/curated/en/633581580714106097/pdf/Outline-for-a-New-Strategic-Plan-Potential-Options-Deliverable-C-1.pdf. [19]

World Bank (2019), *World Development Indicators*, World Bank, Washington, DC. [3]

Notes

[1] Articles 6 and 7 of Legislative Decree No. 1280; Articles 5 and 7 of Supreme Decree No. 019-2017-VIVIENDA.

[2] Legislative Decree No. 1280.

[3] Supreme Decree No. 006-2019-VIVIENDA.

[4] Numeral 3, sub-section 7.1 of Article 7 of Supreme Decree No. 019-2017-VIVIENDA on the regulation of the Framework Law of Management and Delivery of Sanitation Services.

[5] Each JASS is an association that is responsible for the provision of water and sanitation services.

[6] CEPLAN is a specialised technical agency under the PCM that leads the National Strategic Planning System.

Annex A. The Ica River Integrated Basin

The Ica Valley is one of the most important economic areas of Peru due to its booming agro-exports industry, despite its exceptionally dry and desert land. Water resources available are not efficiently managed to meet growing demand and keep up with the pace of current economic growth. In response to this situation, regional water authorities have focused on investments in infrastructure to augment water supply and on exploiting groundwater sources, often at unsustainable rates. The case study provides policy recommendations to shift from a traditional water augmentation approach to innovative water demand management.

Water security for economic growth

The Ica River Integrated Basin is one of the most crucial water resources systems for the Peruvian economy. It supports a regional economy that contributes to over 3% of total production (as measured by gross domestic product [GDP]) and 7% of total exports, despite the small share of the population that lives in the area (2.5% of the total population in Peru) and its small size (the Ica Department represents only 1.7% of Peru's total surface area) (Box A A.1). As of today, the demand for water resources for agricultural use exceeds supply. The reservoirs of the Choclococha System account for an estimated volume capacity of 80 130 million hm3 and an estimated water deficit of 370 hm3, whereas the Ica Aquifer, the valley's main groundwater source, shows a deficit of 52.17 hm^3 per year (ANA, 2017[1]).

Currently, the most important use of water resources in the Ica River Integrated Basin is agricultural use (90% of total water resources). In the Ica Valley, cultivated land covers 1 200 km^2 (approximately 17% of the total land surface of the department of Ica). Three different types of agriculture coexist in the Ica Valley: subsistence, traditional (small-scale farmers) and large-scale agriculture for agro-industrial and export purposes. Since the nineties, the Ica Valley has transitioned from an economic model based on local production to a booming agro-export economy. Yet, most of the water is used by small-scale farms of less than 1 hectare of land (Figure A A.2). It is estimated that there are more than 15 600 small-scale farmers in a harvest area of around 10 000 hectares, whereas 200 companies occupy over 17 000 hectares (63% of total harvest land) (Zegarra, 2018[2]). Out of 120 000 hectares of cultivated land, over 35% are dedicated to export. Many of the cash-productive crops that are being cultivated in the Ica Valley and then exported to the rest of the world are extremely water-intensive, such as grape, potato, asparagus and cotton. According to MINCETUR (2018[3]), Ica was the country's leading producer of grape in 2017 (37% of total grape exports) and is the leading producer of asparagus in 2019 (DRA Ica). The North American and European markets represent more than 45% of Peru's agriculture and livestock export market (PROMPERU, 2018[4]). The main challenge affecting the Ica River Integrated Basin is how to maintain macroeconomic performance (economic growth, employment generation, international competitiveness) as well as private investment in an area under severe water stress, while effectively conserving water resources and promoting social development.

Box A A.1. Key data for the Ica River Integrated Basin

- The Ica River Integrated Basin is situated in the southwest of Peru, between the department of Huancavelica (upper and middle basin) and the department of Ica (lower basin). It extends over 7 889 km^2, covering 25 districts, of which 11 are located in the department of Huancavelica and 14 are located in the department of Ica. The basin is, thus, under the territorial control of two different departments.
- The basin is comprised of the natural watershed of the Ica River, on the Pacific Coast, and part of the upper basin of the Pampas River (Choclococha System), on the Atlantic watershed (Figure A A.1). The Ccaracocha and Choclococha Lakes compose the Choclococha System.

Figure A A.1. The Ica River Integrated Basin

Source: MINAM (2019[5]), *Ficha Técnica "Cuenca del Río Ica y su Trasvase Choclococha"*.

- Over 70% of the land in the Ica Department is characterised by a Pacific Desert climate. Natural plant and animal life in this area of the department, where the Ica Valley is located, are only able to live in the vast green crop areas that have been rendered viable by irrigation.
- In the upper part of the basin, the most important economic activity is cattle farming. In the Ica Valley, situated downstream, the most dynamic sectors of the economy are manufacturing (19.3%), mining (16.1%) and agriculture (13.1%).

Source: MINAM (2019[5]), *Ficha Técnica "Cuenca del Río Ica y su Trasvase Choclococha"*; GORE Ica (2014[6]), *Estrategia Regional de Cambio Climático de Ica*, http://www.regionica.gob.pe/pdf/grrnma/2015/ercc_1.pdf; MINCETUR (2018[3]), *Reporte de Comercio Regional Ica 2018*, https://www.mincetur.gob.pe/wp-content/uploads/documentos/comercio_exterior/estadisticas_y_publicaciones/estadisticas; MINAM (2020[7]), *Diagnóstico de servicios ecosistémicos en la cuenca integrada del río Ica para la implementación de Mecanismos de Retribución por Servicios Ecosistémicos*, https://cdn.www.gob.pe/uploads/document/file/1678130/11.%20Diagnostico-Ica.pdf.pdf .

Figure A A.2. Distribution of agricultural use of water resources in the Ica Valley according to size of land owned

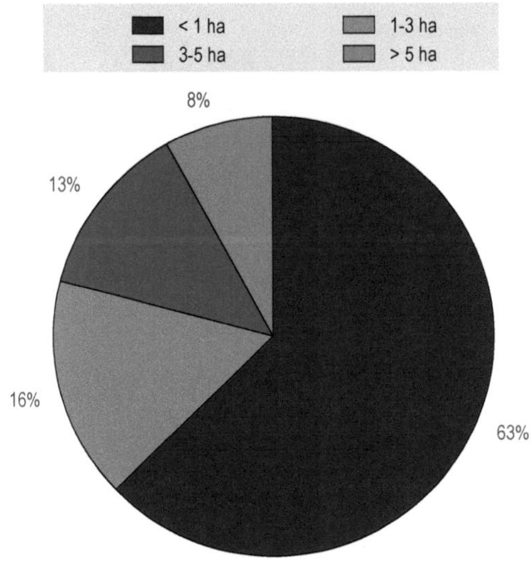

Source: MINAM (2019[5]), *Ficha Técnica "Cuenca del Río Ica y su Trasvase Choclococha"*.

Water resources: The state of play and challenges

In the Ica Valley, which is situated downstream, groundwater takes preference over surface water, especially for the irrigation of agro-export crops. The Ica-Villacurí Aquifer is the most exploited aquifer in Peru with an exploitation rate of 563.35 hm^3, representing 35% of total national groundwater exploitation (ANA, 2013[8]). The groundwater table has gradually receded from 30 metres to 180 metres below ground level, with the growing risk of saline intrusion from the nearby coast. If the speed of depletion of the groundwater table continues according to the maximum tendency observed by the National Water Authority (*Autoridad Nacional del Agua*, ANA) in 2012, then it is estimated that the lifespan of current wells in Ica will only last between 5 and 11 years (ANA, 2012[9]) . In the upper basin (department of Huancavelica), water demand is covered mostly through the use of surface water, while the Choclococha Transfer provides water to the lower basin

The Choclococha Transfer is a diversion project referring to a set of reservoirs and hydraulic works, spanning over the last 70 years, which allows the trans-North American transfer of regulated and natural water resources from a part of the upper Pampas river basin on the Atlantic watershed. This increases the availability of water resources in the Ica River during the dry season in the Ica Valley (spanning from April-October). The transfer carries more than 100 million m^3 of water per year to the coast and is currently being expanded by several different national procurement projects in order to reinforce and increase conveyance infrastructure (GESAAM, 2016[10]). However, while enhancing economic growth, the transfer also caused ecological and social impacts to the five peasant communities established in Ccarhuancho, Choclococha, Pilpichaca, Santa Ana and Santa Inés, areas which are located along the transfer. In the upper part of the basin, there is strong pressure on ecosystems with the result of the acceleration of the degradation of the vegetation cover, which, in turn, results in more water depletion. This circumstance, compounded with the lack of technical assistance from local and regional authorities, increasing plagues and crop disease brought about by climate change, environmental pollution from agrochemical use and informal human settlements, amongst other factors, has increased the rate of and amount of damages created by droughts and floods.

Between 2003 and 2013, the Ica department has experienced an alarming increase in extreme meteorological events as a result of climate change (GORE Ica, 2014[6]), especially from increased rain (49% of total incidents), floods (16%) and *huaycos* (12%), an Andean term for flash floods and mudslides (Figure A A.3). These events have made managing water resources in the area even more challenging.

Figure A A.3. Extreme events associated with climate change in the Ica department, 2003-13

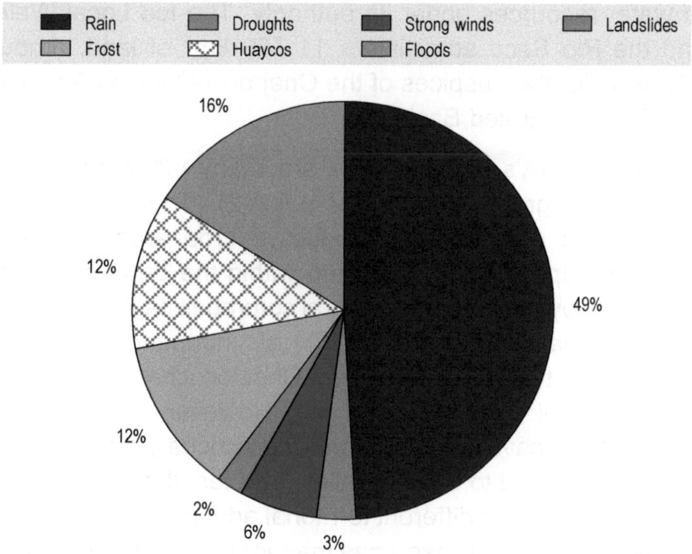

Source: GORE Ica (2014[6]), *Estrategia Regional de Cambio Climático de Ica*, http://www.regionica.gob.pe/pdf/grrnma/2015/ercc_1.pdf.

The population is also growing significantly: more than 50 000 immigrants have moved to the department of Ica, for example from the departments of Ayacucho, Huancavelica y Puno in the last 35 years (GORE Ica, 2014[6]) which puts even more pressure on water resources. A large part of this immigration comes from the rainforest, where people are looking for better living conditions and job opportunities. Immigrants settle on the riverbanks of the Ica River in slums and abstract water from often-illegal wells, with resulting increases in river pollution and pressure on the aquifer.

There is a persisting socio-economic gap between the two departments, with rates of poverty at 3.1% in Ica versus rates of 38.7% in Huancavelica (MINAM, 2019[5]). These gaps also extend themselves to access to universal coverage and child malnutrition, where rates in Huancavelica are much more alarming (Table A A.1). Whereas Ica is one of the most economically well-off departments, Huancavelica, its neighbour and partner in the management of the basin, is one of the poorest departments in the country.

Table A A.1. Rates of poverty, malnutrition and access to water and sanitation services in the Departments of Ica and Huancavelica

Department	Total population (number of inhabitants)	Poverty rate (%)	Households with access to safe drinking water (%)	Households with access to sewerage (%)	Chronic child (under 5 years of age) malnutrition rates (%)
Ica	850 765	3.1	87.3	79	8.3
Huancavelica	347 639	38.7	79.8	41.8	31.2

Source: MINAM (2019[5]), *Ficha Técnica "Cuenca del Río Ica y su Trasvase Choclococha"*.

Institutional features

There are several deconcentrated bodies of ANA in the basin. The Chaparra-Chincha Administrative Water Authority covers 19 hydrographic units and 6 ALAs (ANA, 2019[11]). In terms of the distribution of competencies between both types of bodies, the Chaparra-Chincha Administrative Water Authority, which has a much larger territorial scope, manages and executes the water resources contained within the Ica River Integrated Basin, whereas the Ica Local Water Authority and the Rio Grande Local Water Authority act as administrators of water resources under its authority. The Ica Local Water Authority administers 9 560.01 km^2 of land and the Rio Seco administers 11 756 km^2 of land, amounting to 20% and 24% respectively of the total land under the auspices of the Chaparra-Chincha Administrative Water Authority. This land includes the Ica River Integrated Basin.

Other than the deconcentrated ANA's bodies, there are many other active players involved in water governance in the Ica River Integrated Basin (Table A A.2). The river basin involves two different departments: the Ica Valley, the economically productive crop area downstream, is located in the department of Ica, whereas the upper basin is located within the department of Huancavelica, a much poorer department characterised by the presence of rural communities. The upper basin is also the location of the Tambo-Ccaracocha Special Project (PETACC), an independent public body created in 1990 designed to manage and execute the works within the Choclococha System. This body is now situated administratively within the regional government of Ica. However, its area of physical operation lies upstream in the department of Huancavelica, where the Ccaracocha y Choclococha Lakes are located and from where surface water is transferred to the Ica Valley. The fact that the area of operation and the area of influence of these works are situated in different territorial administrations attests to the imbalance in the management of trade-offs within the water resources management in the Ica River Integrated Basin.

The small-scale farmers in the Ica Valley have collectively organised in three main Water User Boards, which are facing increased difficulties to administer water to their members and collect enough resources for them to maintain operations and finance conveyance infrastructure (Cárdenas, 2012[12]).

Table A A.2. Players involved in water governance in the Ica River Integrated Basin

Location	Player
Upper Basin	• District municipalities (7): Ayavi, Cordova, San Francisco de Sangayaico, San Isidro de Huipacancha, Santiago de Chocorvos, Santo Domingo de Capillas, Tambo) • Local government of Pilpichaca • Peasant communities (5): Ccarhuancho, Pilpichaca, Choclococha, Santa Ana and Santa Inés • Regional government of Huancavelica • Tambo-Ccaracocha Special Project (PETACC)
Lower Basin	• Agency for Environmental Assessment and Enforcement (OEFA) • District municipalities (13): Los Aquijes, Ocucaje, Pachacutec, Pueblo NuevoParcona, Salas, San José de Los Molinos, San Juan Bautista, Santiago, Subtanjalla, Tate, Tinguiña, Yauca • Ica Local Water Authority • Ica public municipal water utility (EMAPICA) • Irrigation Subsectoral Programme (PSI) • National Service of Agrarian Health (SENASA ICA) • National Superintendence of Sewerage Services (SUNASS) • Provincial Municipality of Ica • Regional Directorates (9): Agriculture, Health, Housing, Transportation, Energy and Mines, External Trade and Tourism, Education, Production, Labour • Regional Government of Ica • Rio Grande Local Water Authority

	• Rio Seco Water Authority • San Luis Gonzaga University of Ica • Water User Boards (3): Junta de Usuarios del río Ica, Junta de Usuarios La Achirana, Junta de Usuarios de Aguas Subterráneas del Valle de Ica • Zoning Directorate (AGRORURAL)

Source: MINAM (2019[5]), *Ficha Técnica "Cuenca del Río Ica y su Trasvase Choclococha"*.

Key governance challenges

There is a fragmentation of legal powers between the players based upstream, where the water resources are located, and those based downstream, where the predominant economic demand for that water is located. The administrative players involved in all aspects of water governance are mainly concentrated in the lower basin, in the city of Ica, whereas the upper basin has a much less crowded institutional environment but also a less-advanced stage of water resources management. Some co-ordination mechanisms are in place, such as the Ica-Huancavelica Regional Commonwealth (MANRHI) and the Ica-Huancavelica Bi-regional Dialogue Table. They have been implemented in order to create lines of communication between the departments.

On the other hand, the implementation of the River Basin Council is lagging due to disagreements over its management. Water Resources Act No. 29338 (2009) foresaw the creation of a River Basin Council in the Ica River Integrated Basin. For this purpose, a regional association between the governments of Ica and Huancavelica was created in 2011. The prospect of the creation of a River Basin Council has, since then, become part of the dispute between the two departments. Pursuant to Article 24 of the National Water Resources Act, these councils must be created at the initiative of regional governments. The Ica and Huancavelica regional governments currently disagree about the inclusion of the Choclococha transfer area into the competencies of the council. The escalation of this different views led to the creation of a dialogue table chaired by the Conflict Resolution Division of the Presidency of the Council of Ministers (PCM). However, to date, these disagreements are is blocking the effective implementation of this integrated water resources management tool. Although the Interregional Tambo-Santiago-Ica River Basin Council was created in 2017, there have not been any significant advances towards the effective operationalisation of the council nor a successful implementation of a River basin management plan, which is the main objective behind the creation of the council, as envisaged by the regulatory framework established by the 2009 National Water Law and its implementing regulations.

Another of the main problems in terms of integrated water resources management in the Ica Valley is the weakness of ANA and its decentralised territorial bodies. Despite its new regulatory framework established in 2009 and its position as the governing body of the National Water Resources Management System (*Sistema Nacional de Gestión de los Recursos Hídricos*, SNGRH), it has not yet been able to sufficiently strengthen its capacities to design and implement public policies for regulation, control, co-ordination and planning (Zegarra, 2018[2]). The lack of capacity of the competent water authorities in the region is compounded by the financial and managerial difficulties faced by the main local public water utility, EMAPICA S.A., which are resulting in issues in the provision of water services to its users. The lack of revenues is resulting in increasing difficulties to invest in the maintenance and expansion of water infrastructure, in particular concerning wastewater treatment. For example, the sewerage system in place in the city of Ica includes one wastewater treatment plant that was built in 1971, which is only able to treat 34% of the current demand (Zegarra, 2018[2]). The difficulty to manage this demand and the need for revenues has led EMAPICA S.A. to auction untreated wastewater effluents to agro-food exporting companies. EMAPICA S.A. will be the first water and sanitation service provider (EP) to sell untreated wastewater for reuse. If reused in agriculture, this will increase the agricultural areas of Ica by 600 hectares. It will also contribute to the recharge of the aquifer in times of water scarcity, thanks to the capacity of the soil to purify wastewater (OTASS, 2018[13]).

This effective implementation of the MERESE is uneven in the area. In March 2018, MERESE funds started to be collected in the basin through the water utility EMAPICA S.A. The rates were set by the SUNASS for a total period of five years (2018-22). During the first 2 years, the rate was set at 1% for the first 2 years and increased to 1.5% for the following 3 years. EMAPICA S.A. has reported that PEN 2 million has already been recovered. The Ica-Huancavelica Ecosystem MERESE Committee was established in August 2018 in order to serve as a space for the encouragement and promotion of PES in the Ica River Integrated Basin. The committee is made up of representatives of the regional governments of Ica and Huancavelica, peasant communities and the agrarian water users, and it is currently led by the Ica-Huancavelica Regional Association (MANRHI). However, the Committee is currently paralysed due to the political conflict between the departments and no projects are currently being funded. Despite this situation, JUASVI (*Junta de Usuarios de Aguas Subterráneas del Valle de Ica*) and the community of Choclococha have made progress in the implementation of the MERESE interventions and are currently in the process of signing the agreement. The PES mechanisms aim to increase the availability of water resources, maintain and improve the water regulation ecosystem services and fund conservation efforts to protect the ecosystems that allow ecosystem services to take place, such as Andean forests and pastures.

Ways forward to strengthen water governance

Move from a traditional approach to water supply (infrastructure-intensive) to water demand management and alternative solutions

More demand-driven efforts could be made and alternative solutions could alleviate stress on water resources. In order to confront the expected increase in demand that the agro-export economic model entails, there is a perceived need to significantly invest government funds in more infrastructure. Currently, over PEN 500 million is invested in the execution of water infrastructure, most notably in dams and reservoirs. For the regional government of Ica, the solution seems to be to divert more water to the coast, in particular from the Pampas River and the Atlantic watershed in general. The purpose is to feed the agro-export model that is considered by those downstream as the desirable economic model to establish as a means to secure employment and successful private initiative, in accordance with the economic tendencies at the national scale. Demand management also means effective water pricing, with a differentiated approach taking into account the need for affordability both for subsistence farmers and small-scale farmers. Supply-driven responses are not the only solutions, as demonstrated by international practices (Box A A.2).

Data collection and contingency crisis planning would be needed to reduce many of the risks and help ensure the sustainable use of water resources. Water balances and water quality assessments for the basin (ground and surface water) and long-term projections for the basin for different combinations of climate and socio-economic scenarios can give an overview of the possible long-term futures. This would be necessary to assess the usefulness of long-term investments in public and private infrastructure in the basin and expansion of economic activity in the basin to clarify the issues of risk and resilience that may need to be addressed in contingency planning.

Given the threat in the Ica Valley, innovative solutions to offset soil and groundwater salinity may be essential as salinity, under conditions of very low rainfall, can take generations to be tackled. Salinity increase is linked to other processes such as desertification, soil loss and erosion, which are also either outcomes of groundwater overexploitation or drivers of that increase in salinity that leads to significant negative economic and environmental outcomes. Addressing salinity demands integrated approaches. International experience, mostly in Australia, shows the potential for salinity offsetting mechanisms (Ancev and Azad, 2014[14]). Offsets can be defined as actions that are undertaken off the physical location of an activity to compensate for its negative environmental impact. Offsetting is cost-effective in comparison to the conventional regulatory approaches (e.g. standards) as it allows environmental improvement to be achieved at a greatly reduced cost. The salinity impact of an irrigated agricultural activity can be compensated by establishing new perennial pastures or by revegetation, both of which have an effect of reducing salt loads. Under salinity offsetting, new irrigation enterprises can locate in high salinity impact areas, provided that the salinity impact from these new irrigation developments is offset by reducing salinity impact elsewhere.

Establishing apt financial models to aid farmers in crop planning and encouraging the use of alternative agricultural solutions such as hydroponics could be some other ways forward. Similarly, political will, the collection of updated data and information and appropriate crisis planning and management can help. This is of special importance in an area that is already naturally water-stressed, such as the Ica River Integrated Basin.

Other relevant solution for the water and sanitation related challenges are to design a "water" circular economy approach, for examples through schemes for treating and reusing wastewater in economic activities such as agriculture and to perform water infiltrations into the aquifer using the surplus water (e.g.during the rain season in the Andes).

Promote mechanisms for dialogue amongst the regional governments of Ica and Huancavelica in order to operationalise the River Basin Council and set up natural infrastructure projects, where appropriate

Political responsibility must be assumed by the institutional players in the Ica River Integrated Basin and the clear allocation of powers and responsibilities in water governance should be delineated in order to better deal with the political dispute that is blocking the implementation of more integrated basin management. In 2017, the Ica-Huancavelica Regional Association (MANRHI) was created within the framework of the Ica-Huancavelica Bi-regional Dialogue Table with the objective of providing services and executing public investment works or projects within the territorial scope of the four interregional river basins and transfer areas in the departments of Ica and Huancavelica. This association could act as a basis for consensus to solve the disagreements that are currently blocking the effective operationalisation of the River Basin Council. Incentives from the national government could be needed to ensure that political dispute can be resolved.

Stronger incentives should be produced for the government of Huancavelica to have a greater stake in making sure water resources are managed effectively. This includes implementing measures to distribute the gains and costs of the agro-export model in Ica more equally. This is also crucial for better implementation of MERESE, which depends upon the peasant communities upstream (in the department of Huancavelica) carrying out conservation efforts to improve the quality and quantity of water downstream and making sure that MERESE funds are invested strategically and efficiently.

Strengthen the capacity of water authorities in the departments of Ica and Huancavelica

All levels of government should be equipped with the resources and capacity to correctly enforce policy and work together with private companies and peasant communities to promote improved water governance. This will require an analysis of existing bottlenecks, both in the design of the policy, as well as in its implementation. For the protection of watersheds and the riverbanks and to carry out successful conservation efforts for the aquifer, further efforts in relation to enforcement of existing laws and regulation should be applied, although authorities claim difficulties in widely control the territory and provide an effective response. The full commitment of the national government is necessary to provide the technical assistance and the capacity for regional and local governments to get a better hold on water policy implementation at the right scale and ensure its enforcement in pursuit of the public interest. Ensuring correct policy enforcement will not only improve the management of water resources but also have as a result the improvement of trust and engagement amongst stakeholders.

Box A A.2. International experiences for water management

Techniques such as the use of tariffs or the introduction of more water-efficient fixtures, fittings and appliances, coupled with education and awareness-raising, could all help to create a demand management culture where water is regarded as a scarce and valuable resource. Targets for water efficiency could help to drive action. For this to be effective, however, there needs to be a coherent demand management and communications strategy in place, and agreed mechanisms for equitable allocation and charging.

In **Europe**, the Water Framework Directive is at the heart of European Union policy and practice to safeguard water resources. This regulation introduced an integrated approach based on river basin management plans. Apart from the Water Framework Directive, there are other assessments of water risk, such as for flood risk, in each river basin, which identify areas at risk of inundation. Droughts are also frequent and, in recent years, a series of severe events have affected much of Western Europe. The European Commission has adopted demand management as a priority for water management, including efficiency measures and effective pricing policies. In addition to pricing, various techniques can be used to improve water efficiency in agriculture, such as changing crop patterns and planting dates, and improved irrigation systems.

The region of **Murcia**, in southwest Spain, is informally known as "Europe's garden". One out of every ten agro-food products exported by Spain comes from this region; 21.4% of the wealth of the region and 28.4% of total employment depend directly and indirectly on the agri-food sector. Therefore, this area is very active for agricultural production, despite its location in a traditionally water-stressed area. Like in Ica, most water used for irrigation purposes is groundwater (40.9% of total water resources used by the sector) and a significant portion of the surface water that is used originates in the Tajo-Segura transfer. The estimated water deficit to irrigate the entire agricultural area in the region is 143 hm^3/year, rising to 303 hm^3/per year when accounting for the threshold of natural recharge of the aquifer. Without the Tajo-Segura transfer, both deficit figures increase to 276 hm^3/year (27.7% of the demand) and 436 hm^3/year (43.7% of the demand) respectively. Authorities and research institutions agree that political will is essential to ensure the sustainability of water resources in an economically viable manner while protecting the environment. In the region, good water culture has shaped the lifestyle and way of working, which has led to many efforts in collecting information and reflecting on sustainable demand management, managing incentives for water users and benefitting from technology to increase efficiency in water resources management.

The **State of California** has in recent years endured the longest drought in its recorded history, lasting 376 weeks beginning on 27 December 2011 and ending on 5 March 2019. However, while harvested acreage in California declined during the drought, agricultural revenue remained high, due to a range of response strategies. In particular, growers changed crops, improved their irrigation practices, fallowed land, engaged in water transfers, received insurance payments and pumped more groundwater. These strategies helped buffer the state's agricultural sector from drought-period losses and contributed to far fewer job losses than had been projected.

Source: OECD (forthcoming[15]), "Outcome paper", Workshop #1: Upgrading, Governing and Financing Water Infrastructure, 14-18 October, Brasilia, Brazil; INFO (2019[16]), "El sector agroalimentario regional es el segundo que más exporta de toda España", Instituto de Fomento de la Región de Murcia, http://www.institutofomentomurcia.es/web/portal/noticias/-/asset_publisher/ooaGElmzq1fs/content/el-sector-agroalimentario-regional-es-el-segundo-que-mas-exporta-de-toda-espana; UCAM-Santander (2018[17]), *El Agua en el Sector Agrario de la Región de Murcia*; Cooley, H. et al. (2015[18]), *Impacts of California's Ongoing Drought: Agriculture*, https://pacinst.org/wp-content/uploads/2015/08/ImpactsOnCaliforniaDrought-Ag-1.pdf.

References

ANA (2019), *Administración Local del Agua Ica*, Autoridad Nacional del Agua, http://www.ana.gob.pe/organos-desconcentrados/aaa-chaparra-chincha/ala-ica. [11]

ANA (2017), "Estudio Hidrológico del Acuífero Ica: Memoria Final", Autoridad Nacionaldel Agua, http://repositorio.ana.gob.pe/bitstream/handle/20.500.12543/2490/ANA0001271_1.pdf?sequence=1&isAllowed=y. [1]

ANA (2013), "Situación de los Acuíferos Ica, Villacurí y Lanchas", Autoridad Nacionaldel Agua, http://www2.congreso.gob.pe/sicr/comisiones/2012/com2012ciencia.nsf/0/1187fd07847ff5bc05257b5f00779859/$FILE/07_Situacion_Acuiferos_Ica.pdf. [8]

ANA (2012), *Plan de Gestión del acuífero del valle de Ica y pampas de Villacurí y Lanchas*, http://repositorio.ana.gob.pe/handle/20.500.12543/2284 (accessed on 12 March 2021). [9]

Ancev, T. and S. Azad (2014), "Measuring environmental efficiency of agricultural water use: A Luenberger environmental indicator", *Journal of Environmental Management*, Vol. 145/C, pp. 314-320. [14]

Cárdenas, A. (2012), "La carrera hacia el fondo. Acumulación de agua subterránea por empresas agroexportadoras en el Valle de Ica", Wageningen University, Peru, https://edepot.wur.nl/222566. [12]

Cooley, H. et al. (2015), *Impacts of California's Ongoing Drought: Agriculture*, Pacific Institute, https://pacinst.org/wp-content/uploads/2015/08/ImpactsOnCaliforniaDrought-Ag-1.pdf. [18]

GESAAM (2016), *Gestión del agua en la cuenca del río Tambo Santiago Ica - Pampas*, http://cooperaccion.org.pe/wp-content/uploads/2018/02/Diagnostico-Agua-Ica-Pampas.pdf (accessed on 17 March 2021). [10]

GORE Ica (2014), *Estrategia Regional de Cambio Climático de Ica*, http://www.regionica.gob.pe/pdf/grrnma/2015/ercc_1.pdf. [6]

INFO (2019), "El sector agroalimentario regional es el segundo que más exporta de toda España", Instituto de Fomento de la Región de Murcia, http://www.institutofomentomurcia.es/web/portal/noticias/-/asset_publisher/ooaGElmzq1fs/content/el-sector-agroalimentario-regional-es-el-segundo-que-mas-exporta-de-toda-espana. [16]

MINAM (2020), *Diagnóstico de servicios ecosistémicos en la cuenca integrada del río Ica para la implementación de Mecanismos de Retribución por Servicios Ecosistémicos*, https://cdn.www.gob.pe/uploads/document/file/1678130/11.%20Diagnostico-Ica.pdf.pdf (accessed on 17 March 2021). [7]

MINAM (2019), *Ficha Técnica "Cuenca del Río Ica y su Trasvase Choclococha"*. [5]

MINCETUR (2018), *Reporte de Comercio Regional Ica 2018*, https://www.mincetur.gob.pe/wp-content/uploads/documentos/comercio_exterior/estadisticas_y_publicaciones/estadisticas/reporte_regional/RRC_Ica_2018_Anual.pdf. [3]

OECD (forthcoming), "Outcome paper", Workshop #1: Upgrading, Governing and Financing Water Infrastructure, 14-18 October, Brasilia, Brazil. [15]

OTASS (2018), *Emapica será primera EPS en comercializar aguas residuales crudas*, https://web.otass.gob.pe/noticias/item/579-emapica-sera-primera-eps-en-comercializar-aguas-residuales-crudas.html (accessed on 17 March 2021). [13]

PROMPERU (2018), *Promperustat (database)*, http://www.siicex.gob.pe/promperustat/index.aspx. [4]

UCAM-Santander (2018), *El Agua en el Sector Agrario de la Región de Murcia*. [17]

Zegarra, E. (2018), "La gestión del agua desde el punto de vista del Nexo entre el agua, la energía y la alimentación en el Perú: Estudio de caso del valle de Ica", CEPAL, https://repositorio.cepal.org/bitstream/handle/11362/44219/1/S1800. [2]

Additional references

ANA (2019), *Autoridad Administrativa del Agua Chaparra – Chincha*, Autoridad Nacionaldel Agua, http://www.ana.gob.pe/organos-desconcentrados/autoridad-administrativa-del-agua-chaparra-chincha.

ANA (2016), "Plan de gestión del acuífero del valle de Ica y pampas de Villacurí y Lanchas", Autoridad Nacionaldel Agua, Lima, https://www.ana.gob.pe/sites/default/files/normatividad/files/ica_-_plan_de_gestion_0_0.pdf.

ASBANC (2018), "Financiamiento para el Sector Agropecuario", *ASBANC Semanal*, No. 275, Año 8, https://asbanc.com.pe/Publicaciones/Asbanc-Semanal-275.pdf.

Banco Central de Reserva del Perú (2018), "Caracterización del Departamento de Ica", http://www.bcrp.gob.pe/docs/Sucursales/Huancayo/ica-caracterizacion.pdf.

MINAM (2016), *El Perú y el Cambio Climático: Tercera Comunicación Nacional del Perú a la Convención Marco de las Naciones Unidas sobre Cambio Climático: Lima*, http://www.minam.gob.pe/wp-content/uploads/2016/05/Tercera-Comunicaci%C3%B3n.pdf.

MINAM (2013), *Diagnóstico para la Gestión del Cambio Climático en Ica*.

Muñoz, Ismael (2016), "Agroexportación y sobrexplotación del acuífero de Ica en Perú", *Anthropologica*, Año XXXIV, No. 37, http://www.scielo.org.pe/pdf/anthro/v34n37/a06v34n37.pdf.

Annex B. The Olmos River Basin

The Olmos River Basin hosts one of the largest infrastructure projects in Peru, the Special Olmos Irrigation Project, aiming to transfer water from the Huancabamba River to the department of Lambayeque. The proposal of creating a 20 km-long tunnel across the Andes dates back 90 years. This project turned desert land into productive and fertile soil on which agricultural activity thrives. However, different business models between the "old" and "new" parts of the Olmos Valley and bottlenecks in the implementation of integrated water management reform, require strengthening stakeholder engagement, while balancing contrasting economic and social interests.

The Olmos Irrigation Project

Introduction

The Olmos Irrigation Project (hereinafter, *Proyecto Especial Olmos Tinajones,* PEOT) is a set of engineering works, consisting of 3 main components: i) the transfer of the water through a 20 km Trans-Andean Tunnel and the Limón Dam, which started operating in 2012; ii) the generation of hydroelectric power; and iii) the implementation of irrigation infrastructure for agricultural purposes. The PEOT receives water from the Huancabamba, Manchara and Tabaconas Rivers, located in the Atlantic watershed, transferring it through the trans-Andean tunnel to the Pacific watershed. This project was identified during the early 20th century, mainly to increase production farming on coastal land that, due to low annual average rainfall level and despite the quality of the soils, is considered desert land (Box A B.1).

The PEOT co-ordination body is responsible for the supervision, execution, maintenance and operation of the infrastructure of the project. Created in 2003, it is a decentralised body of the Regional Government of the Department of Lambayeque (GORE Lambayeque) and is considered a budget executing unit that has full management autonomy in technical, economic, financial and administrative aspects. The PEOT co-ordination body depends hierarchically and functionally on the Presidency of the Regional Government and is represented by a board of directors led by a president, which is appointed by the Regional Governor of Lambayeque.

As a result of significant investment in infrastructure and more than 90 years of planning, the authorities in the department of Lambayeque have captured enough water resources from the Andes to irrigate the lands further downstream in the valley (Box A B.2). The project boosted economic development in the area, where important agro export activities take place. However, there is still a gap in terms of economic development between the "old" and "new" parts of the valley.

Box A B.1. Key data for the Olmos River Basin

The Olmos River Basin is situated in the northwest of Peru. The basin extends over an area of 1 082 km^2, of which 90% is situated in the province of Lambayeque within the department of Lambayeque, and the other 10% is situated in the province of Huancabamba, in the department of Piura (Figure A B.1). The Olmos River Basin is composed of the natural catchment areas of the Olmos and Huancabamba Rivers. The basin is subject to a dry climate, with very little annual rainfall, and experiences high temperatures. Originating in the Pacific watershed, the Olmos River is 124 km long and flows from Huancabamba to the district of Olmos in the province of Lambayeque. The average flow of the river is 1.67 m^3/s and its average volume is 52.67 hm^3 (MINAM, 2019[1]), making it a particularly dry river, with intermittent runoff. The river is completely dry for 40% of the time of the total annual runoff and 90% of the total discharge of the river takes place between January and April (MINAM, 2019[1]), attesting to its irregularity and seasonality. Otherwise, it is similar to other rivers on the Peruvian coast, with irregular and strong discharges.

Figure A B.1. The Olmos River Basin

Note: The red dotted lines delineate the departments of Cajamarca, Lambayeque and Piura; the solid black line separates the Olmos River Basin and the Huancabamba River Basin, on which delineation the Limón Dam and Trans-Andean tunnel are located.
Source: MINAM (2019[1]), *Ficha Técnica "Cuenca del Río Olmos;* PEOT (2019[2]), *Proyecto Especial Olmos Tinajones*, https://www.regionlambayeque.gob.pe/web/?pass=MTA1Nw.

Box A B.2. Timeline of the Olmos Irrigation Project (PEOT)

The project included the construction of a 44 million m^3 capacity dam and a 20 km trans-Andean tunnel, with the purpose of transferring the water from the Huancabamba River, on the Atlantic watershed, to the Pacific watershed for agricultural and power generation purposes. The works project consists mainly of two aspects: the Limón Dam collects water from the Huancabamba River and the trans-Andean tunnel transfers it to the Olmos River to irrigate the Olmos Valley. The Limón Dam is managed through a concession awarded by GORE Lambayeque to the so-called Olmos Transfer Concessionaire (*Concesionaria Trasvase Olmos*, CTO). The company carries out the transfer of water from the dam to the new valley through the tunnel and conveys it to users downstream as part of the irrigation component is H2Olmos.

Figure A B.2. PEOT implementation timeline

The main milestones of PEOT are the following (Figure A B.2):

- In 1924, engineer Charles Sutton first proposes the Olmos Irrigation Project to the Peruvian government with the aim of boosting the Lambayeque economy.
- In the 1970s, works start after two engineering companies from the Soviet Union carry out the first technical feasibility plans for the Trans-Andean tunnel. These works soon freeze, due to lack of funding.
- In July 2004, the legal framework for the procurement procedure for the PEOT is set and transfer works are awarded by the Regional Government of Lambayeque (GORE Lambayeque) to the Olmos Transfer Concessionaire (*Concesionaria Trasvase Olmos*, CTO).
- In 2004, the GORE Lambayeque, in the framework of Legislative Decrees No. 994 and 1012 and their respective regulations supporting private investment in irrigation projects, awards the works that allow for the deviation of water from the Atlantic watershed to the Pacific watershed, to the Olmos Transfer Consortium of the Odebrecht Group for a period of 20 years at a cost of USD 185 million, of which USD 77 million funded by the Andean Development Corporation (CAF).
- In June 2010, another concession contract is signed between GORE Lambayeque and H2Olmos, a private company created in 2009, in order to manage the distribution of water for the irrigation component of the PEOT.
- In October 2010, the economic compensation contract is signed between GORE Lambayeque and the private company SINERSA S.A. (*Sindicato Energético*) dedicated to the construction of electricity generation plants, their operation and administration, and the trade of energy (as part of the hydropower component).
- In 2012, the public tendering process is developed by GORE Lambayeque and H2Olmos for the award of the lands of the "new Olmos valley", as part of the irrigation component.
- In November 2014, the irrigation works is inaugurated and the transfer and irrigation works is put into operation.
- New concession contracts for more hydropower plants to be built in the area are being currently planned and negotiated.

Source: Regional Government of Lambayeque, (2019[21]), *Proyecto Especial Olmos Tinajones*, https://www.regionlambayeque.gob.pe/web/?pass=MTA1Nw.

The "old" and "new" Olmos Valley

The Olmos Project aimed since the beginning to contribute towards overcoming one of the main problems in the valley and along the Peruvian coast in general: water scarcity. The PEOT created an additional 43 000 hectares of irrigated agricultural land, 38 000 of which were awarded to the agro-industrial and agro-export sector in the "new" part of the valley further downstream, and 5 500 hectares remained in the hands of the traditional farmers of the "old" part of the valley. The "old Olmos Valley" (referencing the land that was cultivated before the works resulting from PEOT were carried out) is a traditional area of small-to-medium scale agricultural activity in the area. Improved irrigation infrastructures (drip and spray irrigation systems) allowed the development of economic activities in the new valley. The crops that are traditionally sown in the old Olmos Valley only satisfy internal demand (Figure A B.3). In the Olmos District, agriculture and livestock are the foremost sectors of activity, with over 50% of the population working in agriculture, livestock, but also hunting and forestry (Azabache and Quiroz, 2017[3]). Yet, to date, only 25 000 hectares have actually been implemented due to constraints imposed by water scarcity in the area.

The PEOT has encouraged economic development and job opportunities in the area through the productive exploitation of the previously desert land. One of the biggest agro-exporters in Peru, AGROOLMOS, has received a large plot of land from the public tendering process and grows sugarcane in the new part of the Olmos Valley, covering both the exportation quota of sugar to the United States for the country and national demand (43 000 metric tons per year) (MINAM, 2019[1]). As a result of this project, Lambayeque Department is projected as a future hub of agro-industrial development for northern Peru. To date, this project has created more than 9 000 new direct jobs and 10 000 indirect jobs in the transport, infrastructure, manufacturing, fertiliser, machinery, food distribution and uniform sectors, among others (MINAM, 2019[1]). As part of the irrigation component of the PEOT, one of the aims is to create a planned and self-sustaining city in the district of Olmos, province of Lambayeque. The creation of the New City of Olmos is the largest integral urban development project in the history of Peru, which has arisen as a result of the progress and ambition of the PEOT. An area of 734 hectares is projected to house 111 000 inhabitants (MVCS, 2017[4]).

Figure A B.3. Main crops in the old Olmos Valley, in percentage of area cultivated

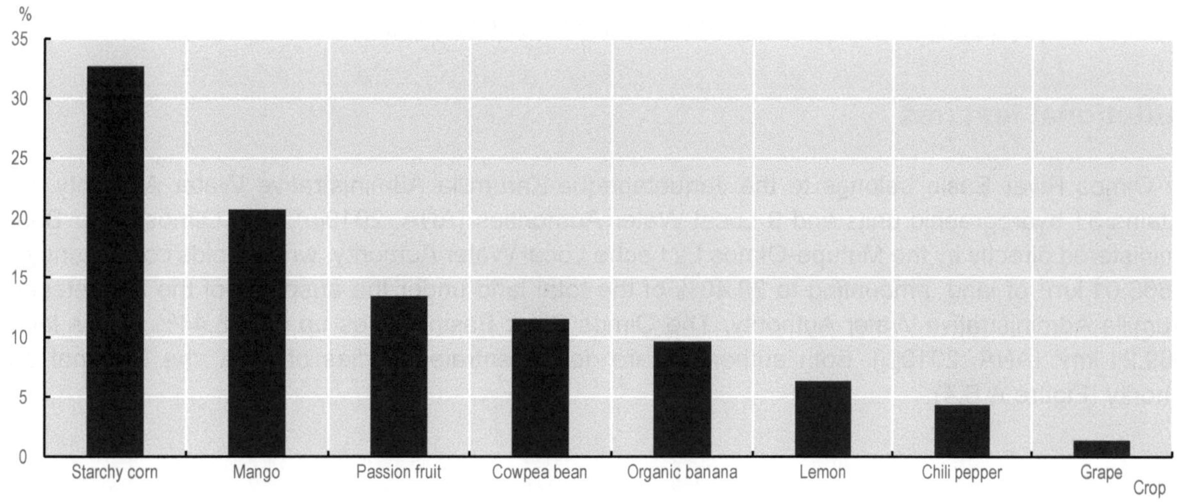

Source: Azabache, L. and S. Quiroz (2017[3]), "Estrategia competitiva para el desarrollo económico del Valle Viejo de Olmos del distrito de Olmos", http://repositorio.uss.edu.pe/handle/20.500.12802/4079.

However, the lack of appropriate water conveyance infrastructure in the old valley undermines the efforts to improve the allocation regime. This has led to growing gaps in per capita income between residents of the old valley and residents of the new valley. The distribution of the water resource in the old valley has become a breaking point in the relationship between the Water User Board (representing the interests of the farmers in the "old" valley) and the national authorities (the National Water Authority [ANA] and the PEOT), as well as with H2Olmos, the company that has been awarded the management of the transfer of water to the valley through the tunnel. This perceived unequal distribution is believed to be the cause of illegal and clandestine access to the La Juliana water intake. Moreover, as a result of the sedimentation affecting the Limón Dam, in which the water from the Huancabamba River is stored, the cost of water in

Olmos is increasing (it is estimated that the treatment of sedimentation increases the cost of bulk water by between USD 0.03-0.07 cents per m^3). The use of flocculants and coagulants to remove microalgae from the water also increases the cost of water in the area. As a result of these technical issues, the price paid for water in Olmos is one of the most expensive in the country, at a rate of USD 0.07 per m^3, in comparison to other areas which have also invested in massive irrigation projects, such as the Chavimochic project in La Libertad, where the average price of water is 4 times lower (USD 0.015).

There is a clear gap in poverty rates and access to services between the inhabitants of the department situated downstream (Lambayeque) and those communities settled upstream, in the department of Piura, especially in the province of Huancabamba, which shows alarming poverty rates (67.8%), according to the National Institute of Statistics and Information Technology (*Instituto Nacional de Estadistica e Informatica*, INEI) (2013[5]) (Table A B.1). In this area of the country, universal access to water and sanitation remains a significant challenge.

Table A B.1. Rates of poverty and access to water and sanitation in the departments of Lambayeque and Piura

Department	Population (number of inhabitants)	Poverty rate (%)	Indicators of access to services		
			Access to public drinking water network and reservoir (%)	Access to public septic tank system (%)	Access to both (%)
Piura	1 856 809	27.5	77	57.1	46.3
Lambayeque	1 197 260	12	86.6	73.1	65.1

Source: INEI (2015[6]) , *Mapa de la Pobreza 2013; INEI* (2017[7]) , *Censo Nacional 2017. Olmos.*

Institutional features

The Olmos River Basin belongs to the Jequetepeque-Zarumilla Administrative Water Authority, which contains 31 hydrographic units and 9 Local Water Authorities (ANA, 2019[8]). The Olmos River Basin is administered directly by the Motupe-Olmos La Leche Local Water Authority, which holds competency over 12 666.01 km^2 of land, amounting to 20.40% of the total land under the auspices of the Jequetepeque-Zarumilla Administrative Water Authority. The Olmos River Basin makes up only 8.44% of this land, or 1 069.21 km^2 (ANA, 2019[9]). Both authorities are deconcentrated bodies of ANA, the National Water Authority (Figure A B.4).

Figure A B.4. Institutional mapping of the Olmos River Basin

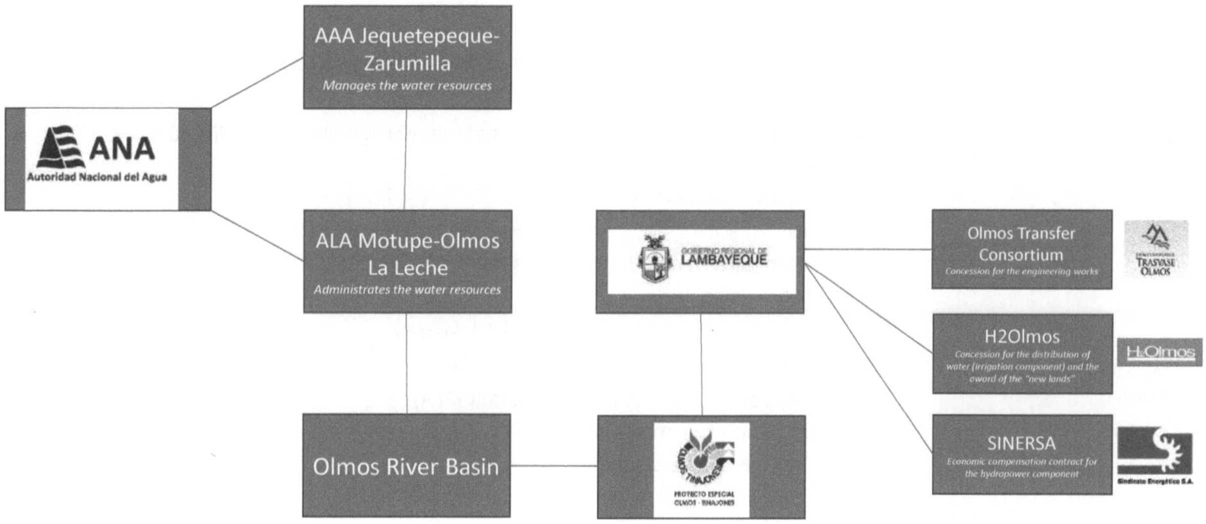

There is a wide variety of players involved in water governance in the Olmos River Basin (Table A B.2), stemming from the differing interests at play between the players situated in the "old" and "new" parts of the valley, as well as the communities established upstream, with respect to the users that are located downstream. The stakeholders can be grouped into four categories (Table A B.2):

- *Direct players*, as those directly impacted by the PEOT, are the main users of the water stemming from the irrigation project. They are water boards, agricultural associations and 20 agro-export companies.
- *Indirect players*, as those indirectly involved in the affairs concerning the PEOT, such as governmental and administrative institutions.
- *Water management institutions*, as those responsible for managing the technical and economic aspects of the physical distribution of the water to the users.
- *Peasant communities*, as those communities situated upstream who have a traditional relationship with the water resources originating in the Andes and with whom PES mechanisms may be established.

Table A B.2. Players involved in water governance in the Olmos River Basin

Type of player	Player
Direct players	• Olmos Water User Board • Agricultural associations of communal landowners: Santo Domingo de Olmos Community • Agro-export companies (20)
Indirect players	• Competitiveness Compensation Programme of the Ministry of Agriculture (AGROIDEAS) • Sub-sectorial Irrigation Project (PSI) • Agricultural Bank (AGROBANCO) • National Fund for Labour Training and Employment Promotion (FONDOEMPLEO) • Ministry of Agricultural Development and Irrigation (MIDAGRI) • National Water Authority (ANA) • Regional Government of Lambayeque (GORE Lambayeque)
Institutions involved with water management	• Special Olmos-Tinajones Project (PEOT) • Motupe-Olmos Local Administrative Water Authority (ALA) • Lambayeque Sanitation Services Provider (EPSEL) • Sub-sectorial Irrigation Project (PSI) • AGRORURAL Piura Zonal Directorate
Peasant communities	• Upper basin: community of Quispampa and Segunda Cajas • Olmos Valley: community of Santo Domingo de Olmos

Source: MINAM (2019[1]), *Ficha Técnica "Cuenca del Río Olmos.*

Key water governance challenges

Some key governance gaps can be identified in the basin, such as:

- **Incomplete institutional framework**: Though efforts have been made to implement a River Basin Council, to date this has still not taken place due to opposition from different stakeholders in the area as to what kind of laws and regulations should govern this council in practice. The main issue is that the PEOT has a large infrastructural component and works extend over several hydrological basins in different departments (Cajamarca, Lambayeque and Piura). Stakeholders ask that the current legislation be adapted to better encompass all the stakeholders involved in the transfer works, which run across several basins. As such, there is the feeling that the current structure of the river basin would not fit this situation and that a specific regulation should be made for Olmos. In addition to the debate on the appropriateness of the river basin councils' current legal framework, there are disagreements as to whether the basin should belong to the existing Chancay-Lambayeque River Basin Council. Some stakeholders feel the territorial scope of this basin council is not appropriate for the demands of the Olmos River Basin.
- **Lack of enforcement and accountability**: Illegal abstraction and a weak water culture are a consequence of the difficulty in enforcing laws and regulations. There is a lack of effective implementation of the laws governing water distribution, water use and concession arrangements. Many stakeholders claim that the concession agreements, especially the most sensitive ones, which governs the distribution of water for irrigation, are not being respected nor effectively implemented.
- **Disputes across users**: In 2018, the Lambayeque department was nearly on the brink of a state of emergency due to the violent protests generated as a result of the blocked dialogue between the representatives of the Water User Board, the agro-exports industry, the regional and local governments and the concession holders. There is room to enhance multisectoral dialogue to address water challenges in relation to water distribution, but also access to water and sanitation.

- **Lack of transparency**: A number of stakeholders complain about the lack of transparency in the technical and financial aspects of the infrastructure works that are being financed by the public sector. Data and information are not always available, nor accessible.

Payments for Ecosystem Service (PES), in the form of MERESE, are not implemented in the whole Olmos River Basin. The Ministry of the Environment (MINAM) is currently encouraging the design and implementation of a PES mechanism in the Olmos River and the Huancabamba River basins, between the companies involved in the PEOT and the peasant communities (who are engaged and committed to conservation efforts) in the transfer area of the Huancabamba River. Indeed, Peru's water and sanitation regulator (*Superintendencia Nacional de Servicios de Saneamiento,* SUNASS) has recently provided technical assistance to the local water operator EPSEL in the municipality of Chiclayo for the implementation of a PES intervention plan, the conformation of a good governance platform and the establishment of a monitoring system (SUNASS, 2018[10]). The objective of this PES mechanism would be to increase the availability of water through conservation efforts in the mountain forests and moorland, mainly in the district of Carmen de la Frontera on Lake Shimbe. The headwaters of the Huancabamba River, where these very humid moorlands are situated, are an area of opportunity to extract more water for its use downstream. In the city of Lambayeque, the water utility EPSEL, whose rate is established at 1% of total tariffs charged, recovers approximately PEN 3 million per year. In the city of Lambayeque, funds are currently being collected. However, they are still not being effectively used upstream for conservation efforts.

Ways forward to strengthen water governance

Encourage dialogue between stakeholders for more integrated and resilient water governance

The creation of a space for dialogue would help manage disputes across stakeholders. The creation of the River Basin Council as a multi-stakeholder platform could help improve plans and dialogues across players in the old and new parts of the Olmos Valley, as well as between the peasant communities established upstream and the water users downstream. Most water users in the Olmos River Basin recognise the need and importance of co-operating to ensure sustainability.

However, stakeholders from the basin have made it clear that if a river basin council were to be created in Olmos, it would have to provide the flexibility to adapt to the specificities brought about by the complex nature of the PEOT. Ways forward could involve a consultation process between stakeholders for the creation of this ad hoc River Basin Council for which a specific legal coverage would have to be given by the national lawmakers. The existing dialogue tables dealing with the conflicts in the area could be used for this consultation process and provide a forum for exchange between all the different parties involved. Ensuring water security in the water-stressed Olmos River Basin requires long-term planning and strong collective action. The development of trust and engagement of all stakeholders in the process is crucial for the success of the department's ambitions and the management of the impending water crisis.

Water users in both the "old" and "new" valley already recognise the need and importance of co-operating across the Huancabamba and Olmos Basins to ensure the sustainability of the water resources. The awarding of two hydroelectric plants through public procurement processes could be a timely opportunity to revisit the first concession agreement for the distribution of the water as part of the irrigation component. The aim would be to ensure participation and inclusion of all stakeholders, effective design and enforcement. The distribution arrangement established in the concession contract between GORE Lambayeque and H2Olmos could be modified in order to accommodate demands from the small and medium-sized farmers in the "old" valley, where appropriate, in order to stimulate economic development across this area of the basin. This represents an opportunity for local, regional and national governments to work together to ensure the legal framework surrounding the PEOT adapts to present and future demands. A water stewardship initiative is taking place in Olmos since October 2020 when the CEOs of 4 Big Agri-Export companies (such as Agrovision, and Agrícola Pampa Baja) signed and announced their Commitment with Water Stewardship and the implementation of the AWS Standard.

Invest in data collection and monitoring

Local, regional and national governments should join forces to ensure greater data collection and monitoring. Water balances and water quality assessments for the basin (ground and surface water) and long-term projections for the basin for different combinations of climate and socio-economic scenarios help to guide authorities in the long term. With regards to the sedimentation issues affecting the Limón Dam, though there is information on how much sediment is invading the river basin. However, there is no information available on where exactly this sedimentation lies or its direct causes, though deforestation in the upper basin is thought to have a great impact. Collecting, using and disseminating more data will not only reinforce the technical solutions but they will also encourage greater transparency and stakeholder engagement. This data and information could be made available to the stakeholders as well as to the general public through a web portal in a clear and timely manner. This may go a long way to aid in the resolution of disputes and increase transparency. However, this measure would require a clear allocation of responsibilities across authorities and agreement on what should be prioritised in terms of data collection, as well as the target groups.

Build capacity

Further capacity and resources are needed to deal with arising technical issues now, before advancing the PEOT's plans any further. The knowledge and expertise that has already been collected during the first years of operation should inform the future projects that are currently being planned. This increase in capacity could help optimise the use of water, aid in the efficient choice of crops and increase profitability for all stakeholders, which will help avoid future social conflicts in the area over acquired rights and water safety, due to non-compliance with granted volumes.

Ensure policy coherence

Water management policies should be accompanied by the implementation of other transversal social policies since the basin headwaters are in areas (such as Huancabamba) where the population mostly does not have access to public services. The regional government of Lambayeque has established a clear economic priority for the department, as is shown by the ambitious reach of the PEOT, its objective of turning the whole of the valley into fertile agricultural land and the recent kick-off of the New City of Olmos project, with aspirations of making Lambayeque the economic hub of the north. Nevertheless, water authorities may consider the re-evaluation of the priorities established in their planning tools and work towards greater cross-sectoral co-ordination and complementarities. This may lead to the implementation of measures to address immediate concerns such as universal access to water and sanitation, especially in light of the objectives recently established by the 2018 Regional Sanitation Plan for Lambayeque, to achieve 100% access to water and sanitation for the urban population and 80.2% and 70.1% for rural populations respectively, by 2021.

References

ANA (2019), *Administración Local del Agua Motupe-Olmos-La Leche*, Autoridad Nacional del Agua, http://www.ana.gob.pe/organos-desconcentrados/aaa-jequetepeque-zarumilla/ala-motupe-olmos-la-leche. [9]

ANA (2019), *Autoridad Administrativa del Jequetepeque-Zarumilla*, Autoridad Nacional del Agua, http://www.ana.gob.pe/organos-desconcentrados/autoridad-administrativa-del-agua-jequetepeque-zarumilla. [8]

Azabache, L. and S. Quiroz (2017), "Estrategia competitiva para el desarrollo económico del Valle Viejo de Olmos del distrito de Olmos", Universidad Señor de Sipán, http://repositorio.uss.edu.pe/handle/20.500.12802/4079. [3]

INEI (2017), *Censos Nacionales 2017*, http://censo2017.inei.gob.pe/publicaciones/ (accessed on 17 March 2021). [7]

INEI (2015), *Mapa de la Pobreza 2013.* [6]

INEI (2013), *Mapa de Pobreza Provincial y Distrital.* [5]

MINAM (2019), *Ficha Técnica "Cuenca del Río Olmos.* [1]

MVCS (2017), *Presentación de la Nueva Ciudad de Olmos.* [4]

PEOT (2019), *Proyecto Especial Olmos Tinajones*, Lambayeque Regional Government, https://www.regionlambayeque.gob.pe/web/?pass=MTA1Nw. [2]

SUNASS (2018), "Lambayeque: Regulador brinda asistencia técnica a Epsel sobre MRSE". [10]

Annex C. The Chillón, Rímac and Lurín River Basins (Chirilú)

The Chirilú River Basin's main users are city-dwellers in the capital city of Lima. It is one of the most important basins in the entire country and its river basin council is in the most advanced stage of implementation compared to others in the country. However, the basin is facing strong water security challenges due to severe scarcity threats, worsened by pollution and climate change. These challenges threaten the ability of the basin to meet the demand for water in the capital city, a conurbation of 10 million inhabitants, representing one-third of the country's total population. The case study provides policy recommendations to strengthen water governance in the basin.

Key facts and features

The Chirilú River Basin, made up of the individual Chillón, Rímac and Lurín Basins, is one of the most critical basins due to its importance for the daily lives of millions of people and the country's economy (Box A C.1). The Chillón and Rímac River Basins contribute the most to supply the water needs of the urban population of Lima, a city of 10 million inhabitants, which represents one-third of the country's total population. A total of 69% of surface water in the area is generated by the Rímac River system, 20% by the Chillón River and 11% by the Lurín River. The latter is smaller in comparison to the other two basins and a less relevant source of water. However, the lower valley of the Lurín River Basin is considered Lima's last "green lung" and is crucial for food supply to the city. It is also essential to the good functioning of the hydrological system in the region because it significantly supports the recharge of groundwater bodies.

This basin supplies most of the water resources for domestic and agricultural use. The main use for the water resources of the Chirilú River Basin is for domestic purposes (69%), followed by agricultural (22%) and industrial (8%) uses (MINAM, 2019[1]). In 2016, the demand for water resources reached 833.7 hm^3. The total volume of available water resources in the 3 basins is 1 109 hm^3, in which the Rímac River, which flows through the city of Lima, plays a very important role. The National Water Authority (ANA) has reported that most of the domestic water licences correspond to the Rímac River basin, due to the fact that it is the closest to Lima. Water licenses in the Chillón and Lurín River basins cover mostly agricultural users. The volume of water used for domestic purposes has significantly increased since 2009, where domestic demand required 753.1 hm^3 and, in 2017, where domestic demand required 833.7 hm^3 (75% of total surface water), which represents an increase of over 10% in less than 10 years. The water in this basin is also primarily used for energy purposes and five of the most important hydroelectric plants in the country are situated there. These plants are situated in the middle part of the Chirilú Basin, where water is harvested for power generation and is then returned to the river.

Groundwater is a much less significant source of water in the Chirilú River Basin than surface water. Approximately three-quarters of this demand is covered through surface water and the remaining 25% is supplied by groundwater (Figure A C.2). The total volume of groundwater provided by the Chillón, Rímac and Lurín aquifers amounts to 310 hm^3, less than one-third of the volume provided by surface water. The Rímac aquifer, like its corresponding river basin, is the most resourceful of the three. Together, the Chillón and Rímac aquifers cover 88% of groundwater demand. According to the Lima Drinking Water and Sewerage Service (*Servicio de Agua Potable y Alcantarillado de Lima,* SEDAPAL), during the period 2006-13, the average abstraction flows fluctuated between 3.5 m^3/s and 4.0 m^3/s. Between 1997 and 2006, the abstraction flows strongly decreased from 8.3 m^3/s to 4.0 m^3/s (SEDAPAL, 2015[2]). Also, in the period between 1969 and 1997, abstraction flows increased from 1.1 m^3/s to 8.3 m^3/s, causing severe overexploitation and a decrease in phreatic strata from 30-40 to 60-80 metres. The Lima Drinking Water and Sewerage Service (SEDAPAL) established in its Optimised Master Plan a maximum abstraction flow of 3.5 m^3/s for the Rímac aquifer, 1 m^3/s for the Chillón aquifer and 0.3 m^3/s for the Lurín aquifer (SEDAPAL, 2015[3]).

Box A C.1. Key data for the Chirilú River Basin

The Chirilú River Basin is located in the department of Lima and the constitutional province of Callao, situated in the mid-west of the Peruvian territory, on the Pacific Coast. The basin spans over 8 050 km^2. Three rivers flow into the basin (the Chillón, Rímac and Lurín Rivers), all of which originate in the Andes and flow along the desert of the Peruvian coast before flowing into the Pacific Ocean. These rivers provide water resources to the metropolitan area of Lima and Callao, the world's second-biggest desert city, located downstream. The annual average total volume of water withdrawal in the basin is 1 484 million m^3, of which 83% is surface water and 17% is groundwater. In terms of groundwater, 90%

of the supply comes from the Chillón-Rímac aquifer and 10% from the Lurín aquifer, in both cases under the assumption of sustainable abstraction. However, data constraints hinder sound analysis.

Figure A C.1. The Chirilú River Basin

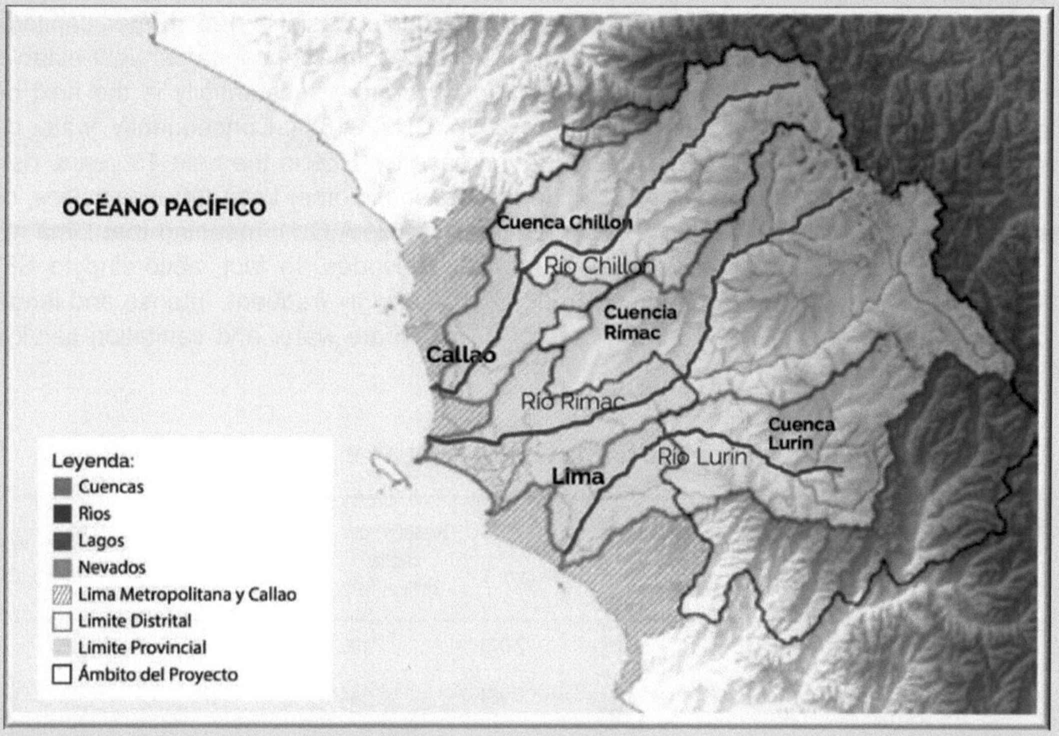

Source: AQUAFONDO (2016[4]), *Estudio de Riesgos Hídricos y Vulnerabilidad del Sector Privado en Lima Metropolitana y Callao en un Contexto de Cambio Climático*, https://aquafondo.org.pe/wp-content/uploads/2016/07/040716-Estudio-de-Riesgos-Hi%CC%81dricos-y-Vulnerabilidad-del-Sector-Privado-en-Lima-Metropolitana-y-Callao-en-un-Contexto-de-Cambi.pdf.

Figure A C.2. Total surface and groundwater volume, in hm^3

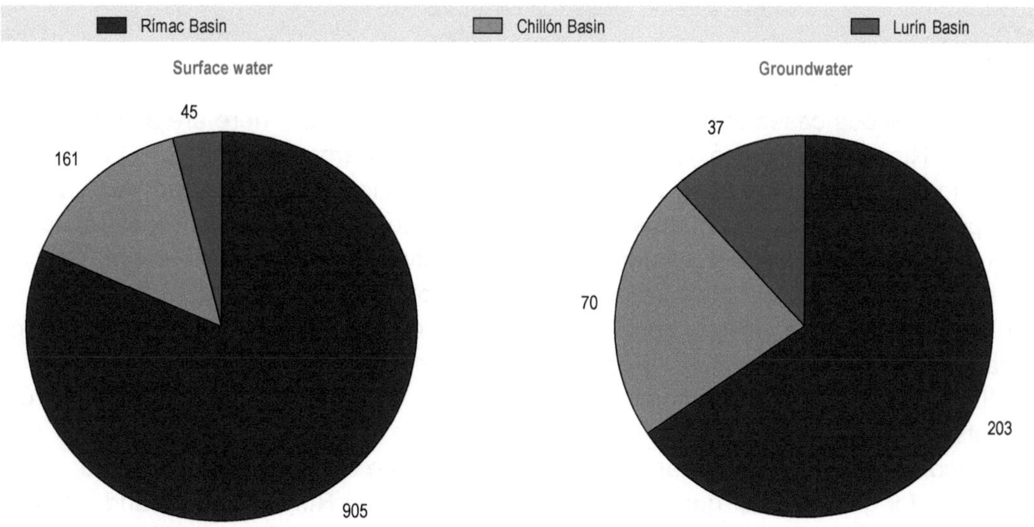

Source: MINAM (2019[1]), *Ficha Técnica "Cuenca de Los Ríos Chillón, Rímac y Lurín (CHIRILÚ)"*.

Water challenges

The amount of water resources available in the basin is currently insufficient to cover the amount of demand from the cities of Callao and Lima. Dealing with the threats posed by the insufficient quantity and low quality of water, in a context of strong anthropogenic pressure and vulnerability to climate change, is Chirilú's greatest challenge. Total water availability in the Chirilú Basin is 125 m³/per capita/per year (AQUAFONDO, 2016[4]), well below the water scarcity rate of 1 000 m³/per capita/per year established by the United Nations (UN). The city of Lima is also expected to grow substantially in the next decades, reaching a population of over 12 million inhabitants by 2030 (UN, 2018[5]). Consequently, water demands for domestic and non-domestic uses are expected to increase by 10% in the next 15 years, rising from 26.8 m³/s to 31.7 m³/s in 2030 (SEDAPAL, 2015[2]). In comparison to other Latin American cities, Lima has one of the lowest per capita water resource reserves rates (Table A C.1), meaning that Lima is also ill-prepared to meet increasing water demand over the next decades. In fact, according to SEDAPAL projections, if Lima were to endure a period of drought (increasingly frequent, intense and lengthy as a result of climate change), it would not be able to provide adequate water and sanitation services to its citizens for more than two years.

Table A C.1. Comparing Lima's resilience to other Latin American capitals

City	Population (millions)	Precipitation (mm/year)	Production capacity (m³/s)	Reserve (million m³)	Reserve per capita (million m³)	Endowment (litre/inhab./ year)	Water that is not charged (%)	Water price (USD/m³)
Sao Paulo	20	1 500	90	2 073	105	222	38	1.03
México	22	1 158	31	984	44	347	40	4.23-9.01
Buenos Aires	14	1 146	19	584	43	613	37	0.50
Lima	9	9	20	330	37	248	29	0.74-2.22
Bogotá	7	800	25	800	117	181	35	1.67
Santiago	5	384	24	900	166	302	29	1.63

Source: AQUAFONDO (2016[4]), *Estudio de Riesgos Hídricos y Vulnerabilidad del Sector Privado en Lima Metropolitana y Callao en un Contexto de Cambio Climático*, https://aquafondo.org.pe/wp-content/uploads/2016/07/040716-Estudio-de-Riesgos-Hi%CC%81dricos-y-Vulnerabilidad-del-Sector-Privado-en-Lima-Metropolitana-y-Callao-en-un-Contexto-de-Cambi.pdf.

Problems in water quantity are compounded by threats to water quality. The pollution of the Rímac River is one of the most serious cases of river pollution on the national scale. There are at least 1 185 sources of pollution in the Rímac River Basin, with 260 (22%) in the upstream area, 336 (28%) in the central area and 589 (50%) in the downstream area, where the urban population is concentrated (ANA, 2015[6]). As for the types of pollution sources, the number of pollution sources related to municipal wastewater is the highest, with 736 (62%), followed by sources of contamination related to solid waste, with 323 (27%), attesting to the magnitude of the city's impact in the pollution problem (K-Water, 2015[7]). In 2016, high levels of metals were detected in the upper Rímac River Basin, mainly arsenic, manganese, iron and lead. The lower part of the Chillón River Basin presents poor water quality, with high levels of biological oxygen demand (BOD), copper, lead and thermotolerant coliforms (i.e. E. coli). The Lurín River Basin, on the other hand, presents excellent quality levels in the upper basin; however, there is a high presence of thermotolerant coliforms in the lower basin, presumably from the dumping of solid waste (ANA, 2018[8]). Monitoring results for groundwater quality show better results. The Rímac, Chillón and Lurín aquifers all generally show normal to high-quality results at the different measuring points. However, quality decreases on approach to the coastal area, where the city of Lima and the district of Callao are located (ANA, 2018[8]). In order to reach target water quality levels, ANA has put into place a Water Pollution Prevention Plan for the Rímac River (*Plan Maestro para la Restauración del Río Rímac*). This plan includes both structural and non-structural measures.

One of the main issues affecting the health of the rivers in the Chirilú Basin is the outcome of the informal human settlements that have appeared along the riverbanks and that contribute heavily to pollution levels, increase illegal abstraction and depletion of the aquifers, and hamper the recuperation of riparian ecosystems. One of the best-known cases is the left bank of the Rímac River (*Margen Izquierda del Río Rímac*, MIRR), where more than 80 000 people reside (IDRC/CRDI, 2012[9]). This area faces myriad vulnerabilities in the form of social, economic and environmental issues. Due to their proximity to the riverbank, the geophysical conditions of the terrain, seismicity and precarious constructions, these areas are much more vulnerable to water erosion and flooding, which result in many instances of houses being washed away. The lack of adequate sewerage systems leads to the dumping of untreated domestic wastewater directly into the Rímac River. Informal settlements are the result of complex social, economic and political factors that require sensible solutions for the effective disassembling of the settlements and relocation of the communities living there to improved living quarters.

Institutional features

The Chirilú River Basin belongs to the Cañete-Fortaleza Administrative Water Authority, which contains 17 hydrographic units and 5 Local Water Authorities (ANA, 2019[10]). The Chirilú River Basin is governed by the Chillón-Rímac-Lurín Local Water Authority, which holds competency over 9 384.61 km^2, amounting to 23.50% of the total land under the auspices of the Cañete-Fortaleza Administrative Water Authority. The basins that concern Chirilú concern 78.1% of the land governed by the Chillón-Rímac-Lurín Local Water Authority, amounting to 7 329.68 km^2 (ANA, 2019[11]), making this basin system the most important under its control.

Key actors in the water management system are the following:

- The Chillón-Rímac-Lurín Local Administrative Water Authority (ALA) is a deconcentrated organ of the National Water Authority (ANA) charged with the operational management of the water resources found in the basins that constitute the Chirilú system. Given the importance of domestic use in the basin, its main function is managing the supply of drinking water.
- The Lima Drinking Water and Sewerage Service (SEDAPAL) is the main water operator in the Chirilú Basin and the most relevant water utility in Peru. Its main mission is the provision of sanitation services such as drinking water and sewerage. It is also charged with executing sectorial policy in the operation, maintenance, control and development of basic services, with specific functions in aspects of regulation, planning, programming, project development, financing, execution of works, advice and technical assistance. It can also engage in other related and/or complementary activities. Like other urban water operators, SEDAPAL is regulated by the National Superintendence of Sewerage Services (SUNASS). Its main purpose is to regulate and supervise the provision of sanitation services by providers, independently, objectively and in a timely manner. An annual rate of 1% of total revenues from SEDAPAL's service provision was established for the collection of PES (Box A C.2).
- The Chillón-Rímac-Lurín River Basin Council, founded in 2016, is a space for consultation in which the institutions and other organisations of the region linked to the integrated management of water resources can present their needs, projects and claims, in order to plan and co-ordinate the sustainable use of water in the basin.
- The Sub-sectorial Irrigation Program (PSI) is a decentralised organ of the agricultural sector. Its main objective is to promote the sustainable development of irrigation systems in the coast and

mountains, the strengthening of user organisations, the development of management capacities, as well as the dissemination of the use of modern irrigation technologies to contribute to increasing agricultural production and productivity. Its overall mission is to improve the profitability of agriculture and raise farmers' living standards.

- The Agricultural Regional Directorate of the Regional Government of Lima (GORE Lima) is a decentralised body of the Regional Government of Lima that promotes agricultural productive activities at the regional level and depends technically and functionally on the Ministry of Agriculture.

Box A C.2. Payment for ecosystem services (PES) in the Chirilú Basin

In order to protect the headwaters, a PES scheme is in place. In 2015, SUNASS published a binding decision that state the management objectives, tariff formulas and structures that SEDAPAL, Lima's water utility company, has to comply with in 2015-20. In this decision, the creation of a PES fund was prioritised. An annual rate of 1% of total revenues from SEDAPAL's service provision was established for the collection of PES. The tariff formula contemplated funding a portfolio of projects for a total amount of PEN 38.5 million, dedicated to the repairing and conservation of ecosystems and environmental services in the Mantaro and Rímac Rivers, mainly responsible for the supply of water to the city of Lima and under severe threats of pollution. Since 2015, approximately PEN 90 million (almost USD 26 million) have been collected for investment in conservation projects by SEDAPAL.

Starting in 2018, several tariff studies were carried out to determine what the potential beneficiaries and contributors to PES could be in both the Chillón and Lurín River Basins. According to SEDAPAL, a total of 32 projects have been identified. The most advanced projects are the following:

- Recovery of the water regulation ecosystem service in the Milloc, in the district of Carampoma, province of Huarochirí, department of Lima: This project is expected to cost a total of PEN 1 811 355 and it was designed by AQUAFONDO, a multisectoral articulation platform with the objective of promoting the conservation, recovery and sustainable use of water sources for the cities of Callao and Lima.
- Recovery of the water regulation ecosystem service in the community of Huamantanga, Lima: This project is expected to cost a total of PEN 2 007 132 and it was designed by CONDESAN, a civil society organisation committed to the conservation of mountainous ecosystems in the Andean region.
- Recovery of the water regulation ecosystem service in the Laraos inter-basin, in the district of Laraos, Huarochirí Province, in the department of Lima: This project is expected to cost a total of PEN 1 994 773.20 and it was also designed by AQUAFONDO.

The MINAM is currently co-ordinating with SUNASS and SEDAPAL in order to execute these projects with SEDAPAL's funds. Technical assistance for the formulation and design of these projects in accordance with the MINAM's guidance is also being provided. Even though PES are being collected by SEDAPAL, Lima's main water operator, the funds have not yet been operationalised due to institutional bottlenecks that delay their use for conservation efforts upstream.

Source: MINAM (2019[1]), *Ficha Técnica "Cuenca de Los Ríos Chillón, Rímac y Lurín (CHIRILÚ)"*.

A River Basin Council is in an advanced implementation phase to ensure the provision of continuous and quality basic water and sanitation services to the bustling City of Lima and the District of Callao. The River Basin Council for the Chillón-Rímac-Lurín basin was formally created in 2016 by the Supreme Decree 009-2016-AG. Yet, its operationalisation was not secured until 2018. The initiative was spearheaded by ANA, with the support of the regional government of Lima and Callao, which grouped potentially interested stakeholders and proposed their inclusion as members of the council. The scope of the Chirilú Council is broad: it covers 15 hydrographic units totalling 9 384.6 km². It is composed of 19 representatives and currently contains 8 working groups (Table A C.2).

The council representatives hail from a variety of organisations and institutions, including regional governments, the Cañete-Fortaleza Administrative Water Authority, universities, agricultural and non-agricultural water user boards, local governments, peasant communities and professional associations belonging to the water sector. The council is currently presided by the Regional Government Programme of the Metropolitan Municipality of Lima.

The first objective of this council, which has been functioning for over a year, is the elaboration and successful implementation of a Water Resources Management Plan (PGRHC), which has been designed by the Technical Secretariat and is now pending approval. This plan will be the council's main management and operating instrument. There is not yet a Chirilú PGRHC, approved by ANA. What has been advanced is the creation of working groups such as the Natural Infrastructure and Water Conservation Group, the Water Culture group, the Chirilú water observatory group, among others. Thematic groups are soon to be formed to put together the management plan. Of particular interest in this council is the extent to which its operations have advanced, including the creation of working groups with specific objectives and scopes of action (Table A C.2). The working groups not only gather council representatives but also non-governmental organisations (NGOs), private sector companies and other types of organisations in order to advance work in key areas of interest. No other River Basin Council in Peru has established working groups with the amount of outreach and institutional development as those that have been established within the Chirilú River Basin council.

Table A C.2. Composition and main objectives of the Chirilú River Basin Council

Working group	Composition	Main objectives
Water, Climate and Development Programme (PACyD)	Members of the Chillón-Rímac-Lurín River Basin Council: • Lima Drinking Water and Sewerage Service (SEDAPAL) • National Water Authority (ANA) Other consultative members: • Biosfera Association • Catholic Pontifical University of Peru (PUCP) • Consortium for Sustainable Development • Energy consortium of Huancavelica S.A. (CONENHUA) • Global Water Partnership (GWP) South America • La Molina National Agrarian University • Ministry of Agricultural Development and Irrigation (MIDAGRI) • Ministry of Energy and Mines (MINEM) • Ministry of Environment (MINAM) • Ministry of Housing, Construction and Sanitation (MVCS) • Municipal Association of the Santa Eulalia Valley • NGO "Agua Limpia" • Peasant Intercommunity Association Nor Huarochirí • Peruvian Water Forum – GWP Peru • Yacuñahui Association	• Developing and proposing the strategy for the implementation of integrated water resources management in the Santa Eulalia River sub-basin. • Promoting the sustainable use of its associated resources, as well as the efficient use of water with the participation of organisations and institutions that use water in the area of the Santa Eulalia sub-basin.
Water Observatory Chillón-Rímac-Lurín	Members of the Chillón-Rímac-Lurín River Basin Council:	• Exchanging and sharing data and information on water resources between players in the basins.

Working group	Composition	Main objectives
	• Lima Drinking Water and Sewerage Service (SEDAPAL) • National Water Authority (ANA) • Regional Government of Callao • Regional Government of Lima • UNACEM S.A. <u>Other consultative members</u>: • EDEGEL S.A.A. • Geological, Mining, and Metallurgical Institute (INGEMMT) • Metropolitan Municipality of Lima • National Meteorology and Hydrology Service of Peru (SENAMHI)	• Generating secondary information and knowledge about water resources and the impact of climate change. • Collaborating in the monitoring and complete evaluation of the water resources in the basins. • Encouraging the development of studies and research about water resources in the basins, extreme hydrological events, the impact of climate change and climate change adaptation measures. • Providing technical and scientific support to water policy and climate change adaptation decision-makers. • Educating basin players in integrated water resources management.
Conservation of Water and Natural Infrastructure in the Chillón-Rímac-Lurín Basins (GT CAIN CHIRILU)	<u>Members of the Chillón-Rímac-Lurín River Basin Council</u>: • National Water Authority (ANA) • Lima Drinking Water and Sewerage Service (SEDAPAL) • UNACEM S.A.A. • Regional Government of Lima • Callao Association of Biologists • ENEL Generación Perú <u>Other consultative members</u>: • Board of the Nor Yauyos Cochas Landscape Reserve • EMG HUANZA • ESSEI CONSULTING SAC • Geological, Mining, and Metallurgical Institute (INGEMMET) • Global Green Growth Institute Peru (GGGI) • Global Water Partnership (GWP) Peru • HELVETAS Swiss Intercooperation • Metropolitan Municipality of Lima • Ministry of Environment (MINAM) • National Environment Fund (FONAM) • National Superintendence of Sanitation Services (SUNASS) • Peruvian Association of Environmental Engineering (APINAM) • Peruvian Society of Environmental Law (SPDA) • Pontifical Catholic University of Peru (PUCP) • The Nature Conservancy Peru (TNC) • Water Fund for Lima and Callao (AQUAFONDO)	• Planning and co-ordinating the sustainable use of water resources in the interregional basin.
Multi-sectorial Working Group for the Lurín River Basin (GTM Lurín)	..	• Planning and co-ordinating for consolidation of integrated water resource management in the Lurín River Basin.
Multi-sectorial Working Group for the Santa Eulalia Sub-basin (GTM Santa Eulalia)	..	• Planning and co-ordinating actions for the sustainable use of water resources in the Santa Eulalia sub-basin.
Working Group for the Water Use Plan (GT PADH)	<u>Members of the Chillón-Rímac-Lurín River Basin Council</u>: • ENEL Perú • Lima Drinking Water and Sewerage Service (SEDAPAL) • Water User Board of the Chillón, Rímac, Lurín-Chilca Hydraulic Sector	• Planning for the integrated use of surface and groundwater in a multisectoral manner.

Working group	Composition	Main objectives
	Other consultative members: • Chillón-Rímac-Lurín Local Administrative Water Authority (ALA) • Technical Secretariat of the Council • National Meteorology and Hydrology Service of Peru (SENAMHI)	
Working Group for Water Culture	..	• This thematic group is co-ordinated by SUNASS and is intended to support the council. It is based on the scope of the Chilca, Chillón, Lurín and Rímac River Basins. Its objective is to plan, co-ordinate and arrange inter-institutional actions so that through integrated management, the culture of water is promoted within the scope of the council.
Multi-sectorial Working Group for the Lurín River Basin (GTM Lurín)	..	• Its main objective is to plan and co-ordinate the actions for consolidation for integrated water resource management in the Lurín River Basin.

Source: MINAM (2019[1]), *Ficha Técnica "Cuenca de Los Ríos Chillón, Rímac y Lurín (CHIRILÚ)"*.

Key water governance challenges

In the Chirilú Basin, institutional fragmentation and lack of effective cross-sectoral co-ordination make it difficult to align policy with objectives across several institutions and sectors. For example, the issues of water quality in the city of Lima should be dealt with through the engagement of actors from the sanitation and health, housing, education and waste management sectors.

The authorities in the metropolitan area of Lima have made great progress in the use of legal and economic instruments in order to achieve more articulated and integrated basin management. However, the main planning tool is still pending approval, despite the fact that the council has been operating for over three years. The successful creation of the Chirilú River Basin Council is the clearest example of these efforts of stakeholders coming together to discuss and agree on joint objectives for better water governance. However, this process required a significant amount of time for all stakeholders to gather and agree on the fundamental structure and operation of the basin council, and while its operation has somewhat advanced, there are still impediments when it comes to the operative instruments of the council, such as the PGRHC.

Data and information on the state of water quality in the Chirilú Basin is lacking given that information is not collected every year. Moreover, there are gaps in the territorial scope of the collection, in particular in the Lurín River Basin. In addition to the lack of frequency of data collection, the data collected by ANA on groundwater quality in Lima only show an assessment of the presence of salts. Therefore, there is a lack of information regarding other pollution indicators such as pesticides, hydrocarbons, benzene, toluene, ethylbenzene and xylenes (BTEX) and heavy metals. As such, the full extent of the quality of groundwater sources is unknown.

Technical capacities are pending regarding the implementation of projects related to the MERESE funds (mentioned above as PES). As such, SEDAPAL opened a call for projects to fill this gap. MERESE funds have been collected for over 4 years in the region and a sizeable amount of funding (an estimated PEN 90 million) is available for upstream ecosystem protection. However, the operative use of these funds is lagging. There is some evidence of MERESE operating to serve the district of Callao but no projects have been implemented for Lima. SEDAPAL is in charge of collecting the funds but, due to its nature, it is not necessarily equipped with the capacity to effectively co-ordinate with upstream players and design conservation projects in order of priority.

There is a deficit of social legitimacy of some charges. Mostly industrial users paying SEDAPAL to the groundwater monitoring and management tariff in Lima have been complaining or expressing their doubts about the actual use of collected revenues. Sometimes this has even implied litigation between those users and SUNASS. Unless the necessary provisions are made, social issues may emerge due to the lack of management of the expectations of taxpayers and those implementing water management projects. In that sense, it is important to keep actors involved informed and ensure their participation in the various stages. It should also be acknowledged that the water and sanitation service company's (EP) regulatory tariff update every five years tends to create a climate against private engagement in water services delivery and in favour of considering affordability concerns.

Ways forward to strengthen water governance

Improve policy coherence across sectors

Co-ordination across sectors is needed to collectively deal with the problems of water scarcity and pollution in the Chirilú Basin. Institutions and operators could jointly elaborate a catalogue of issues that should be addressed and/or explored and, where possible, indicate actions that could be taken in this respect. Negative externalities on the water sector often stem from other sectors, like solid waste. As such, members of the manufacturing sector can also be involved, given the amount of waste that is produced through their activities.

Improve the collection of data and information

More relevant and up-to-date data and information are needed for basin authorities to make efficient policies and plan for effective implementation. There is a consistent lack of updated, concise and easily accessible environmental information related to the environmental status of the Chirilú Basin and its conforming elements, including a wider variety of indicators on pollution and consumption of water resources. The difficulties in the quality of information are coupled with the fact that many institutions are in charge of collecting data. Addressing this issue to provide timely, easily accessible and transparent data should include careful consideration about what administration should be responsible for this data collection and establish priorities in terms of what categories of data need to be collected and who the target groups for such data collection should be, taking into account the economic, social and financial implications of these decisions. The creation of a water observatory as one of the working groups within the Chirilú Basin Council that has as one of its aims the collection and exchange of information is a promising initiative that will hopefully grow once the mandate of the basin council is effectively operationalised through the approval of the PGRHC.

Building capacities

The expertise and knowledge of private companies could be tapped to ensure more effective PES structures. Challenges showed by SEDAPAL in using the revenues from the MERESE funds effectively are an example of a capacity gap. To fill this gap, the operator is involving the private sector and associations able to implement projects related to the preservation of the basin. In fact, some of the most advanced PES projects in the Chirilú Basin are being co-ordinated through AQUAFONDO, a multisectoral platform containing members from academia, the private sector and civil society. This organisation is carrying out conservation projects both in the upper and lower basins. NGOs such as Forest Trends are also at the forefront of co-operation with SEDAPAL, especially in projects involving natural infrastructure, Furthermore, the expertise that has been generated by the *Siembra y Cosecha* scheme driven through the Sierra Azul Programme by the Ministry of Agriculture could be of inspiration to SEDAPAL and its partners for the design and implementation of its portfolio of conservation projects. Furthermore, there is a growing dynamism within the private sector in the region that is resulting in conservation efforts being increasingly embedded in their corporate social responsibility programmes in their respective areas of influence, beyond the actions foreseen through the PES funds. Many companies already invest private funds into the recuperation and conservation of the aquifers.

Engaging stakeholders

The involvement of wider civil society such as NGOs, academia and the private sector could act as a catalyst for the MERESE to take off. Actively engaging citizens in the recuperation and conservation efforts of the waters in the Chirilú Basin and empowering them as agents of change will be essential for the full recovery of the rivers' vitality and health. Some work is already underway through their participation in the working groups (see Table A C.2). The practice of creating specific working groups to tackle areas or subjects of interest within the council is a good way to focus on specific problems and solutions while keeping the motivation high (see Table A C.2). However, particular attention should be devoted to the implementation phase and to the co-ordination across the working groups to avoid duplication and overlaps.

Promote investment in green infrastructure

The public investment system needs to be adapted to these new forms of green infrastructure, as the system is designed to build rather than to conserve. As such, the releasing of the funds take place too slow to be able to effectively address the conservation efforts needed as part of the green infrastructure schemes. Financing and investment schemes should be adapted to the characteristics of natural infrastructure so that projects can be designed and implemented successfully. Transitioning from grey to green infrastructure has been flagged as an issue of national priority, especially in the Chirilú Basin where one of the working groups within the River Basin Council works specifically on the conservation of water and natural infrastructure (GT CAIN CHIRILU). Natural ecosystems – which provide key services and benefits such as the regulation of flows and erosion prevention – are indispensable in the fight against water stress in the region. Green interventions could substantially contribute to addressing the current dry season flow deficit experienced by the city of Lima at costs that are lower than, or competitive with, proposed grey infrastructure projects (Gammie and De Bievre, 2015[12]). Several civil society organisations and NGOs work with SEDAPAL to create and implement natural infrastructure projects. These interventions range from the conservation of wetlands and forests to the restoration of pre-Incan infiltration channels and the improvement of grazing practices, incorporating this issue as a pillar of the sustainable management of water resources. The development of a specific regulatory framework, new technical tools and the allocation of financial resources, are recent advances that help shift attitudes towards integrated and sustainable management of water resources.

References

ANA (2019), *Administración Local del Agua Chillón-Rímac-Lurín*, Autoridad Nacional del Agua, http://www.ana.gob.pe/organos-desconcentrados/aaa-canete-fortaleza/ala-chillon-rimac-lurin. [10]

ANA (2019), *Autoridad Administrativa del Agua Cañete-Fortaleza*, Autoridad Nacional del Agua, http://www.ana.gob.pe/organos-desconcentrados/autoridad-administrativa-del-agua-canete-fortaleza. [11]

ANA (2018), *Estado Situacional de los Recursos Hídricos en las Cuencas Chillón, Rímac y Lurín*, ANA Repository, Autoridad Nacional del Agua, http://repositorio.ana.gob.pe/handle/20.500.12543/2902. [8]

ANA (2015), *Plan maestro del proyecto de restauración del río Rímac: informe final*, http://repositorio.ana.gob.pe/handle/20.500.12543/637 (accessed on 12 March 2021). [6]

AQUAFONDO (2016), *Estudio de Riesgos Hídricos y Vulnerabilidad del Sector Privado en Lima Metropolitana y Callao en un Contexto de Cambio Climático*, https://aquafondo.org.pe/wp-content/uploads/2016/07/040716-Estudio-de-Riesgos-Hi%CC%81dricos-y-Vulnerabilidad-del-Sector-Privado-en-Lima-Metropolitana-y-Callao-en-un-Contexto-de-Cambi.pdf. [4]

Gammie, G. and B. De Bievre (2015), "Assessing green interventions for the water supply of Lima, Peru", Forest Trends, https://www.forest-trends.org/wp-content/uploads/imported/assessing-green-interventions-for-the-water-supply-of-lima-peru-pdf.pdf. [12]

IDRC/CRDI (2012), *Sistematización: Una experiencia de investigación acción participativa de reducción de la vulnerabilidad en la Margen Izquierda del Rio Rímac del Cercado de Lima, Proyecto Ciudades Focales*, https://ciudadesfocalesmirrlima.files.wordpress.com/2012/08/sistematizacion-experiencia-de-accion-participtiva-de-reduccion-de-vulnerabilidad-mirr1.pdf. [9]

K-Water (2015), *Plan Maestro para el Proyecto Restauración del Río Rímac: Informe Final*, ANA Repository, http://repositorio.ana.gob.pe/handle/20.500.12543/637. [7]

MINAM (2019), *Ficha Técnica "Cuenca de Los Ríos Chillón, Rímac y Lurín (CHIRILÚ)"*. [1]

SEDAPAL (2015), *Afianzamiento hídrico para el abastecimiento de agua para Lima Metropolitana*, http://smia.munlima.gob.pe/documentos-publicacion/detalle/79 (accessed on 12 March 2021). [2]

SEDAPAL (2015), *Afianzamiento Hídrico Para el Abastecimiento de Agua para Lima Metropolitana*, http://www.sedapal.com.pe/c/document_library/get_file?uuid=0aa74785-edf2-47f8-a750-48aace398c67&groupId=10154. [13]

SEDAPAL (2015), *Plan Maestro Optimizado 2015 - 2044*, https://repositorio.minagri.gob.pe/bitstream/MINAGRI/714/1/ANA0001523.pdf (accessed on 12 March 2021). [3]

SEDAPAL (2015), *Plan Maestro Optimizado 2015-2044*, http://www.sedapal.com.pe/plan-maestro-2015-2044. [14]

UN (2018), *The World's Cities in 2018*, United Nations, https://www.un.org/en/events/citiesday/assets/pdf/the_worlds_cities_in_2018_data_booklet.pdf. [5]

Annex D. List of stakeholders consulted during the policy dialogue

Institution	Name
2030 Water Resources Group	Emi Yamamura Patrick Huggard-Caine
AAA (*Autoridades Administrativas del Agua*, Water Administrative Authorities)	Elmer García Jose Muñiz Miroquezada Luis Yampufé Morales Neptalí Sánchez Sixto Celso Palomino Garcia
ABRESA (*Asociación de la Industria de bebidas y refrescos sin alcohol*, Soft Drink Industry Association)	Ernerto Dávila Taboada Maria Luisa Ángeles Maria Luisa Málaga Verónica Bonifaz Masías
AECID (*Agencia Española de Cooperación Internacional para el Desarrollo*, Spanish International Cooperation Agency)	Fernando Bonilla
AFIN (*Asociación para el Fomento de la Infraestructura Nacional*, Association for the Promotion of National Infrastructure)	Juan Pacheco
AGAP (*Asociación de Gremios Productores Agroexportadores del Perú*, Association of Peruvian Agro-exporting Producers' Guilds)	Edwin Córdova Pérez Gabriel Amaro Alzamora
Agua Limpia ONG, Agua Limpia NGO	Alejandro Conza Salas Mercedes Castro
ANA (*Autoridad Nacional del Agua*, National Water Authority)	Adolfo Toledo Carlos Perleche Enrique Meseth Macchiavello Esar Baslio Jairs Miranda Jenny Katy Huamán Jorge Ganoza Juan Mariluz Juan Sevilla Luis Prado Rebeca Uribe Del Aguila
ANGR (*Asamblea Nacional de Gobiernos Regionales,* National Assembly of Regional Governments)	Mesías Guevara Amasifuén
ANEPSSA (*Asociación Nacional de Entidades Prestadoras de Servicios de Saneamiento del Perú*, National Association of Sanitation Service Providers of Peru)	Juan José Quintanilla Tuppia Luis Vilca Ochoa
ANUPP (*Asociación Nacional de Universidades Públicas del Perú*, National Association of Public Universities of Peru)	Carlos Silvestri Somontes
AQUAFONDO (*Fondo de Agua para Lima y Callao*, Water Fund for Lima and Callao)	Mariella Sanchez
Asamblea Nacional de Gobiernos Regionales, National Assembly of Regional Governments	Eduardo Rubira Acosta
Asociación AGUA-C, AGUA-C Partnership	Fanel Guevara

Institution	Name
Asociación de Agricultores de Ica, Ica Farmers' Association	Manuel Olaechea
Asociación de Comunidades Campesinas de Santa Eulalia, Association of Farming Communities of Santa Eulalia	Faustino Guzmán Freddi Gutierrez Loyola
Asociación Pro-Olmos, Pro-Olmos Association	José Lecaros De Marz
CCL (*Cámara de Comercio de Lima*, Lima Chamber of Commerce)	Alejandro Conza María Luisa Angeles
Centro de competencias del Agua, Water Competence Centre	Bram Leo Willems Rossi Taboada Hermoza Walter Martín Leyva Molina
Centro de Investigación de la Universidad del Pacífico, University of the Pacific Research Centre	Elsa Galarza José Luis Ruiz
CEPLAN (*Centro Nacional de Planeamiento Estratégico*, National Centre for Strategic Planning)	Jorge Abugattas Fatule
Comunidad campesina Sallique, Sallique farming community	Luis Huancas Concha
Comunidad campesina San Felipe, San Felipe farming community	Elzer Ibañez Huaman
Comunidad campesina Segunda y Cajas, Segunda y Cajas farming community	Hilario Peña Huamán
Concesionaria Trasvase Olmos, Olmos Water Diversion Concessionary	Ántonio Araujo Javier Montenegro Montoya Juan Soria Casaverde
CONCYTEC (*Consejo Nacional de Ciencia, Tecnología e Innovación*, National Council for Science, Technology and Innovation)	Miguel Ayquipa Elguera
CONDESAN (*Consorcio para el Desarollo Sostenible de la Ecorregion Andina*, Consortium for the Sustainable Development of the Andean Ecoregion)	Cecilia Ginella
COSUDE (*Agencia Suiza para Desarrollo y Cooperación*, Swiss Development Agency)	Kenneth Peralta Martin Jaggi
CRHCs (*Consejos de Recursos Hídricos de Cuenca*, Basin Water Resource Councils)	Abner Zavala Jerónimo Chiarella Nilton Buguña Ronal Fernández
CTB (*Cooperación Técnica Belga*, Belgian Technical Cooperation)	Patrick Gaudissart
Defensoría del Pueblo, Office of the Ombudsman	Lily Ku Yanasupo Luis Alberto Alvarado
DGAEICYP (*Dirección General de Asuntos de Economía Internacional, Competencia y Productividad*, Directorate-General for International Economic Affairs, Competition and Productivity)	José La Rosa Milagros Gonzales Natalia Alayza
DGPI (*Dirección General de Política de Promoción de la Inversión Privada*, Directorate-General for Private Investment Promotion Policy)	Armandina Guevara Lenin Mayorga
DGPIP (*Dirección General de Política de Ingresos Públicos*, Directorate-General for Public Revenue Policy)	Ernesto Bazán Miguel Gargate
Embassy of Canada	Amélie Geoffroy Rafael Galván
Embassy of the Kingdom of the Netherlands	Synara Sanchez
EMAPICA	Carlos Casalino Uribe Juan Carlos Barandiarán Rojas
ENEL Generación Perú	Liliana Crudo Vera
EPSEL (*Entidad Prestadora de Servicio de Saneamiento de Lambayeque*, Lambayeque Sanitation Service Provider Entity)	Lorenzo Bocanegra Campos
EU (European Union)	Tatiana Garcia Alfaro
Gobierno Regional de Ica, Regional Government of Ica	Carlos Guillermo Avalos Castillo

Institution	Name
	Javier Gallegos Barrientos María Aragones Vente Víctor Eduardo Injante Palomino
Gobierno Regional de Lambayeque, Regional Government of Lambayeque	Teolinda Aurora Pizarro
FAO (Food and Agriculture Organization of the United Nations)	Alberto García de Romaña María Kattia Escudero Rodríguez
FEMA (*Coordinación Nacional de Fiscalías Especializadas en Materia Ambiental*, National Coordination of Specialised Environmental Prosecutor's Offices)	Nora Vasquez Paucar
Forest Trends	Gammie Gena Gabriel Rojas Liseth Pilar Asto
GIZ (German Cooperation Agency)	Carmen Zegarra Hans-Werner Theisen
GORE Callao (*Gobierno Regional de Callao*, Regional Government of Callao)	Dante Mandriotti Castro Enzo Elguera Echegaray Raúl Zarate Rendón Rozana Pareja Sagasti
GORE Lima (*Gobierno Regional de Lima*, Regional Government of Lima)	Diana Sanchez Nunez Julio Antonin Castillo Correa Karina Takashi Santos Ricardo Chavarría
H2Olmos	José Salinas Saavedra
IDB (Interamerican Development Bank)	Santiago J. Bucaram
INEI (*Instituto Nacional de Estadistica e Informatica*, National Institute of Statistics and Information Technology)	Jose Luis Huertas
INSH (*Proyecto Infraestructura Natural para la Seguridad Hídrica*, Natural Infrastructure for Water Security Project)	Fernando Momiy Isabel Calle
Instituto de ciencias de la naturaleza, territorio y energias, Institute for Nature, Territory and Energy Sciences	Teresa Oré
Instituto de Promoción para la Gestión del Agua, Institute for the Promotion of Water Management	Andrés Alencastre Catherine Alva Montoya Laureano del Castillo Pinto Lorenzo Chang Navarro Lévano Manuel Paulet Iturri Víctor Alarcón Jibaja
Instituto Geofísico del Perú, Geophysical Institute of Peru	Elisa Armijos Cárdenas
Instituto Nacional de Investigación en Glaciares y Ecosistemas de Montaña, National Institute of Glacier and Mountain Ecosystems Research	Jesús Gómez López
JICA (Japan International Cooperation Agency)	Mario Arriaran La Torre
JUASVI (*Junta de Usuarios de Aguas Subterráneas del Valle de Ica*, Board of Groundwater Users of the Ica Valley)	Alfredo Sotil
Junta de Usuarios del Sector Hidráulico Rímac, Board of users of the hydraulic sector *Rímac*	Cipriano Sullca Juan Cabrejos Ypanaque
Junta de Usuarios del valle de Olmos, Board of users of the Olmos Valley	Ales De la Cruz Daniel Manrique
Junta de Usuarios Subdistrito de Riego Lurín – Chilca, Board of users of the Irrigation Subdistrict Lurín - Chilca	Teodoro Marengo Rivera
KfW (German Financial Cooperation)	Ignacio Santamaria
LIS-Water	Rita Amaral

Institution	Name
Mancommunidad Lima Norte (Community of Lima Norte)	Nelly Coaguila Rennán Espinoza
Mancomunidad de Lurín (Community of Lurin)	Alcalde de San Damián Eder Pinaud Ochoa
MEF (*Ministerio de Economía y Finanzas*, Ministry of Economy and Finance)	Daniel Peñaflor Dayana Lizbeth Cuba Ernesto Bazán Miguel Gargate Sandra Ramos Flores
MIDIS (*Ministerio de Desarrollo e Inclusión Social*, Ministry of Development and Social Inclusion)	Rodrigo Salcedo Du Bois
MIMP (Ministerio de la Mujer y Poblaciones Vulnerables, Ministry of Women and Vulnerable Populations)	Alejandro Vilchez De los Ríos Elena Rosa Ramos Tenorio Elmer Galván Bermudez Silvino Cueva Sánchez
MIDAGRI (*Ministerio de Desarrollo Agrario y Riego*, Ministry of Agricultural Development and Irrigation)	Emerson Salinas Caparachín F. Javier Martinez Fabiola Hernández Borja Jorge Saenz José López Jurado Laura Avellaneda Nilda Vásquez Paula Carrión Wilder Chancafé
MINAM (*Ministerio del Ambiente*, Ministry of the Environment)	Amalia Cuba Analía Alejandra Aramburu Carlos Rojas Carmen Mejia Christian Lopez Coral Calvo Cristina Díaz Cristina Rodriguez Daniel Matos Daniel Nuñez Edgar Palomino Erasmo Otárola Fabiola Nuñez Fausto Hinostroza Gabriel Quijandría Giovana Egas Gladys Talledo Jesús Gómez Jhaqueline Contreras Jorge Benites José Miguel Pajuelo Juan Lao Olivares Karina Montes Tapia Luis Bravo Luis Ledesma Luis Marino Nava Luisa Elena Guinand María del Carmen Quevedo

Institution	Name
	Mariana Llona Martha Cuba Villafuerte Omar Ruiz Zumaeta Sandro Dominguez Susana Saldana Verónica Villarreal Serpa
MINCETUR (*Ministerio de Comercio Exterior y Turismo*, Ministry of International Trade and Tourism)	Josefina del Prado Chávez Herrera Lourdes Loayza Bellido Victor Eduardo Bullon Alcala
MINCUL (*Ministerio de Cultura*, Ministry of Culture)	Mayra Contreras
MINEM (*Ministerio de Energia y Minas*, Ministry of Energy and Mining)	César Ulloa César Ulloa Arteaga Enrique Puente Ferroñay Gina Castillo Leon Iriarte, Yuri Pinto Ortiz
MINSA (*Ministerio de Salud*, Ministry of Health)	Aldo Persival Dalia Suarez Diego Enrique Sime Rendon Llimi Renzo Lopez Cruz Percy Montes Rueda Teófilo Baltazar Jirón Estela Victor Zamora
Municipalidad de Lima, Municipality of Lima	Rocio Aparicio, Diana Porlles, Jorge Muñoz Wells Alcalde
Municipalidad Provincial de Ica, Provincial Municipality of Ica	Rodrigo Zavala
Municipalidad Provincial de Huancabamba, Provincial Municipality of Huancabamba	Adán Campos Flores
MVCS (*Ministerio de Vivienda, Construcción y Saneamiento*, Ministry of Housing, Construction and Sanitation)	Abel Pedro Bellido Torres Mabel Juana Morillo Viera Max Carbajal
Organización Panamericada de la Salud, Pan American Health Organization	Hildegardi Venero Magaly Guevara Rubén Mayorga Sagastume
OSEI (*Organismo Supervisor de la Inversión en Energía y Minería*, Energy and Mining Investment Supervisory Agency)	Abel Rodriguez Gonzalez
OTASS (*Organismo Técnico de la Administración de los Servicios de Saneamiento*, Technical Agency for the Administration of Sanitation Services)	Felix Marmanillo Bustamante Mabel Juana Morillo Viera
PERU 2021	Aracelli Ramos Micaela Cortes Micaela Rizo Patrón
PETACC (*Proyecto Especial Tambo Ccaracocha,* Tambo-Ccaracocha Special Project)	Edwin Manchego Meza José Ghezzi Hernández
PNSR (*Programa Nacional de Saneamiento Rural*, National Rural Sanitation Programme)	Gina Santa María Cabrera Hilario Wilder Aguilar Marco Antonio Mauricio Tixe Víctor Luis Cabrera La Rosa
PNSU (*Programa Nacional de Saneamiento Urbano*, National Urban Sanitation Programme)	Humberto Gustavo Tipiani Rodriguez Yesenia Gladys Capcha Espinoza
Pontificia Universidad Católica del Perú, Pontifical Catholic University of Peru	Maria Tere Oré
Presidencia del Consejo de Ministros, Presidency of the Council of Ministers	Bratzo Bartra

Institution	Name
	Brenda Ormea Alcazar Juana Kuramoto Nathalie Carolina Tejada Meza Rafael Suarez
PRODUCE (*Ministerio de la Producción*, Ministry of Production)	Edgar García Carbajal Joannes Diaz Buendia Jorge Zuzunaga Maria Paliza Maria Ysabel Valle Martínez Richard Alca Rosa Zavala, Sharon Dale González
Profonanpe (*Fondo de Promoción de las Áreas Naturales Protegidas del Perú*, Fund for the Promotion of Natural Protected Areas of Peru)	Fernando Momiy Hada
PEOT *(Proyecto Especial Olmos Tinajones,* Special Project Olmos Tinajores)	Juan Carlos Escalante Medina
Red de Municipalidades Urbanas y Rurales del Perú, Network of Urban and Rural Municipalities of Peru	Flavio Mamani Hancco Javier Peralta Huanca Víctor Villar Narro,
SEDAPAL (*Servicio de Agua Potable y Alcantarillado de Lima*, Lima Drinking Water and Sewerage Service)	Alonso Zapata Alvaro Jesús Torres Jorge Rucoba María del Pilar Acha Polo Agüero Yolanda Andía
SENACE (*Servicio Nacional de Certificaciones para las Inversiones Sostenibles*, National Certification Service for Sustainable Investments)	Jenny Corman Morales Verónica Villareal
SENAMHI (*Servicio Nacional de Meteorolgia e Hidrologia del Peru*, National Unit for Meteorology and Hydrology)	Juan José Ordoñez Galvez
Servicio Nacional Forestal y de Fauna Silvestre, National Forestry and Wildlife Service	Leopoldo Rocca Calienes
SNI (*Sociedad Nacional de Industrias*, National Society of Industries)	Patricia Valdez Rolando Piskulich
SNMPE (*Sociedad Nacional de Minería, Petróleo y Energía*, National Society of Mining, Petroleum and Energy)	Enrique Ferrand Jacqueline Villanueva Lesly Zamora
SNP (*Sociedad Nacional de Pesquería*, National Fisheries Society)	José Villarán
Sociedad Minera Cerro Verde, Cerro Verde Mining Society	Miluska Cervantes
SUNASS (*Superintendencia Nacional de Servicios de Saneamiento*, National Superintendence of Sanitation Services)	Cynthia Huayta Sánchez Diana Miranda Frans Pezo Ruiz Ivan Lucich José Manuel Zavala Juan Andrés Soto Guevara Luis Acosta Mauro Gutiérrez Rodrigo Chirinos Roger Loyola Sandro Huamaní Ximena Quiroz Zoila Avilés
The Nature Conservancy	Alberto Limo

Institution	Name
	Aldo Cárdenas Fernando Ghersi
UNDP (United Nations Development Programme)	Camilo Huneeus
UNICEF (United Nations International Children's Emergency Fund)	Juan Carlos Valencia
Union Andina de Cementos, Andean Cement Union	David Cueto Sánchez
USAID (United States Agency for International Development)	Dirk Ten Brinck Gina Cady
Water for People	Juan Francisco Soto Hoyos
World Bank	Gustavo Saltiel
World Wildlife Fund	Mariela Canepa Montalvo

Printed by Libri Plureos GmbH in Hamburg,
Germany

9 789264 955691